Shield: River Witham (Lincs.). Upper (A) and lower (B) roundels (½).
The positions are as seen by the owner glancing leftwards and downwards. (Pp. 26, 27.)

Photograph: British Museum.

NATIONAL MUSEUM OF WALES

PATTERN AND PURPOSE

A SURVEY OF
EARLY CELTIC ART
IN BRITAIN

BY

SIR CYRIL FOX

CARDIFF
Published by
THE NATIONAL MUSEUM OF WALES
1958

WILLIAM LEWIS (PRINTERS) LTD., CARDIFF

PREFACE

The National Museum of Wales is fortunate in possessing a considerable number of objects made by Celts who, coming mainly from Gaul, were established in Britain in the mid-third century B.C.; none is later than the completion of the Roman Conquest in A.D. 80. These are of bronze and iron, and many may fairly be described as works of art. They come mainly from sites in Anglesey and on the coasts of Wales, and, having long been exhibited in the archaeological galleries, are well known to visitors.

The chief centres of Celtic culture in Britain were, however, in what is now England, and the works of art from its various regions are for the most part preserved in the British Museum and the local museums of the country.

Wishing to extend the knowledge and appreciation of Celtic achievement in this field of creative activity throughout its range in this island, the Museum Council invited Sir Cyril Fox, Director of the National Museum of Wales from 1926 to 1948, to supplement his study of the Llyn Cerrig finds (1946) by a complete survey. This book is the outcome : the Museum Council is glad to add it to the distinguished works by Sir Cyril Fox which it has previously published.

The Museum Council and the author are deeply grateful to all who have lent blocks for illustrations and to those who have helped in other ways. The source of each borrowed block is shown in the list of plates and figures on pp. xiii–xix.

D. DILWYN JOHN,
Director.

National Museum of Wales,
    August 1, 1958

FOREWORD

The writer's active interest in Early Celtic art in Britain began in 1920, in the course of a survey of the Early Iron Age in the Cambridge region. It was continued in Wales, intermittently from 1926 to 1943, when the discovery of the Llyn Cerrig, Anglesey, metal-work gave me fresh impetus. Several papers were published in archaeological journals, on aspects of the art there represented, in addition to their study in the Museum publication of the Collection: these are listed in an Appendix. In the latter book, *A Find of the Early Iron Age at Llyn Cerrig, Anglesey*, I benefited from the late Dr. Paul Jacobsthal's knowledge of the continental background and from his comments on individual British pieces: the detailed analyses of art forms and sequences it contains are not yet outmoded.

Thereafter, in 1951, a presidential address to the Anthropology and Archaeology Section of the British Association at Edinburgh was devoted to this subject, the need for further research, brought home to me during these years, being strongly urged.

Early Celtic art is distinctive; technique and design in gold, bronze, or iron are often masterly, but there is nothing of "Fine Art" about it; the incised patterns and the relief ornament are on purposeful things—torcs and brooches and bracelets, weapons and drinking vessels, for example. It was not only a decorative art; useful things were well-shaped, with a sense of style, so a beautiful or well-balanced form often sufficed, satisfying the bronze-worker's critical sense, as it does ours. When the Council of the National Museum of Wales invited me to write a book on the subject, therefore, I had a title ready: "Pattern and Purpose".

Though chronological symbols are used throughout the book, the treatment is essentially stylistic, for the period covered, from the entry of Celts into Britain in mid-III B.C. down to the Roman Conquest (A.D. 43 in the south, A.D. 80 in the north of England) is almost entirely proto-historic. Text and illustration deal mainly with Britain up to the Tyne–Solway line, but a few of the greater works of art that drifted into northern Britain are also described, and the continental background is discussed. A series of distribution maps clarifies or defines many geographical problems.

When the number of finds in a given style or sub-style of our Celtic tradition is considerable, or the quality of a few exceptional, I have discussed the possibility of locating the area in which the workshop or workshops were situated. The comparative ease of travel in the Lowland Zone along such routes as the "Jurassic" and Icknield Ways and such a river as the Thames—maybe also Trent and Great Ouse—would seem to allow wide distribution of bronzes within the creative area, which is the east and south of Britain. Many important examples have been dredged up from river-beds, particularly the Thames above London Bridge and the Witham below Lincoln: these present a special problem.

The northern limit of our creative art was probably in Yorkshire, but this *may* have extended into north-west Britain—near the Solway Firth in Kirkcudbright and Dumfries—at an early date. It is unlikely that any creative centres lay to the west of the Severn or the lower Dee: nevertheless, the number of examples of fine metal-work discovered in Wales is remarkable, as will be seen in the text and illustrations of this book; many are on view in the National Museum. The rarity of such works of art in the tin-producing south-western peninsula will be a subject for discussion.

I have tried to see, and examine again, every important piece that comes into the text of the survey, and to obtain photographs or drawings of these. Much is owed, of course, to other workers in the same field of study, many of their illustrations having been kindly lent to me, and their recorded views not infrequently adopted.

Readers of this book previously interested in Early Celtic art in Britain may not find, then, many outstanding pieces new to them among the eighty plates or in the equally numerous figures: the late E. T. Leeds's *Celtic Ornament* has a fine series of plates, a recent picture book organized by competent scholars has skimmed the cream, well-illustrated papers in learned journals are widely read, and good photographs of fine pieces in the great collection at the British Museum are familiar to interested people. They will be invited, however, to appreciate the character and quality of many works of Celtic art made in this country not of the first rank, and to examine the links in pattern and detail which bind such pieces to the great achievements, and enable us to envisage schools of craftsmanship in Britain, and even to suggest the districts wherein they flourished.

Furthermore, the influence of continental art has been much in the writer's mind, and the probable succession of British styles has been closely studied; efforts have, moreover, been made to extend the knowledge already attained in this field, as to how new styles have arisen and techniques modified in Britain. The relation between asymmetric and symmetric patterns is of interest, and the reasons why, in given instances, such changes take place will be discussed. The relation of ornament to function, again, is a matter which has been, up to the present, inadequately examined. A Grammar of Celtic Ornament, moreover (Figures 82–3), is an essential part of the book. Here the influence of Dr. Jacobsthal will be apparent.

The book, then, has been organized to bring the known pieces of quality or character into a (necessarily tentative) stylistic and regional succession which, beginning in mid III B.C., extends in south Britain down to the Claudian conquest in A.D. 43 and in the Brigantian region, or beyond, down to A.D. 80. After this, it is unlikely that an effective demand for, or supply of, works of art or use other than trinkets, in the Early Celtic or Belgic tradition, here existed. Early Celtic art in Scotland generally presents a special problem: it will, I hope, be dealt with by Professor Stuart Piggott, one of the many friends whose published work I have drawn upon, and whose illustrations therein I have borrowed. Professor C. F. C. Hawkes, among other kindnesses, sent me an important paper in advance of publication. I am also particularly indebted to the helpful courtesy of Directors and Curators of museums possessing treasures of Early Celtic art all over my allotted country-side: particularly to Mr. J. W. Brailsford, Keeper of the Sub-department of Prehistory and Roman Britain in the British Museum, who has so often been approached, and to my former colleagues in the Department of Archaeology in the National Museum of Wales, the late Dr. V. E. Nash-Williams—whose sudden death was so grievous a loss—and Dr. H. N. Savory, his successor in the Keepership. I am much indebted to Miss E. H. Edwards, the Museum Librarian, for compiling the Index. To Aileen Fox I owe much; she is my most acute and helpful critic. Above all, I would wish gratefully to acknowledge the action of the Council of the Museum in commissioning the work, and the continued interest taken by the Director, Dr. D. Dilwyn John, in the project and its progress.

March 1, 1958.

CONTENTS

CONTENTS—*continued*

CHAPTER III

BRITISH SCHOOLS OF CELTIC ART: THE FIRST PHASE (commencing c. 230 B.C.)

NORTHERN SCHOOLS

CHAPTER IV

BRITISH SCHOOLS OF CELTIC ART: SECONDARY PHASES, c. 100—1 B.C.

CONTENTS—*continued*

PART II

ASPECTS OF CELTIC AND BELGIC ART IN BRITAIN, *c.* 20 B.C.—A.D. 80

CONTENTS—*continued*

MAPS AND DIAGRAMS

LIST OF ILLUSTRATIONS

On the dustjacket is a restoration, by Richard Atkinson, of the Ashmolean triskele.

PLATES

FIGURES

INTRODUCTION

(i) THE HISTORICAL AND CULTURAL BACKGROUND

(a) On the Continent

Iron-working, by tribes on the Continent north of the Alps, began in IX B.C., and groups well-acquainted with the technique spread into Britain about 450 B.C., establishing our Iron Age "A" culture (see accompanying diagram). These folk practised a simple farming economy, their most flourishing centres in Britain being on the chalk downlands in the south, where they long dwelt in contact with the later Iron Age people—Celts—whose artistry we are to consider in this book.

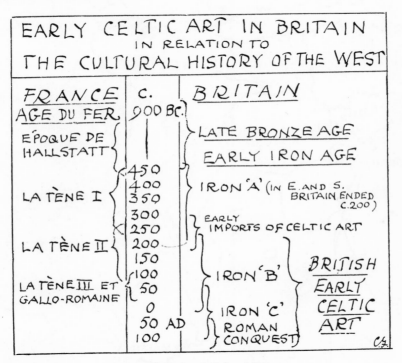

Chronological and Cultural Diagram.

Our Celts seem to have come from the uplands of Champagne, watered by the river Marne, from about 250 B.C. onwards, possibly in small bodies; the culture they brought over (styled "Iron 'B'" in our insular nomenclature) is known as "La Tène", from a settlement on the shores of Lake Neuchâtel in northern Switzerland where "Celtic" arts and crafts were first located, studied, and defined: it is shown on Map A. Now the Marne joins the Seine just above Paris, and a late classical reference to the "*Parisi*" in eastern Yorkshire suggests that this was one of the tribes or groups whose achievements, more than three hundred years earlier, we shall be discussing.

This La Tène culture of the Celtic peoples originated in the Middle Rhinelands in V B.C. Its art was a remarkable amalgam of the earlier Iron Age ornament (Hallstattian), with new motifs and patterns derived from Greek art. A third element is eastern "animal" art, primarily that of Scythian and other peoples in the area of Greek settlement on the shores of

MAP A.—Western Europe in III and II centuries B.C.
La Tène art reached Britain mainly from the Marne and Seine region.
(Arrows indicate possible routes of invaders into Britain and Northern Ireland.)

the Black Sea. The classical "orientalizing" art-phases of late VIII to VI B.C. in Greece and Italy—particularly Etruria—were, however, the *proximate* source of the patterns and forms met with in this Early Celtic art on the Continent, even of most of the Hallstattian motifs, northern Italy being the intermediate region whence came the imported works of art[1] that inspired the barbarian craftsmen.

The three stylistic elements referred to, united in a manner seen by later examples to be characteristically Celtic, are distinguishable in the magnificent bronze wine flagons from Basse-Yutz, Thionville, Lorraine (the Moselle region), now in the British Museum,[2] dating from the beginning of IV B.C., one of which is illustrated on *Plate 1a*. Their prototypes go by the Greek name of *oinochöe*, but these have a high shoulder and slender outline, not met with in classical examples. A classical feature is the "palmette", a famous pattern of Greek origin derived from the honeysuckle, seen (with other forms) as white settings (becoming red if wetted, and identified as coral) in the decoration of the flagon's throat in *Plate 1b*.[3]

As for the "Hallstatt"—earliest Iron Age—background, the "duck with coral eyes" that "sits on the beak-tip" is characteristic. Its alert posture is paralleled in a later, British, piece (*Plate 42b*). Orientalizing features are the wolf-like animals crouching on the lid and forming the handle; their hollow eye-sockets were once filled with coral. Dr. Jacobsthal cited close Persian parallels for the character of these beasts, and for their spiral "ears" and joints—Siberian and Chinese—remarking that he would expect to find Scythian prototypes. He stressed also a "geometric" element in the art, seen in the central zone in *Plate 1b*. Lastly, the cap or lid of the flagon has red enamel, run-in (champlevé), to define a pattern on the bronze.

In the compounds of the rich Celtic chieftains on the upper and middle Rhine, then, barbarian craftsmen and their apprentices gloated over art-works of varied origin and use, unloaded from north Italian packmen's ponies:[4] and they wrought, as every creative group does, their own adaptations of form and pattern associated with some modifications of technique, which together constitute the new style, "Early Celtic Art": at first, no doubt, local, then regional, extending thereafter in Europe as the Celtic tribes spread, east and west and south. The older name of the style "La Tène", is too local for use in our text-books today.

The reader may wish to go further than the study of a single piece in this continental La Tène style offers; if so, my suggestion must be—look at Jacobsthal's survey; failing that, Déchelette has a good range of illustration in the text of his *Manuel d'Archéologie*. Since the former's *Early Celtic Art* (1944) is almost unobtainable, a brief summary of his stylistic analysis in the relevant phases is here given:

1.	Early style	*c.* 425–300 B.C.		La Tène I
2.	Waldalgesheim style	*c.* 325–250 B.C.		
3.	(*a*) Plastic style	*c.* 275 B.C. onwards		La Tène II
	(*b*) Sword style	*c.* 275 B.C. onwards		

Of these styles, the first is still "strongly classical": it is not represented in Early British art, although an occasional piece was imported. The second includes the Cerrig-y-Drudion scrolls, coils on the Standlake scabbard, and scrolls and hollow-sided triangles in low relief as on the Newnham Croft bangle (Figure 6a, an import) and the Beckley, Oxford, brooch (Figure 9b). In the third (*a*) the relief forms burgeon; the "snaily coil" on the Danes' Graves brooch (*Plate 9, e, f*) is a good example. The third (*b*) style supplies the (rare) ornament aligned diagonally on British works of art (*Plate 22b*).

The "spread" of Celtic peoples should be more clearly indicated; the western-most concerns us, for the Celts occupied all Gaul, northern Italy (invaded and occupied from 380 B.C. onwards), and north-west Spain at the time of their intrusion into Britain (Map A). To the eastward their movement was down the Danube, Hungary being particularly rich in characteristic Celtic antiquities; the thrust reached Asia Minor, where in Roman times the province of Galatia marked the extreme, and isolated, limit of Celtic settlement. Despite the loss of homogeneity which might in such an expansion be expected, through absorption of conquered peoples, Dr. Jacobsthal found himself able to say, in concluding his study of the art of this people on the Continent, that "the whole of Celtic art is a unit: it is the creation of one race, the Celts". Such a result was possible because it was in the highest degree an art of the princes rather than the people:[5] aristocrats are mobile and their craftsmen may be peripatetic; if so, the result will be widespread uniformity in culture.[6]

The Marne region (Champagne) was the most important countryside in France in early La Tène times, as the distribution of cemeteries and isolated burials, some of chieftains, in Déchelette's map of the period indicates.[7] Illustrations, in his book, of rich Celtic burials in which the warrior was laid on his chariot in a grave with his treasured possessions, at Somme-Bionne and La Gorge-Meillet, are famous early records of such interments.[8] The distribution of these extends to the adjacent sea-coast and makes it highly probable that most of our invaders embarked at the mouth of the Seine (Map A). It is well to remember that the adventure was not undertaken until long after the Celtic exploitation and settlement of the Seine–Marne region, and the beginnings of the art the Celts invented and practised. The phase then reached is known as La Tène II—"Iron 'B'" in our insular nomenclature. We are, however, not to assume that the Marne region was the only source of our Celtic culture.

(b) In Britain

This departure of Celts from northern Gaul to Britain in the mid-III century—as well as to northern Ireland, with which we are not concerned—is likely to be connected with the ending of Celtic expansion in western Europe—when its culture indeed was on the defensive in the Marnian area. Pressure from mixed Teutonic and Celtic breeds, later known as the Belgae, was probably the cause of this principal migration of Celtic stock.

The Belgae. During Caesar's conquest of Gaul, 58–51 B.C., the Belgae, in their several tribes, were occupying the continental sea-coast from Rhine-mouth to Seine-mouth, and the Meuse valley; Catuvellauni and Suessiones are named tribes in the Marne region. The older (La Tène II) culture had been absorbed and modified by the new-comers—at a time earlier than the lifetime of Caesar's informants. Cremation was the burial rite of these more advanced groups, and the "pedestal urn" their principal pottery form.[9] The culture thus represented is known as La Tène III; it was in touch with and influenced by the contemporary Mediterranean civilization, as a result of the annexation of southern Gaul—The Province, by the Romans in 120–118 B.C.

Some of the Belgic peoples referred to above had moved about 75 B.C. into Britain (initiating "Iron 'C'" in our parlance): occupying the east Kent and Hertfordshire districts, they brought in their modified La Tène culture, their intensive agriculture and a modified "Early Celtic" art.

The completion of Caesar's conquest of Gaul in 51 B.C. set in motion further Belgic intrusions into south Britain—Hampshire, the Isle of Wight, and south Wiltshire—one group being Atrebates, and the leading adventurer Commius. An implacable enemy of Rome, he founded a dynasty whose principal town partly underlies the Roman (Claudian) city at Silchester (Hants), where a levelled ring-work has recently been found.

This is the stage where the tribal pattern in southern Britain, familiar to us from the text-books, began to take shape (Map C); but the tribal boundaries are conjectural.

Celtic contacts with south-west Britain. Celtic peoples (κελτοί) were established in Spain in the time of Herodotus, and the peninsula was named κελτική until the third century: Livy names "Celtiberians" (folk of mixed blood) as living in 218 B.C. on the eastern border of the Castilian plateau: grave-goods confirm.[10] These people undoubtedly had connections in early times with inhabitants of our south-western peninsula; the bronze cult-figurine (*Plate 2f*) found beside the Severn estuary at Aust in Gloucestershire, a well-known landing place for seamen, is important testimony for early traffic up the Bristol Channel, and Celtiberian brooches have been found in Cornwall (Harlyn Bay) and south-west Devon (Mount Batten, Plymouth, *Plate 31*). The Celtic tribes of western Gaul, also, had contacts with Cornwall and south Devon because Cornish tin was brought by sea to Corbilo on the estuary of the river Loire, or to the Garonne-mouth, for transport overland to Mediterranean coastal cities, Greek and thereafter Roman, near the mouths of the Rhône. The Veneti, well-known sea-traders living in Brittany (Map A), will doubtless have supplied the shipping required. (They defied Caesar, it will be remembered, and their fleets were destroyed in 56 B.C.) As a result of this indirect commerce with the Mediterranean, a large number of coins of Greek city states, and some of Republican Rome, have been found widely distributed from Dorset to Cornwall, but particularly in the former county.[11] Two large hoards of gold coins found in Cornwall, mostly of Gallic imitations of Philip II of Macedon's Greek "*staters*", came from one fortified site, Carn Brea. Hengistbury (Hants), a fortress on a spit of land between the sea and Christchurch harbour, in the territory of the Durotriges, illustrates wealth (possibly of a small merchant class) similarly obtained: a gold bracelet and fragments of torcs came from a well-known excavation by the late J. P. Bushe-Fox, covering only a small part of the occupied area.[11a]

Not only Brittany, but the whole of Armorica (the coastal region between Seine and Loire), is likely also to have been the base for traffickers carrying trade goods and seeking metals (gold and copper) on the *western* sea-route to which we have not yet drawn attention (up St. George's Channel to the Irish Sea). A famous bronze "hanging-bowl" found 10 miles from tidal water at the mouth of the Clwyd in Denbighshire, dating about 300 B.C., is explained in this way.[12]

The economics of the Early Celtic settlements in Britain. The Marnian culture in Britain was primarily pastoral, coming, as most of our first settlers apparently did, from the open uplands of Champagne. Pony breeding is evidenced by the famous chariot burials on the Wolds of Yorkshire, and by metal harness fittings, widely distributed; and cattle-ranching may be inferred. Pig breeding, usually associated with woodland areas, is indicated on the Wolds by the joints of meat in pots beside the humbler burials in the cemeteries mentioned above. Some agricultural communities must be assumed in the eastern, as in the southerly settlement areas,[13] but no isolated dwelling sites of this early period have yet been located in eastern Britain, nor have hill-forts which they built or occupied (such as Hunsbury, Northants) been effectively excavated. Some two hundred years after the first settlers arrived, Caesar, as we well know, described the intensive agriculture of the coastal region (Kent) of south-east Britain, a Belgic area ; but when he moved up towards the Thames, he mentions woodland, and, later, tells us that Cassivellaunus's stronghold (in Hertfordshire) was in forest country. Cassivellaunus, he notes, used both chariotry and cavalry: the former had then been superseded, in Gaul.

Distribution of works of art. The distribution map (B) of find-sites of early Celtic metal-work of character illustrates the geographical aspects of Celtic (and Belgic) settlement (in so far as chance finds can provide evidence of such) and the student wishing to have some knowledge of the prehistoric background could, with advantage, compare with it the physical map in *Personality of Britain* overprinted with Bronze Age finds, also published by the Museum.

The "Jurassic Zone" on which there was a prehistoric upland traffic route[14] from the Mendips (Somerset) to Lincoln Edge and the Humber, and thereafter, it may be, along the (western) scarp of the Yorkshire Wolds, was, I consider, the approximate western boundary of the principal area of Celtic occupation (except in the middle Trent Valley), and the Vale of Pickering, in the North Riding, close to its northern limit.

The "Midland Plain" from the river Avon to the Mersey, mostly consisting of heavily forested red-lands is, of course, largely barren. Important Early Celtic finds on the sea-margins of south and west Wales, dating from II B.C. onwards, may be held to represent localized settlement of chieftains and their followers which resulted, after the Roman conquest, in the whole of "Wales" being parcelled out in cantons, like eastern Britain; but except, perhaps, in the south-east, the country of the Silures, there must surely have been a massive survival of earlier inhabitants.

Anglesey is a special problem; it is historically a religious centre, and the great collection of art and craftwork found at Llyn Cerrig, though proved[15] to have been derived almost entirely from Dobunic and Catuvellaunian sources, is held to have been a Druidic deposit. The concentration of finds of Celtic art in or near the Vale of Clwyd on the north coast, again, may be connected with a gold trade from Ireland (p. 56).

A few important works of art found near the Solway Firth, in Kirkcudbright and Dumfries, dating both at the beginning of the period and its close, provide unsolved problems of the origin of this (surely Celtic) settlement, and of the geography of later contacts.[16] In the south-west the stimulus of contacts with western Gaul should have brought Cornwall and west Devon into the orbit of early Celtic continental culture, but despite its mineral wealth this region yields few works of Celtic art until the last century of freedom; these are mostly coastal, and the survival, inland, of a late Bronze Age folk is possible.

It should be noted that, far up the Bristol Channel, a "B" culture related to the Marnian and called "Severn B" has been isolated and studied; there is Hallstatt "duck" pattern on some of its pottery, among other simple motifs; but it has yielded no comparable art. It is probable that the bronze bowl from Hunsbury fort illustrated on *Plate 77* with its three rows of "duck" ornament belongs to this intrusion, and is not earlier than I B.C. in date.[17] Barren areas on the map in Wiltshire and Hampshire indicate long-continued survival of the artistically-backward Iron "A" culture already referred to.

Lastly, there is the rich Iron "B" art in northern Ireland: it is not dealt with in this book. It may be the result of an independent move from Gaul up the western sea-route, or (less probably) a colonization from north-eastern Britain. Though the art is closely related to British in character and technique, it is perceptibly different. Students should test this for themselves: so I include, on *Plate 73*, a scabbard with incised ornament in Belfast Museum, drawn for me by Mr. E. M. Jope, which may be compared with the Bugthorpe scabbard on Figure 26. This difference is not surprising: for if the British environment can produce first-class work recognizably not continental in a half-century or so, why should not the Irish limestone country, good chariot-land, have a cognate effect? The character of a country and of the exceptional people it breeds—craftsmen, in this case—is what influences, and ultimately controls, an intrusive art.[18]

The making of works of art in Britain. Since the art we shall study in this book is mainly aristocratic, workers in metals (and wood) may have been attached to the households of leading chieftains (and, later, kings); but it is likely that semi-independent workshops of long standing, well known throughout Celtic Britain, were present here and there in the chief centres of power or settlement. Smithies such as are here in mind are pictured on Egyptian reliefs and Greek vases; and fragments of crucibles for melting, or alloying, metal have been found on Early Celtic sites in Britain. There were no less than thirty-seven such vessels in the Glastonbury Lake village: small, triangular, with a spout at each angle, made of clay which had been mixed with chopped straw or chaff.

Continuity in certain features of design and in technique, suggesting one tradition covering a century or more (which we shall in due course discuss), can thus be best accounted for.

We are, however, not to suppose that all metal-workers served noble households, for brooches, pins, and the like are spread widely through the commonalty, of metal-workers themselves, of farmers, herdsmen, stablemen, chariot drivers, and household servants— judging by the numerous poorly-furnished graves in the Yorkshire cemeteries.

Celtic art in Britain, then, will be found to have, like most art-styles in emergent communities, a threefold purpose: first to decorate functional things needed in the household, for the persons and the toilet of women: the brooch, the pin, the necklace, and the mirror. The men also used brooches, and fine ones too, no doubt for their cloaks, but their particular interest was elaborately garnished war panoply: decoration on the helmet and the shield, the scabbards of sword and dagger, the chariot and the pony harness.

The third purpose will, surely, have been the elaboration of the interiors of the chieftains' guest-houses or halls, for reasons of prestige and hospitality. Of this—since it should be mainly wood carving—we have very little evidence;[19] what there is will be brought out as the survey proceeds.

(ii) THE PRESENTATION OF CELTIC ART

It will be found difficult, as in the case of other societies at the same stage of development to distinguish between works of art and of "craft". Objects in general use, such as firedogs and buckets, pot-hooks and cauldrons, will be included if they have ornamental features— ox-heads and other masks (of man or animals) on some, twists and coils of metal on others. Consideration of the decoration of the chariot, moreover, will involve the structure; this was one of the most striking technical skills practised in Britain, as was demonstrated in 1947.[20]

Since, moreover, we are writing an account of the development of art styles and techniques in our region, starting before history began therein, we must provide a *grammar* of the art— and also work out a sequence with its approximate chronology, and with suitable "labels". The scheme summarized below will, it is hoped, be found satisfactory: a change of treatment halfway, which the fusion of Celtic and Belgic styles rendered necessary, enforced the two-part organization of the book.

As for the chronology, that adopted should be a fairly close approximation to accuracy from c. 60 B.C. onwards. Phases of style in art or craft, it may be remembered, always overlap in time: this overlap is usually reckoned as one generation—thirty years or so—but may be more extended. A terminal date for the survey at c. A.D. 70–80 is indicated for historical reasons. The inevitable end of all art styles not cut short by circumstance—over-ripeness— is not noticeable in Celtic art in Britain up to the Claudian conquest of the south in A.D. 43: it continued to develop in the comparative freedom of the north, under the stimulus of Roman contacts, in the next twenty-five years, reaching a brilliant end (up to the Tyne–Solway line, that is) in the luscious curves of the Aesica brooch-style, of about the date suggested. The reader may find the distribution map, already referred to, at this stage useful: it shows the areas in Britain significant for our studies.

Lastly, in discussing a Regional art, reference will sometimes be made to objects found in another region; the implication being that the pieces in question have travelled, and that their provenance is not, in this respect, relevant. The scheme of the book, then, is as follows:

PART I

Imported bronzes, III and early II B.C.
Art associated with settlement and burials (mostly Marnian), late III and II B.C.
British Schools of Celtic Art c. 250–1 B.C.: Primary and Secondary Phases.
Historical "Interlude". The invasion of Julius Caesar and the settlement of the Belgae.
The Art of the Belgae, c. 75 B.C.–1 B.C.

PART II

Aspects of Celtic and Belgic art in Britain, c. 20 B.C.–A.D. 80.
"Peasant art" in Britain.
The art of the Coinage, and the Tribal pattern.
Reflections.

Grammar of Celtic ornament. Two Figures, 82 and 83, placed for convenience of reference at the end of the book, with their own index, provide illustrations of the principal motifs seen in works of Early Celtic art in Britain. Some are represented by two or more variants, the majority by one example only. A list of sources will be found on pages 149–50. The richness of our art is foreshadowed by this extensive, but necessarily incomplete, array of primary (or near-primary) forms: those most frequently used are the palmette with the associated lyre-pattern, and their derivatives. A Greek form of this famous motif is shown on Figure 82, A1: it is remarkable how close to the type such British forms as A5 and A6 are, and how persistent contortions of the pattern like A4 (from a continental import, the Cerrig-y-Drudion bowl) are, in Britain: the student will see, in B13 and 14, how little may survive at the very end of our Early Celtic period.

The sub-triangular motifs in Row C, with two coiled tips and a stem, are early (III and II B.C.). The duck-head on C22 is rare in Britain, but characteristic of the Early Celtic style in general.

From this series, in our "middle phase", come the "domed trumpet" forms initiated in B23 (river Witham dagger) and developed in D24–29, 31. The trumpet almost always has a curved stem, and the "dome" curls round a boss—but sometimes the boss is associated with the stem (D28), or there may be a boss at both ends (D29). A triple structure tends to develop out of this series, here illustrated by D30.

The E series dominates the primary phase of our art (late III and early II B.C.) and then fades out: the tight spirals of 36 and 41, the bat-wings of 35 and 38, and the incomprehensible irregularities of 40 are characteristic.

Turning to Figure 83: the few rectilinear forms met with include swastikas (44–45), triangles (48–49), and a whirligig (47). Other patterns, whose only unity is that their character is governed by circles or segments of circles, are set out in Rows G and H. The Celtic tendency to create complexes approximating to circular form is illustrated (55). No. 52 suggests that the Celtic comma-form, one side of which is formed by a double curve—as pattern 59 on this sheet—may arise from a wave-like division of the circle; this is seen also in No. 57. Further analysis is here unnecessary: the last five shapes on the Figure are voids commonly met with; 98 and 99 show the care frequently taken by the craftsmen in secondary aspects of their designs; 100–101 are less happy.

Many of the motifs here set out recur century after century, and their continued presence helps to maintain the unity of the style; others have a very short life in our art—such as the tight spiral (41) which is almost entirely confined to the Marnian phase, round about 200 B.C.

Again, when two or three motifs merge to form a pattern, they decay or are transformed, or lost, as readily as any other larger complex the art provides. This is well shown in Figure 56, where the fan, the comma, and the circle are united as a two-dimensional pattern in B^1 and B^2; decay and elimination follows, and only the fan survives recognizably in the third "generation" thereafter.

Figure 52 illustrates the reverse process; the enrichment of a comparatively simple palmette form common in continental art (and present as such in Britain, e.g. on the Desborough mirror) into a complex pattern (Polden Hill).

A motif called "primary" is not necessarily early: it is just an elementary form (such as K84 which does not appear until late I B.C.). Some long-lived forms continually breed novelties—such as series C23–D28, followed by L92–96. Lastly, this collection is partly subjective, since it includes forms with two elements which for one reason or another have impressed the writer, perhaps unduly. Now a start has been made, later workers may well improve it, both by addition and subtraction.

NOTES

[1] Primary references:—

    (*a*) Déchelette, *Manuel d'Archéologie*, Paris: Premier Age du Fer, 1913—Second Age du Fer, 1914.

    (*b*) Dr. Paul Jacobsthal, *Early Celtic Art*, Vol. I, text; Vol. II plates. Oxford University Press, 1944.

    (*c*) J. M. de Navarro, "Survey . . . on an Early Phase of Celtic Culture", *Proc. British Academy*, Vol. XXII, 1936, *esp.* pp. 5 and 29–30: and his chapter on "The Celts of Britain and their Art", in *Heritage of Early Britain*, Bell and Sons, 1952, pp. 56–82.

    (*d*) R. J. C. Atkinson and Stuart Piggott, "The Torrs Chamfrein", *Archaeologia* 96, 1955, pp. 197–235.

[2] R. A. Smith, *Archaeologia LXXIX*, pp. 1–12, *Plates I–IV*; Paul Jacobsthal, op. cit., *Plates 178–83*, pp. 24, 27, 37–8, 90, 153 ff., and *esp.* 200–1. Several of these flagons are regarded by P.J. as of Etruscan origin, but though he includes the associated "jar" in this category, he omits the flagon.

[3] The technique is remarkable. A pattern of *voids* is cut in a prepared sheet of thin bronze; coral plates are fixed at the back, covering all the voids, and the sheet is then fixed to the body of the flagon at throat and foot.

[4] Déchelette, op. cit., p. 912. The Brenner pass was the chief route across the Alps (see Map A).

[5] Sir Thomas Kendrick, *Anglo-Saxon Art*, p. 3. "Celtic society in Britain seems to have been essentially oligarchic."

[6] The Swedish elements in the Sutton Hoo treasure in the British Museum, accumulated by an East Anglian royal family in early VII A.D., afford a later demonstration of such aristocratic culture and wealth in Britain.

[7] Déchelette, op. cit., II, p. 1060.

[8] Figure 124, p. 1024, and Figure 125, p. 1025.

[9] The Belgae of Gaul and Britain, C. Hawkes and G. C. Dunning, *Arch. Journ.* 1930 (LXXXVII), pp. 150–335.

[10] P. Bosch-Gimpera, "Two Celtic Waves in Spain", *Proc. British Academy*, 1940 (but he regards Late Bronze Age folk as Celts; p. 30 ff.). For a summary of the evidence in Britain for the prehistoric tin trade, see Hencken, *Archaeology of Cornwall and Scilly*, chapter V, pp. 158–88, particularly Figure 46.

[11] J. G. Milne, *Finds of Greek Coins in the British Isles*: Aileen Fox, "Two Greek Silver Coins from Holne, South Devon", *Ant. Journ.*, 1950, pp. 152–5.

[11a] *Excavations at Hengistbury Head, Hants.* Soc. Ant. Lond., 1915.

[12] See p. 2 below. Works of art and craft may have reached our western coastal districts by this sea-route in earlier centuries, and the Clwyd estuary may have been a port-of-call. The remarkable and unique hoard of bronze horse-trappings from Parc-y-meirch, Denbighshire, well represented in the Museum, comes first to mind; the site is only a mile from the estuary. Its date will be *c.* VII B.C. (T. E. Sheppard, *Arch. Camb.*, 1941, pp. 1–10). The wealth of the region in the 1st millennium B.C. is illustrated by the famous gold corslet found in a burial mound at Mold, Flintshire (T. G. E. Powell, *Proc. Prehist. Soc.*, 1953, pp. 161–79). But see my p. 56 where its importance is tentatively held to be due to its position on a gold route.

[13] Plough agriculture was probably introduced into south Britain about 800 B.C., and in an intensive form into south-east Britain by the Belgae about 75 B.C. (p. 59 below). See J. G. D. Clark, *Prehistoric Europe*, p. 106.

[14] First defined by myself in 1927 in *Arch. Camb.*, pp. 96 ff. See also the study by W. F. Grimes in *Aspects of Archaeology*, 1951, pp. 144 ff.

[15] "Llyn Cerrig", Anglesey, Report, 1946 (National Museum of Wales), Figure 34.

[16] These settlers may have come by the western sea-route up the Irish Channel: or they are an offshoot of the Yorkshire folk; or, landing at Tynemouth, they took the Bronze Age route (crossing the Pennines south of Bell Crags to the Solway Firth region (*Personality of Britain*, Map B). The scattered finds of Celtic art in Scotland, mostly late, are not *systematically* discussed in this book: Professor Stuart Piggott is working on them.

[17] See "Sutton Walls, Herefordshire"; K. Kenyon, *Arch. Journ.*, 1953, p. 1 ff.

[18] The Cuchullain Saga, product of this region, represents to perfection the kind of human society we are discussing in this book.

[19] See my p. 110 below, and Hawkes and Hull, *Camulodunum* (Society of Antiquaries), 1947, p. 46.

[20] Fox, *Ant. Journ.*, 1947, *Plate XVIII* and Figure 1.

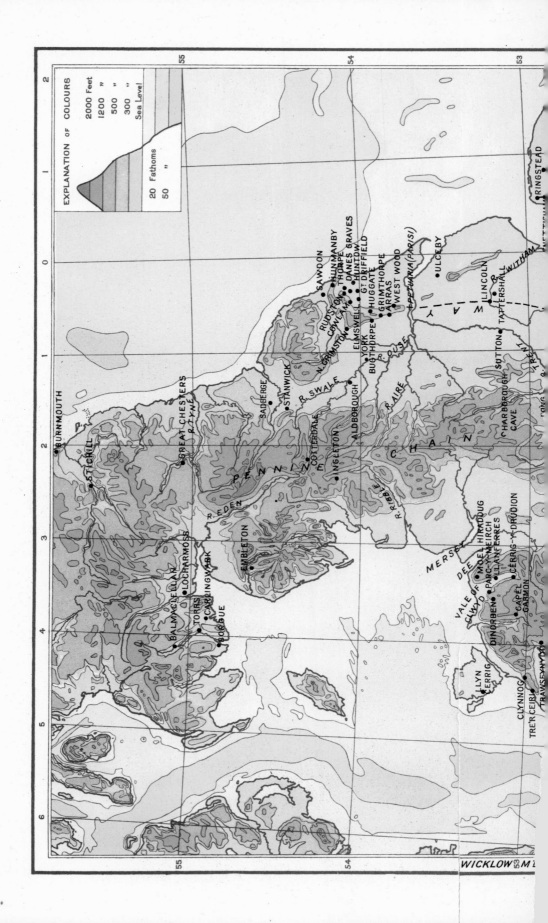

LONDON RIVER SITES:
BATTERSEA
BRENTFORD
CHELSEA
GT. TOWER ST.
HAMMERSMITH
HOUNSLOW
RICHMOND
WANDSWORTH
WATERLOO BRIDGE

1 Long. West of Greenw. 0 Long. East of Greenw. 1

MAP B. EARLY CELTIC ART: SITES REFERRED TO,
NO COINS INCLUDED.

W. & A. K. Johnston & G. W. Bacon Ltd. Edinburgh & London.
Natural Scale 1 : 2,534,400 or 40 miles to one inch
Simple Conic Projection

English Miles
Kilometres

Part I

CHAPTER I. BRONZES HELD TO BE IMPORTED : III B.C.

The first examples of the brilliant art of the Celts to reach Britain are important; they will have set a fashion, or created a demand among the Iron Age "A" folk, which may account for some later pieces in areas not occupied by the "B" invaders. Sixteen objects—a bowl, a horn-cap, and dagger or sword sheaths—are here discussed.

(i) BRONZES WITH INCISED PALMETTE-AND-SCROLL PATTERNS

Hanging-bowl, Cerrig-y-Drudion, Denbighshire

The finest of all presumed imports from Gaul in this early period is the bronze hanging-bowl[1] "found in a stone cist at Cerrig-y-Drudion" (Map B), in our Museum; a reconstruction and carefully detailed record of the ornament is reproduced here (Figure 1: see also Figure 82, 4). It is designed to hang by four chains, high up, since the ornament on flange and base can only be seen from below; in the remote corner of the world whereto it came, it may have been suspended from the roof of a large hut—such as those at Holyhead, Anglesey—as a lamp carrying oil and a "floating" wick. The round base was artistically the most important part; only a fragment survives, suggesting bold scrollwork of continental (Waldalgesheim) style (p. xxiii above). Two "palmette" forms, derived from an Italo-Greek source (Figure 82, A1), alternate on the underside of the surviving portion of the flange, and bold "acanthus" half-palmettes are also prominent; the ribbons linking all these are broad, with central rib,[2] and the background is filled with an irregular "basketry" pattern. The complete design of the base cannot be reconstructed; a more elaborate side may have been intended to face the place of honour in any room in which it came to be hung. The character of "palmette" patterns when elongated as they are on the rim is difficult to grasp; in a later illustration (Figure 54) the design is compressed, and the ribbons are seen as opposed scrolls, shaped like a Greek musical instrument, the lyre.[3]

"Lyres" and "palmettes", then, are often associated in Early Celtic art; we shall, indeed see such motifs recurrent through the centuries—sometimes dominant, sometimes recessive; a never-failing stimulus to the Celtic bronze-smith's pattern-making, as the series AB1–15 on my Figure 82 demonstrates.

The closest parallel to the palmette ornament on our bowl is on a pottery vase from Finistère (Brittany),[4] and it probably came from western Gaul (Map A), not later than 300 B.C. Students of post-Roman art will observe, then, that it precedes the remarkable series of hanging-bowls found in Anglo-Saxon contexts in Britain by some 800 years.

Scabbard-plate, Wisbech, Cambridgeshire

A second probable import, with similar but simpler ornament, is the Wisbech (Cambs.), scabbard made to house a short sword, part of which survives (Figure 2).[5] The ladder of

FIGURE 2.—Scabbard plate: Wisbech (Cambs.) (⅓).

I

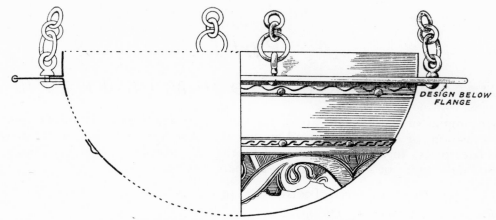

Elevation and section of bronze bowl from Denbighshire (½)

Decoration and details of bronze bowl from Denbighshire ½ with restoration ⅙

FIGURE 1.—Hanging-bowl, Cerrig-y-Drudion (Denbs.).

linked palmettes and fat scrolls, seen by the owner (looking down his thigh) as a vertical and diminishing pattern is an attractive ornament. Each palmette is thus seen upright, within a lyre-shaped frame;[6] the geometric border pattern of hatched triangles (Figure 83, F48) has a long history on the Continent, and the piece may also be dated in the mid-III century. Its relation to the Cerrig-y-Drudion bowl is illustrated in Figure 82, A5; and it forms an important link with later (British) works such as the Colchester mirror (Figure 51).

Horn-cap, the Thames at Brentford, Middlesex

An elegant waisted cast-bronze cap from the lower Thames at Brentford (*Plates 3, a, b, c,* and *4*) has a circular saucer-shaped top with a finely-wrought triple palmette pattern linked to hollow-sided triangles, with tendrils approximating to duck-heads; the palmettes (Figure 82, B10) are more conventional than those of the Cerrig-y-Drudion bowl. Movement is expressed by the inner tendrils (Figure 82, C22) bending in the same direction, but the outer, being opposed, are static: it is a carefully balanced three-way design in the Waldalgesheim style.

R. A. Smith[7] in his account of this Thames find refers to "traces of red enamel": of this, one blob—almost microscopic—remains to prove his statement. The pattern is smoothly finished, the background dull, but not visibly striated; the relief slight.

The ornament as it now is therefore needs close scrutiny for full appreciation: with a bright red background and with the golden bronze polished it would, as the enlarged and finely detailed drawing prepared for me suggests, be delicately lovely. The enamel will have been "run in" (since the relief is so slight) and then rubbed down. Dr. Jacobsthal noted that it is of his Waldalgesheim style; enamel is used on early helmets on the Continent, and the technique required is present on the enamelled stud of the lid of the Lorraine flagon (*Plate 1*); the piece, then, is continental, early III B.C.

If the reader wonders why the metal cap of a hand-hold was so delicately waisted, its base so amply moulded, and its incurved top so beautifully patterned, a glance at the model (*Plate 6*) of the vehicle the Celtic aristocracy used in peace and war will, I suggest, supply the reason. Art was one of the delights they cultivated; and each time our owner, standing in his swaying, creaking chariot—his charioteer bent low over the flying ponies—looked toward his hand-grip, the gold and vermilion pattern will have gleamed bright beside his forearm.

Note on a primary motif. The importance of the palmette forms present in each member of this group has been stressed; the wide range of the motif, as seen in the associations of Figure 82, 4, 5, and 10, is significant.

(ii) DAGGERS WITH DECORATED SHEATHS

A group of early bronze dagger-sheaths of continental origin, with variant forms of the ring-ended, knobbed chape has been found in Britain.[8] Some of the sheaths are plain, as *Plate 10a* from the river Thames at Wandsworth; others have elaborate ornament, usually geometric and in lateral bands. An example from Minster Ditch, Oxford (*Plate 10d*) shows a delicate pounced pattern—parallel strings of hollow-sided lozenges, rings, and a "spear-head"—not represented in our British art; together with a modified ring-chape in openwork, with dainty knobbed ends. Another well-known dagger-sheath in the British Museum from the Thames at Wandsworth (*Plate 10b*) has a formal lozenge pattern on either side—invisible on the only photograph obtainable—which is related to the shaded triangles of the Wisbech scabbard. It also has an elaborate oval chape decorated with linked "S-curves" in openwork starred with concentric circles: similar circles, larger, are placed centrally, top and bottom. Another British Museum photograph of a dagger from the Thames at Richmond (*Plate 10c*) ought to show the bands of zig-zag ornament with pounced background. The chape is a knobby structure in openwork, contrasting almost too strongly with the incised detail.

The distribution of these early weapons is striking, no less than eleven being concentrated in about 4 miles of the gravel-bordered reaches of the lower Thames just above London, from Chelsea to Richmond. The three others are in the middle Thames Valley (Cookham and Oxford) and in Somerset (West Buckland near Taunton).

The existence of a III century trading station on the tidal river above Westminster (at Wandsworth or Brentford?) is a possible explanation: alternatively, we may see here evidence for a Thames Valley intrusion, or invasion, by a warrior group not yet correlated with any other material culture.[9] The date of the activity this attractive series represents, whatever it be, will be in mid-III B.C.[10] A few other continental pieces associated with Marnian settlement will be discussed in the next chapter.

NOTES TO CHAPTER I

[1] R. A. Smith, *Ant. Journ.*, 1926, p. 276 ff.; see also Paul Jacobsthal, *Early Celtic Art*, p. 95; and W. F. Grimes, *Prehistory of Wales*, p. 119. An excellent general survey of the Continental background is that by J. M. de Navarro in pp. 56–74 of *The Heritage of Early Britain*, Bell and Sons, 1952.

[2] As Jacobsthal, op. cit., *Plate 278*.

[3] *Proc. Prehist. Soc.*, 1952, p. 50.

[4] R. A. Smith illustrates this: loc. cit., p. 280.

[5] Based on Stuart Piggott, *Proc. Prehist. Soc.*, 1950, p. 5.

[6] Compare similar scroll forms in Jacobsthal, op. cit., *Plates 272–3*. Two studs, of coral (?), ornamented this scroll near the mouth.

[7] R. A. Smith, *Archaeologia 69*, 1918, p. 22, Figure 22. The piece was probably found when Brentford Dock was built in the nineteenth century. Smith's figure is not quite accurate; my illustrations have been produced at the Brentford School of Art.

[8] The form, on the Continent, is seen in Jacobsthal, *Early Celtic Art*, *Plate 62* (No. 100), from Weiss-kirchen, Sarre, Germany, the ring-chape in *Plate 56* from Vert la Gravelle, Châlons-sur-Marne. Simple geometric ornament is lifted on to the plane of art on the latter scabbard. For lozenge patterns in general see *Plate 268* (*213, 217–18*), for *pointillé* ornament *Plate 58* (*94*) from Somme-Bionne, and *Plate 268* (*205, 207*, etc.).

[9] It is accepted that Iron Age "A1" settlement at Long Wittenham, Oxon., "was reached direct from the Continent by way of the Thames" (*Oxoniensia XVI*, 1951, p. 22). Our group, it is held, also came this easy way.

[10] Four are illustrated in *Proc. Soc. Ant. XXV*, opposite p. 58; three in *Arch. Journ.* 86, p. 87; three in *The Early Iron Age Guide*, B.M., 1925, *Plate IX, 1*, and Figures 119–20; and three in *Later Prehistoric Antiquities of the British Isles*, B.M. (Figure 22). The group is summarized by Stuart Piggott in *Proc. Prehist. Soc.*, 1950, pp. 3 and 4.

CHAPTER II. THE MARNIANS IN BRITAIN

We now turn to the definite beginnings of our insular Celtic culture, the importance of which, for us, is the acclimatization and modification in Britain of La Tène I art, Styles II (Waldalgesheim) and III (Plastic and Sword), brought by settlers from the Marne region—almost certainly including the Parisi, from the middle, as we now judge, of III B.C. onwards. Jacobsthal called this modification "Style IV", but we shall describe it simply as our British Iron "B" art.

The earliest of such pieces are not likely to be older than c. 230 B.C.: fine craftsmen (bronze-workers) in the retinue of invading chieftains, or brought in from overseas when the new régime was established, would have to grow into the new milieu before an insular art could arise—but the distinctive work thus envisaged would include elements, necessarily out-moded, of continental design and character.

Fine unassociated bronzes held to be British await our study and appreciation, but the evidence of lesser works associated with settlement or burials (including a few significant imports) must come first, and a picture of this chariot-culture given. Chance—or an unexplained limitation of settlement—has provided most of the evidence from north-eastern Britain (Yorkshire).

(i) The Yorkshire Wolds (East Riding): Arras, Danes' Graves, and other Cemeteries. The North Riding: Sawdon

The chalk uplands of east Yorkshire (Map B) were extensively settled; two large and several small cemeteries, marked by small mounds, have been discovered and investigated, partially and intermittently, from the early XIX century onwards. The principal sites are near Arras, a hamlet 4 miles east of Market Weighton, on the edge of the Wolds overlooking the plain of York, and "Danes' Graves", $3\frac{1}{2}$ miles north of Driffield. Cowlam is $6\frac{1}{2}$ miles north-west of the latter town. *Petuaria*, at Brough, on the Humber estuary, the capital of the *Parisi* in the Roman period and probably the original focus of their settlement, is also indicated.[1]

There were said to be up to 500 mounds in the Danes' Graves, and the Arras cemetery was comparable in extent: nothing of them is visible today. The only reasonably competent record is the well-known survey *Early Iron Age Burials in Yorkshire*, by William Greenwell,[2] in which excavations carried on in each of these throughout the XIX century and his own work at Danes' Graves are summarized, and finds from lesser cemeteries referred to. Greenwell provides no plan of any one of the numerous barrows opened by him, and there is, indeed, only one published "sketch" of an excavated barrow of the period in this rich area, in Mortimer's *Burial Mounds of East Yorkshire*; it is one of that important type in which parts of a chariot, and (or) chariot fittings are found in the grave. These rich barrows (very scarce) were interspersed with smaller mounds, some of which contained only a skeleton; in others this was associated with a jar of coarse pottery and a bone representing a joint of pork.[3] Such joints, even a whole pig, were placed with the aristocrats, as with the commonalty: their burial ritual must have been basically similar.

We are, then, studying communities consisting of chariot-using chieftains and their followers or subjects (many of the latter being probably natives of the region, since similar cemeteries occur in the adjacent Cleveland Hills). The invaders seem to have been mainly a pastoral folk, pony and pig-breeders; not necessarily numerous, for the cemeteries may cover as long a period as two hundred years, c. 250–50 B.C. We shall have cause to think that after a phase of achievement, the Wolds became a cultural backwater.

The earliest approximately dateable object is a small damaged brooch associated with a necklace of blue glass beads some with opaque white inlay, and a bronze armlet, in the grave of an old lady under a barrow in the Cowlam cemetery (*Plate 2a, d*). The brooch has a spring with external chord (as the writer noted from the broken portion in 1955), and an undecorated flat disc terminating the reverted foot, which approached the bow at a slight angle, as Figure 13 (*b*) from Wood Eaton (Oxon). That the owner brought it with her in mid-III B.C. is likely;[4] the same applies to a possibly identical, damaged, brooch from another Marnian settlement at Worth, Kent.[5]

The country thus entered was probably, then, much like the upland of Champagne the intruders had left; but to get a mental picture of it, as I found in an extensive traverse, is very difficult today. The former open downlands with close-cropped turf can only be seen here and there on marginal scarps (western and northern), and on the slopes of little combes too steep to plough; elsewhere there is now intensive cultivation, arable and ley. The chalk formation, of which this is the northernmost outcrop, ends at Flamborough Head; hence, perhaps, the limitation of intensive settlement at this period to the East Riding.[6]

Bronze was the metal the local aristocracy prized, having had plenty in the homeland, but it was hard to come by in north-eastern Britain; the fittings of the chariots and the harness, nave-hoops, and linch-pins—as well as, of course, wheel-tires, terrets for the reins, and bridle-bits—are mostly of iron, the smaller objects being usually coated with molten bronze, a technique commonly seen in the later Llyn Cerrig find, in Anglesey. The Celtic chariot— already referred to—was, of course, geared to the tractive power available, ponies the size of the Shetland breed, and so is surprisingly small; the Danes' Graves wheels, for example, are from 2 ft. 5 in. to 3 ft. only in diameter. The construction of such chariots, now fairly well understood, is illustrated in a scale drawing (Figure 40) as well as on *Plate 6*.[7]

From four of the chariot burials works of art and craft survive, and understandably colourful titles were provided for three by the excavators; it is from the Charioteer's, the King's, and the Queen's barrows (and, I would add, the Lady's) in the Arras cemetery that most of our information about this Celtic art and British life of late III and early II B.C. in north-eastern Britain derives.

Three objects coming from the Charioteer's barrow will first be described. Two of them are tines of red-deer antler, crudely ornamented with criss-cross incisions and with rounded tops hollowed at the lower end and with a lateral hole for a wooden pin: they were exactly the size and shape required for the hand-grasp to mount a chariot, and their surfaces were polished by use.[8] They were placed on the body together with the bronze reinforcement

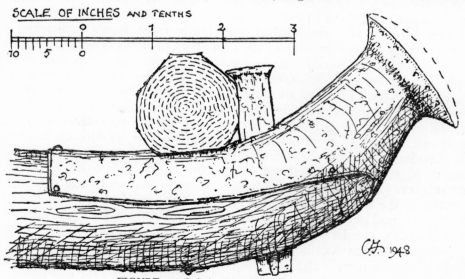

SCALE OF INCHES AND TENTHS

FIGURE 3.—Poletip, bronze: Arras (Yorks.).

6

of the tip of the chariot pole (Figure 3) which formerly had a decorative head (of shell or paste, bright red).[9] The Figure shows its relation to the yoke (lashed to an iron pin, for which a hole was provided).

The slenderness of the charioteer's pole as indicated by this sheath is a remarkable feature. It was about 1.7 in. in greatest diameter, the Llyn Cerrig[10] pole-tip being 2.4 in. It had been used and damaged, and was most carefully wrought; it was not a part of a light funerary vehicle.

How then are we to account for such a difference? It may be that there were two classes of chariot in use in Britain, a light chariot for ceremonial parade or social occasion and a heavier chariot for war (p. 59 below—a likely state of affairs where a military aristocracy was concerned.)[11]

In the King's Barrow an old man was buried with chariot-wheels on either side of him— that is, he lay, like the Marne chieftains, stretched out on the floor of the vehicle: the iron hoops of the naves were coated with bronze. The skeleton of a "horse" (pony) lay partly under each of the wheels; both ponies were under thirteen hands. The bridle-bits were of iron, bronze-coated; one is figured here (*Plate 5a*). Note the narrow projection and hollow moulding on the central link: they are early features. The joins of the bronze sheet are along the outer faces of the rings; the iron, rusty and proliferating, has burst this casing in places.[12] Another Arras barrow yielded a bit-ring of unusual character, lipped: this detail is sketched in Figure 83, K91.

The Lady's Barrow contained much chariot furniture, notably a bridle-bit wholly of bronze, light in weight and dainty in shape, and a nave-hoop of bronze, with internal, central iron band. Her mirror (*Plate 7a*) is of iron, bronze-mounted; the lobes above the loop, and at the junction of handle and disc, are typically Marnian. The comparable ornaments of a mirror from La Motte St. Valentin, Haute Marne, are inset.[13]

The fourth barrow in this series, the "Queen's Barrow", yielded a remarkable variety of interesting things; there was a necklace of glass beads, up to $\frac{3}{4}$-in. in diameter, and parti-coloured, greenish-blue in two shades, with white annulets (*Plate 8a*); and a brooch (*Plate 9cd,*) with reverted foot joined to the bow—of early La Tène II character, ornamented with bosses and bars of shell, probably coral.[14] The radial plan of the foot is notable; the pin is hinged, the ribbed crossbar simulating a coiled spring. There is also a circular pendant (*Plate 9a*) with three zones of encrustation, and a ring-headed shouldered pin (*Plate 9b* and Figure 83, H69) with embossed "spokes", similarly decorated.[15] The "Queen" also had a circlet of amber, but the most rare and dainty of her possessions is a gold finger-ring (*Plate 8b* and Figure 82, A8). This imported (?) III century piece is built up of two parallel strips of stout gold wire expanding at the front into looped coils whose salients are decorated with three gold balls. Coils of the same character are prominent in the ornament of the diadem of Vix[16]

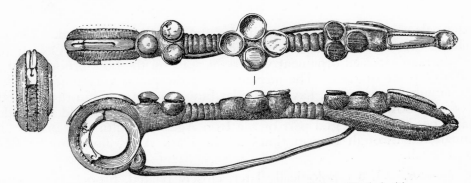

FIGURE 4.—Brooch, bronze: Danes' Graves, Kilham (Yorks.). ($\frac{1}{1}$)

(Chatillon-sur-Seine). A delicate "twist" fills the V-shaped hollow of the ring structure, the whole of which is fused into a smooth flat on the inner face. Bronze bracelets of Marnian type and a pin with free-moving ring-head completed this—for the region—uniquely rich burial.

Brooch-development. An example of the brooch-form with nearly flat bow (Figure 4) comes from the Danes' Graves cemetery. It is a clumsy piece, enriched with cup-shaped seatings, some retaining their ornamental bosses of "white stone, tufa or travertine". The ring at the head is functionless; the pin is hinged.[17]

Flat-bowed brooches. The flattening of the bow referred to above became absolute, as the Yorkshire series shows. A badly eroded iron example from the Danes' Graves is known, and a barrow at Huntow, near Bridlington, also in the East Riding, yielded a bronze specimen together with two massive penannular brooches. From the North Riding, at Sawdon, comes a similar flat-bowed brooch, and another penannular brooch.

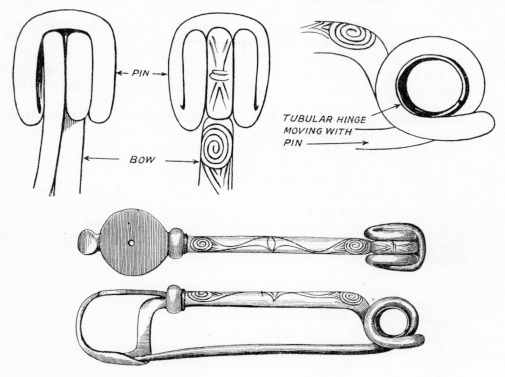

FIGURE 5.—Brooch, flat-bowed: Sawdon (North Riding, Yorks.). (¼) detail enlarged ⅔/₁

The latter pair, now in the Scarborough Museum,[18] is here illustrated. The photograph (*Plate 11a*) shows the character and patina of each, the line-block (Figure 5) early (*c.* 200 B.C.) curvilinear "Marnian" incised ornament with tight coils on the bow-brooch, and the seating for a lost boss of paste or tufa. The mechanism of the pin is very ingenious. The outer linked loops, simulating a spring, have a tubular hinge moving within the decorated central unit, part of the bow structure. The penannular brooch, it should be added, is not a continental type, but an integral part of the Iron Age "B" culture in Britain: it survived practically unaltered through Roman times to the Dark Ages, flowering in Celtic lands: e.g. the Tara brooch.

Involuted brooches. Of a typologically later, closely related, brooch type, with incurved bow peculiar to Britain, two examples come from the Danes' Graves cemetery. The more

8

elaborate—a showy, coarse piece (*Plate 9e, f*)—has bossy applied ornament in vitreous paste which is typically continental: lobes derived from the palmette, and elements of Jacobsthal's Waldalgesheim and Plastic styles, coily "snailshells", are present (Figure 83, H61). The pin moves on a pivot, and the decorative flower-like moulded cap, shown separately, fits on the hinge-plate. There was a smaller brooch of the same involuted character in the grave, but its pin is hinged on an open ring. The type illustrates the tendency of fashion in all societies to go to extremes before revulsion sets in.

Bracelets. Mention has been made of bracelets in this account of the Yorkshire burials: no group of women's gear in the barrows exceeds in technical quality the best of such. The example from an Arras grave now in York Museum (*Plate 11b*) is 2½ in. in diameter. The smooth internal face of half-round section slides easily on the wrist. The ovoid knobs, each ⅝-in. long, finely polished, are seen, by the wearer, to be linked by the narrower basal structure of the piece; each interspace has two delicate, exactly parallel, striations at right-angles to the plane of the bracelet. It is probably an import from Gaul, like those found in south-west Britain (p. 14).

Character and time-range of the Yorkshire culture. Such is the character of the Marnian settlement as illustrated by the British development of Marnian art and craft in Yorkshire (Map B): the importance of the chariot burials, and the absence of offensive weapons[19] have been commented on by students of the period. The showy brooches encrusted with coral or paste seem to represent a distinct north-eastern style, but the existence of a pin from the river Thames at Hammersmith (*Plate 2, E*), formerly decorated with knobs and bar of similar material, suggests a wider distribution of the technique in Britain.

Covering, as the known burials in the extensive cemeteries may have done, well over a hundred and fifty years, from *c.* 250 to 100 B.C.,[20] we may have to regard the northern culture as representing, towards the close, an archaic survival.[21] Most of the works of art described and illustrated, however, belong to the creative phase.

Nothing has hitherto been said in this chapter about the incompetence of early nineteenth-century diggers in the Wold barrows, Arras in particular, nor has the division of unstudied, unrecorded loot of numerous graves among the participants been mentioned: at its close it is better to dwell on the sociologically interesting facts which their wholesale methods (and those of their successor and chief chronicler, Greenwell himself, who opened sixty-four barrows) revealed, of the close and apparently unmindful association of prince and peasant in death: rich and poor, one with another: and to emphasize the mass of information and illustration embodied in the discursive pages of Greenwell's classic record.

(ii) DERBYSHIRE

Numerous objects of bone and antler, a few of bronze, and one of gold, have been found with other signs of occupation in Harborough Cave, The Peak, Derbyshire (Map B). Some are of early Iron Age date, such as a bronze bridle-ring with stop-knobs, and a brooch. The latter is of outstanding quality,[22] resembling the one from the Queen's Barrow: the illustration (*Plate 8c*) which shows both its present appearance and original character, will help the reader to appreciate the damaged Yorkshire example of the type. The radial display of ornament (coral) at the foot will have been a striking feature, if as is likely the brooch was worn, as a fastening for the cloak, on the breast. Though the cave can hardly have been other than a refuge for robbers, the costly ornament suggests a wider distribution than the known burials indicate for the aristocratic Yorkshire culture in the north, and may have some bearing on later activities in the west, the Clwyd region.

9

Slight evidence from burials, or other concentrations of this culture, comes from Suffolk and Cambridgeshire: it is likely that Marnians came into the Wash at the same time as they entered the Humber, pushing up the rivers Ouse and Cam (Map B).

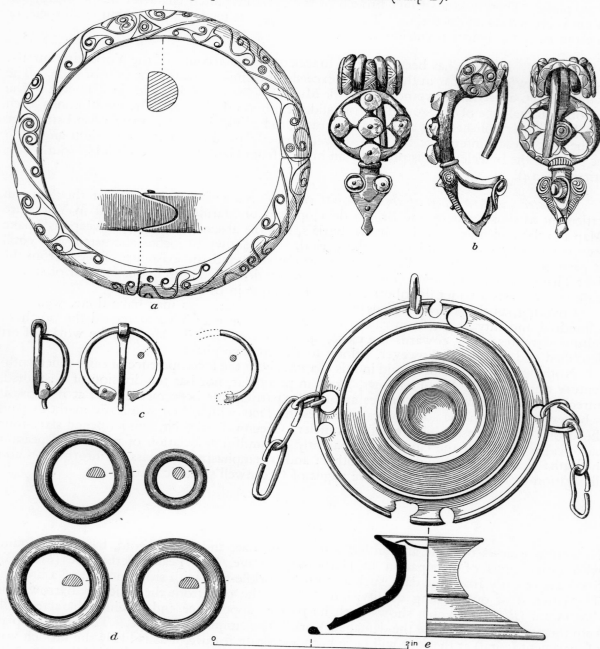

FIGURE 6.—Bronzes: (*a*) arm-ring; (*b, c*) brooches; (*d*) rings; (*e*) pony-cap with dingle-dangles. Chariot burial, Newnham Croft (Cambs.). ¼

At Mildenhall in the former county a chieftain had been laid in a grave between two "horses" (ponies, no doubt); he was equipped with an iron sword and axe, and had a "gold torc". None of these is preserved.[23]   At Icklingham, Suffolk, an early bronze bracelet, ribbed, was found in a child's burial.

At Newnham Croft, Cambridge, the well-known rich burial was of a middle-aged man; he had an imported arm-ring of cast bronze.   The delicate Marnian running ornament thereon, which becomes an important element of our insular tradition, consists of wandering scroll forms, defined diagonally by more purposeful stems: at one point a triangle-with-circle intrudes (Figures 6 and 82, C16 to 19).   The technique is masterly.   The warrior also had a brooch; beset with knobs of shell on the wheel-shaped bow, geometric incised ornament of "Waldalgesheim Style" on bow and spring, with relief work in the "Plastic Style" (snaily coils) on the triangular foot[24] (Figure 6).   It is very delicately wrought, and in structure unlike the northern brooches.   A bronze ornament with chains, probably for making a cheerful tinkle above a pony's head-harness, as in examples from Denmark,[25] suggested that much of the associated deposit (? a chariot) had been overlooked, or destroyed before the burial was discovered.[26]   Earlier imported bronzes (of Hallstatt character) probably designed for the same noisy purpose, but hung on the pony's breast, are in our Museum.   This rich burial is later than it looks; the brooch, being transitional (to La Tène II) dates it in II B.C.[27]

(iv) Northamptonshire and Nottinghamshire

Hunsbury. We know little of the dwelling places of the chieftains whose possessions we are studying, but the plateau of Hunsbury (Northants), where a ring-work of considerable strength was built, seems to have been settled by Marnians who, entering from the Wash by

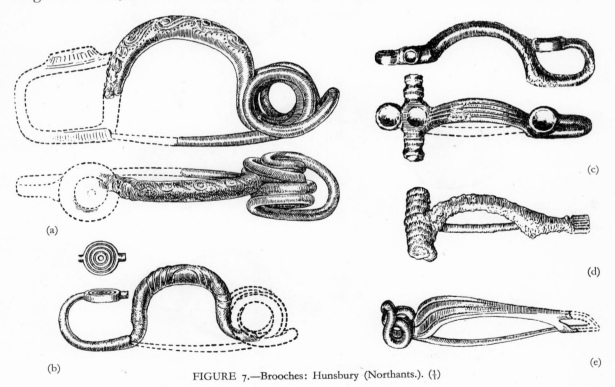

FIGURE 7.—Brooches: Hunsbury (Northants.). (½)

the river Nene (?) and attracted by the accessible iron-bearing deposits, evicted, or lorded over, earlier (Iron "A") occupants.[28]   It is situated on a dominant ridge near Northampton, on the "Jurassic highway" (mentioned in the Introduction and shown on Map B) which provided good communication from the south-west (the Mendips and beyond) by way of

Lincoln Edge and a Humber "ferry-crossing", to the Yorkshire Wolds. This upland probably forms—except in the middle Trent region—the western flank of the country occupied by the newcomers.

Hunsbury ring-work and its immediate neighbourhood has yielded a chariot burial with terret-rings of iron bronze-coated, like several from the Yorkshire graves, and two early II century brooches closely resembling my Figure 13d. One of the latter (Figure 7a) shows a series of enclosed palmettes on the bow: the second has simpler curvilinear ornament.[29] A bronze bowl from the site with three zones of "duck-pattern" is illustrated on *Plate 77B*: it is a survival of Iron Age "A" technique.

This pattern was persistent; it is seen on a I A.D. casket at Winchester only slightly modified (*Plate 77, A2*).

Red Hill. A bird-brooch from a site at Red Hill on the bank of the river Soar near its confluence with the Trent, in south Nottinghamshire, originally embellished with coral, and of Marnian character, is illustrated on Figure 8[30]; its originality and significance is well brought out in the reference indicated, but the damage it has suffered seriously reduces its interest as a work of art. Dating about 220 B.C., it suggests early settlement at a point important for east–west communications.

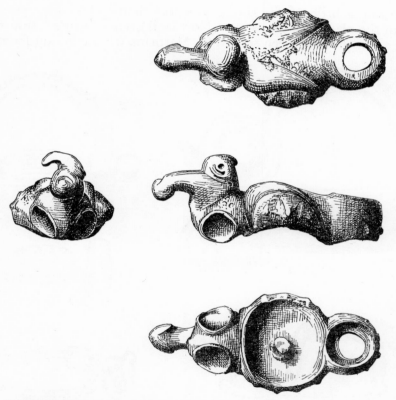

FIGURE 8.—"Bird" brooch, four aspects of: Red Hill (Notts.). Pin and spring structure missing; also settings. ($\frac{2}{1}$)

(v) The "Oxford" Region

River routes were probably used by the Marnian invaders, the Thames in particular; we recall the earlier series of daggers, examples of which came from both tidal water and the middle reaches. Works of art from the former zone will be discussed in the next chapter;

we are here concerned with the middle Thames valley, the "Oxford region", as a possible area of Marnian settlement. It was fully occupied in the Bronze Age, and Iron Age "A" settlement is established. A little brooch from Wood Eaton[31] closely related to the Red Hill example, and two involuted—and therefore British-made—brooches have been found hereabouts, one being the famous early example from Beckley in the Ashmolean Museum. This is illustrated by a photograph (*Plate 12a*)—which shows the patina of the piece and its

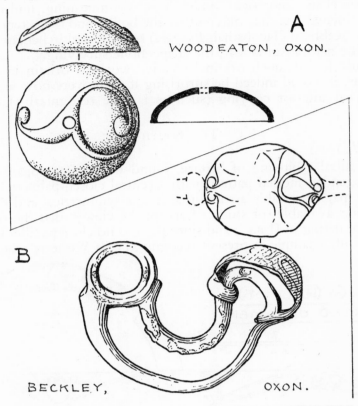

A

WOOD EATON, OXON.

B

BECKLEY, OXON.

FIGURE 9.—A. Bronze disc: Wood Eaton. B. Brooch: Beckley (Oxon.).

finely adjusted proportions—and by a drawing (Figure 9b)[32] which brings out all that can be known of the much-worn group of "hollow triangles" linked in pairs and with knobbed terminals, that forms the ornament (Marnian in character) on the strangely-expanded foot. This decoration is an insular interpretation of the Waldalgesheim style to be dated as early (*c.* 200 B.C. ?) as the novel form of the brooch permits. How attractive the open ring and the shining curve of the ornament would be if, as is likely, the dainty piece were set upright on a lady's bosom as a dress fastener!

The Standlake Sword-scabbard. Another and more important piece is the sword-scabbard from Standlake (Oxon), illustrated on *Plate 22a*; the striking ornament is on both locket and chape.[33] The former shows, *to the wearer*, a loop in bold relief with stem expanding into a broad head of semi-circular outline with pointed tips and hollow centre; it is no doubt derived from the closed palmette (Figure 82, A7*b*). There is a matted background: not the formal chequer-work of a later period, but an irregular series of incisions in the bronze (Figure 83, K81), more like those on the Cerrig-y-Drudion bowl, defining a "flat" pattern in smooth metal which is closely related to, and so enriches, the relief work. This secondary pattern is shown independently in Figure 82, A7a.   The bronze chape extends from the tip to half-way up the scabbard; the same secondary pattern, more elaborately developed (Figure 83, K90), is here, with its matted background faintly apparent (the scabbard had long service and the metal is worn smooth).   Outlined in sinuous coils, this is a coarsened version of Continental ornament, as a glance at *Plates 96* to *99* of Jacobsthal's corpus, illustrating the chariot-burial of Waldalgesheim, will show the enquiring student.   The sub-angular openings on either side of the chape, moreover, which look so unmeaning, find close parallels at an earlier stage in Continental art; they differentiate the bodies and the extended heads and necks of flying ducks, as a scabbard (Jacobsthal, *Plate 62*) from Weisskirchen, among others, shows. In our later piece the naturalism is lost, the shape alone surviving.

We have already found much original creative work in Britain in this early phase of Iron "B" settlement; it would indeed be surprising if there were now no derivative pattern-making, or somewhat inferior copying (such as is here recognizable), carried out in the insular workshops.

(vi)   THE SOUTH-WEST

Bridle-bit ring, Yeovil (Som.)

One-half of a tubular bit-ring of bronze, found with other objects at West Coker, in Somerset, has an extended incised pattern with a central closed-palmette feature (Figures 10 and 82, B15).   We may reasonably assume that it was symmetrical and that all the elements of the design are thus available for study.   I accept the view[33a] that the running scroll-work is of Marnian origin, dating in II B.C.; and since there is no close parallel it may provisionally be regarded as the only example at present recognized of a Western School of the period.

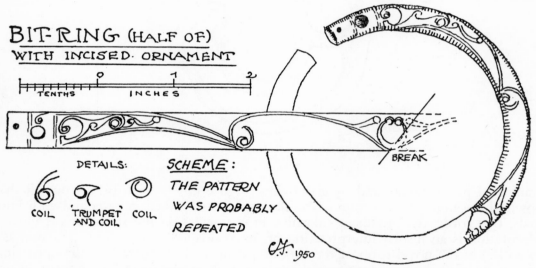

FIGURE 10.—Bit-ring, West Coker (Som.).

Finds at Mount Batten, Plymouth (Devon)

At a few south-west coastal sites, the chief of which is "Mount Batten"[34]—the rocky promontory which flanks the natural harbour of the Cattewater at Plymouth—the objects from burials and middens discovered in the nineteenth century include bracelets and armlets imported from Gaul as well as the Spanish brooches already mentioned.   No. 21 on *Plate 31* is identical with that illustrated in *Plate 11b* from grave 43 at Arras, and others (22 and 23) are similar.   Part of an elaborate armlet, No. 28, is designed as a succession of domes; it also is almost certainly an import.   These exotic objects—destroyed during the War, and surviving

14

only in poor illustrations—should represent contacts effected by the tin trade, at landing places convenient for early traders from Western Gaul; settlement, by a Marnian group, cannot be excluded, for there are British brooch-types in the collection (Nos. 26–27: compare (*a*) and (*c*) in Figure 13).

An extensive cemetery of the period has been examined at Harlyn Bay, north Cornwall, the scarcity of bronze in which underlines the comparative poverty of the native Cornish folk.[35]

Traffic up the western sea-route may be held to account for a collar of the same type as the armlets found at Mount Batten, reaching Clynnog (Caerns.).[36]

(vii) KENT

The invaders did not, apparently, develop a wide-spread culture in Kent, as might have been expected: it was an obvious landfall, and localized settlement in east Kent and the Medway valley, contemporary with those we have been considering, is proven. At Worth, near Sandwich, fine pottery, carinated like the ware found in the homeland, together with an early brooch with large spring coils and high-arched bow, as my Figure 13f, are on record,[37] but the material is very fragmentary.

(viii) INTERPOSED: THE MAIDEN CASTLE, DORSET, BROOCH: WITH OBSERVATIONS ON EARLY BROOCHES AND PINS IN BRITAIN

From a workshop in the middle Thames region, probably, comes a very remarkable brooch illustrating Marnian artistry modified in Britain; its find-spot was, surprisingly enough,

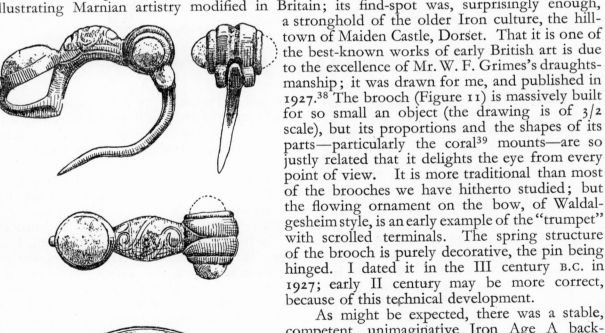

a stronghold of the older Iron culture, the hill-town of Maiden Castle, Dorset. That it is one of the best-known works of early British art is due to the excellence of Mr. W. F. Grimes's draughts-manship; it was drawn for me, and published in 1927.[38] The brooch (Figure 11) is massively built for so small an object (the drawing is of 3/2 scale), but its proportions and the shapes of its parts—particularly the coral[39] mounts—are so justly related that it delights the eye from every point of view. It is more traditional than most of the brooches we have hitherto studied; but the flowing ornament on the bow, of Waldal-gesheim style, is an early example of the "trumpet" with scrolled terminals. The spring structure of the brooch is purely decorative, the pin being hinged. I dated it in the III century B.C. in 1927; early II century may be more correct, because of this technical development.

As might be expected, there was a stable, competent, unimaginative Iron Age A back-ground to the virtuosity, technical skill, and ingenuity shown by the Marnians in this minor field of artistry and craftsmanship; this will be briefly recorded.

The well-known evolution of the brooch in western Europe between 500 and 100 B.C.—

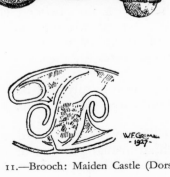

FIGURE 11.—Brooch: Maiden Castle (Dorset). $\frac{3}{2}$

the key to which is the development of the "foot"—is illustrated in Figure 12.[40] The stage reached on the Continent in the III century B.C. at the time of the Marnian invasion is lettered D, but phase C long continued in use in the less advanced districts of western Gaul, and it is likely to have been the commonest type made in Britain for the first half-century or so after the arrival of the Marnians.

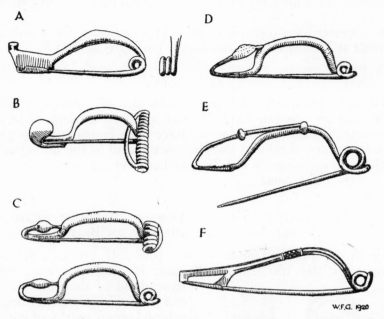

FIGURE 12.—Evolution of the brooch in Western Europe, *c.* 500–1 B.C.
(After W. F. Grimes.)

These phases, C and D, are summarily illustrated in Figure 13 by British examples; the change is, as will be seen, very gradual. The coil spring of the pin does not vary much in structure; the loop is almost always external.[41] The omission of the spring in the Maiden Castle brooch, is, as we have seen, characteristic of the specialized work of the settlers (*Plates 8c*, *9d* and *e*, and *12a*: also Figure 4).

The knobbed foot, and the linear and dotted ornament on the bow of the Blandford brooch (*a*) are associated in several brooches; equally characteristic is the disc terminating the foot of, and the later decoration on, the Wood Eaton example (*b*).

A beaked or knobby foot-terminal then develops: (*c*), (*d*). The Avebury (Wilts.) brooch carried a setting of coral or paste, the Box (Wilts.) brooch has a curvilinear pattern on the bow like one from Hunsbury (p. 11 above), while the river Thames broad-bowed specimen has a vesica-like decoration. The series is also represented by a fine brooch (*f*) from the Hammersmith reach of the Thames, which retains not only the red stud (of shell (?) imitating coral) on the foot, but also the thin bronze plates which fitted into each end of the large coil-spring, thus closing the openings. The attachment of these plates, by means of a cylinder of wood and a rivet, is illustrated in the sketch.

The last brooch to be illustrated here (*g*) is the latest typologically: flat-bowed, massive, with triangular foot, it comes from a famous Iron Age hill-fort—Ham Hill in Somerset. It is suitable for fastening a cloak.

The study of these early brooches of simple type in Britain is complicated in some cases by the difficulty of deciding whether we are dealing with an insular product or an import, in other cases by the problem of date. In south Britain (Wessex) which, apart from small pockets

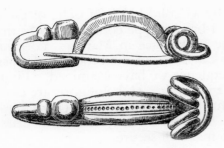

a. Blandford (Dorset).

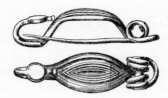

e. River Thames ("London").

b. Wood Eaton (Oxon.).

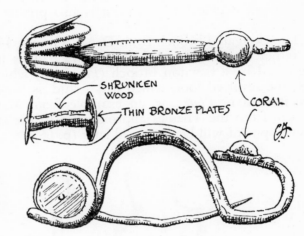

SHRUNKEN WOOD
THIN BRONZE PLATES
CORAL

f. River Thames (Hammersmith).

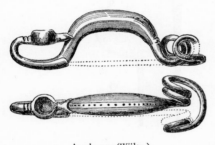

c. Avebury (Wilts.).

d. Box (north Wilts.).

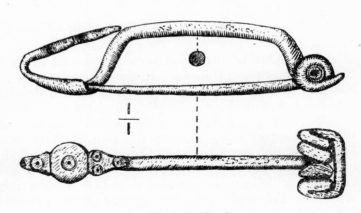

g. Ham Hill (Som.).

FIGURE 13.—Early brooches in south Britain, *c.* 250–150 B.C. (*d.* $\frac{2}{3}$, others $\frac{1}{1}$)

17

of Marnian intruders on the south coast, was occupied by a "solid block of Celts of the old Hallstatt tradition", it is certain that the simple La Tène I brooch type continued to be made and used long after the change to the La Tène II type took place in Marnian Yorkshire, Cambridgeshire, and elsewhere. Let us now glance back at some of the brooches discussed earlier in this record, and place them in or beyond the sequence we have examined. First of all, the two La Tène brooches at Mount Batten, 26 and 27 on *Plate 31*, belong, or are closely related, to Type C on Figure 12. The fine brooch from the Queen's Barrow (*Plate 9c*) has a bent-back foot touching the bow, rather like "*c*" from Avebury (Wilts.): the heavy mass of ornament is pinned through the foot to the pin-catch, to make all secure.

The design of all the other brooches goes further than any we have noted here, entering the "La Tène II" phase wherein the bent foot is attached to, or merged in, the bow. This is well seen in *Plate 9e*, the involuted brooch from Danes' Graves, and is elaborated in the brooch from Beckley, *Plate 12a*: it is also present in the Newnham Croft (Cambs.) brooch, Figure 6.

The elongated brooch from Danes' Graves, Figure 4, has a "ring" hinge and a reverted foot rather clumsily merged in the bow. This inadequacy is averted in the development represented by a Sawdon brooch (*Plate 11a*) which becomes standard practice in these flat types; the reverted foot, which had a stud, is fixed by a ring to the bow. The transitional shape is seen in *Plate 26e*, an example from Maidstone (Kent): the handsome brooch in *Plate 41a* from the Thames approximates to the last, La Tène III form, F on the diagram: its development will be discussed later (p. 66).

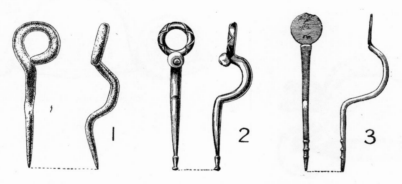

FIGURE 14.—Pins, bronze: Cold Kitchen Hill (Wilts.). (1 and 3, ⅔; 2, ¼.)

Pins. One of these has been mentioned in the survey of sites; a brief survey of the contemporary types follows. In the III century B.C., pins, like brooches, had a long history behind them in the west. The type used and developed by the newcomers to Britain was ring-headed with bent shoulder, "twisted out of wire". The development thereafter is two-fold: the pin is cast, and the head becomes loaded with ornament. Here two of our British examples come in, very different in character: *Plates 2e* and *9b*, from the Thames at Hammersmith, and a burial at Danes' Graves, Yorkshire. The showy panel, bar, and circle of coral (or paste) of the former—all lost—will have been lightened by the open-work cresting—a delicate succession of linked scrolls: the latter, daintier in design, retains its settings. The angle of the stem carries a knob, pinned to its curve; the wheel-head (Figure 83, H62) is starred with five insets of coral (?) on spokes expanded to carry them, and ringed with a narrow continuous band, inset, of the same material.

A dress-pin, involuted like these two, and so resembling a modern scarf-pin, is met with in south Britain; three specimens are shown in Figure 14. No. 2, from Cold Kitchen Hill (Wilts.), is perhaps the most interesting; "its small size and delicacy represent a triumph of craftsmanship". The head is incised with a series of semi-circles, and the small stud (of coral) is attached by a pin. On the point is a moulding with terminal knob which seems to represent the point protector sometimes found with long pins of the Hallstatt period.[42]

The distribution of these Iron "B" pins generally, follows a familiar pattern, being mainly in the Lowlands and the north-eastern coastal areas; the technical links with northern Ireland—a contemporary but presumably independent settlement—are notable.

GENERAL COMMENT. The Marnians on the Yorkshire downlands and elsewhere were pony, pig and probably cattle breeders. As late as 55 B.C. they were possibly one of the iron-using non-agricultural tribes referred to by Caesar. The works of art from their graves, dating probably from mid-III to the end of II B.C., range from competently wrought pieces barbaric in character to objects illustrative of a more refined cultural tradition. The earliest examples of the latter were imported. The difference is, as a study of the surviving pieces in our Museum shows, not one of skill but of outlook. Some of the skilled craftsmen in Britain were working in a baroque tradition; the showy pieces referred to have a Continental background in decoration, though not in form. The most curious features, for example, of the involuted brooch from Danes' Graves (*Plate 9e* and Figure 83, H61) are the knobs ("snaily coils") on bow and foot; these are paralleled on brooches from Hungary and bracelets from Switzerland, and form a persistent element of design in Britain. The elongated brooch, again, from Danes' Graves, with a row of seatings for paste or glass mounts, stems from a type known from a Lake Neuchâtel, Switzerland, site. The Continental styles involved are the Waldalgesheim (II) and the Plastic (III).

A very attractive group of British grave-goods is the bracelets. Their rounded, smoothly-polished, internal faces, well shown in the example from Arras (*Plate 11b*), make them comfortable to wear. Such a design is seen in examples from Hungary and Switzerland, and our finest specimens are undoubtedly imports. The daintiest of the finds, however, is the imported finger-ring from the Queen's Barrow (*Plate 8b* and Figure 82, A8), the loops of which reflect a Continental goldsmith's motif, shown on the grand scale in the ornament of the famous diadem found with a burial at Vix, near the source of the river Seine.[43]

No sites comparable in extent to those on the Wolds have been discovered elsewhere in Britain, and no extensive field research has been devoted to the early Marnians, but the series of bracelet types from Mount Batten (*Plate 31*) provides an impressive picture of early trade, here interlocked, possibly, with very localized Marnian settlement.

This is by no means the whole picture: in mid-Britain, from the Trent to the Stour, minor arts of great refinement, Continental and (later) insular, are illustrated in the brooch and arm-ring from the Newnham (Cambs.) chariot burial, and by chance finds of brooches at Beckley, Wood Eaton and Standlake (Oxon), Maiden Castle (Dorset) and the Soar valley (Notts.). Brooches of simple types, and pins, have also been discussed.

These widely scattered works of art and of craft provide a broad and colourful background for the study of six famous bronzes which cover, with one exception, a similar range of time, and which to most students epitomize "Early Celtic art" in Britain.

[1] It is not necessary to suppose that all the invaders in Yorkshire came direct by sea: finds of early date are too widespread in southern Britain for this. Those interested should read Professor Hawkes's remarks in *Ant. Journ.*, 1940, p. 118.

[2] *Archaeologia* 60, pp. 251 ff.

[3] Lincolnshire provides a burial with an associated pot similar to those found with pig-bones in the Yorkshire graves, which, while Iron "A" in origin, has been given a "new look" under the influence of the invading groups. "Prehistoric Lincolnshire", *Arch. Journ.*, 1946, p. 14, Figure 4.

[4] *Arch. Camb.*, 1927, p. 67 ff. Later research sustains the typology of this paper, but the provisional dating (p. 73) has long needed drastic revision. See C. F. C. Hawkes, *Ant. Journ.*, 1940, pp. 115–21 (*esp.* p. 119, where a similar brooch to the Cowlam example is dated) and 276–9; Mortimer Wheeler, 1943, *Maiden Castle*, p. 251 ff; and Miss M. J. Fowler in *Arch. Journ.*, 1953, p. 88 ff.

[5] C. F. C. Hawkes in *Ant. Journ.*, 1940, p. 120.

[6] There is one chariot burial in the North Riding, at Cawthorn Camps (Mortimer, *Forty Years*, p. 358 ff.) and a few finds of British bronzes are on record, e.g. at Sawdon, p. 8 below.

[7] Reconstructed from Llyn Cerrig, Anglesey material. The swingle-tree in this model, looped for a trace on each side, should have been bolted to the chariot-frame. *Ant. Journ.*, 1947, pp. 117–19.

[8] Compare the example, also polished, in *Glastonbury Lake Village* II, Figure 156, from Gough's Cave, Cheddar, Som. These simple types have no decorative "caps".

[9] C. Fox, *Ant. Journ.*, 1949, pp. 81–3.

[10] Studied in 1946: see Figure 40. The best nineteenth century commentary on these chariot burials is in Mortimer, *Forty Years*, already referred to, p. 358 ff. Chariot construction and detail of fittings, as here, is discussed in the "Llyn Cerrig" Report.

[11] Cf. Eddius Stephanus, *Life of Bishop Wilfrid*, XXXIV (Colgrave, 70–1), which describes Ecgfrith's queen as riding abroad in her chariot (*in curru pergens*) with the bishop's (looted) reliquary worn as an ornament.

[12] Arras is the type-station for bits of this class, see *Llyn Cerrig*, p. 30, Figure 15.

[13] See Déchelette, *Manuel d'Archéologie* II, p. 1286, and G. C. Dunning, *Arch. Journ.* LXXXV, 1928, pp. 72–3. Mr. Dunning, who drew the piece for me, rightly thinks that this Arras mirror enters into the ancestry of the British series; it had a bone- or ivory-plated handle. A second iron mirror was found in one of the Yorkshire graves, but is now lost.

[14] The island of Hyères, off the coast of Provence, is the nearest source for this precious material.

[15] For a parallel wholly of bronze and the history of this type of pin, see G. C. Dunning in *Arch. Journ.* XCI, 1934, p. 269 ff., *esp.* Figure 4, 10.

[16] *Le Trésor de Vix* (near Châtillon-sur-Seine), *Plate XXXII*. René Joffroy, 1954.

[17] The remarkable elaboration of such brooches is discussed by C. F. C. Hawkes, *Ant. Journ.*, 1946, p. 187 ff.

[18] W. Watson, *Ant. Journ.*, 1947, p. 178 ff.

[19] A later burial in the region, isolated, with sword and shield, is referred to on p. 33 below.

[20] Additional information will be found in J. R. Mortimer, *Forty Years' Researches . . . in East Yorkshire*, 1905, Part II, pp. 353 ff. and frontispiece, and in Frank Elgee, *Early Man in North-East Yorkshire*, 1930, pp. 186 ff.

[21] There was a fresh art style in this area in I A.D. See p. 73 below.

[22] *Proc. Soc. Ant.*, 1908, p. 142.

[23] Mildenhall is in the region where the Iceni, who may have come in at this time, first settled. The warrior's gold torc is significant. See R. Rainbird Clarke, "Archaeology of Norfolk", *Arch. Journ.*, 1939, p. 1 ff., and my p. 45.

[24] A common Continental motif. See Figure 83 (61, 69–70), and Jacobsthal, *Celtic Art*, p. 92 ff, *Plates* 270–2. The brooch is later in character than the arm-ring: the discovery was accidental, and the positions of the finds not recorded in detail.

[25] T. Sheppard, *Arch. Camb.*, 1941, *Plate VII*.

[26] V.C.H., *Cambs*. I, p. 294, Figure 26.

[27] *Arch. Camb.*, 1941, p. 2, *Plate I*.

[28] Clare Fell, *Arch. Journ.*, 1936, p. 63, *Plate II*. W. F. Grimes, "The Jurassic Way", *Aspects of Archaeology*, *Plate VI* and pp. 164–6.

[29] *Celtic Ornament*, Figure 8, pp. 23–4.

[30] C. F. C. Hawkes and Paul Jacobsthal, *Ant. Journ.*, 1945, p. 117 ff, and *Plate XI*.

[31] Hawkes and Jacobsthal, loc. cit., *Plate XI*.

[32] I am indebted to Mr. Humphrey Case for this fine drawing. See J. S. P. Bradford, *Oxoniensia* VII, 1942, p. 41.

[33] Brief notes in *Proc. Prehist. Soc.,* 1950, p. 4: since this was written Stuart Piggott has assigned the piece to a Continental workshop: I am not sufficiently convinced to alter the text—see *Archaeologia* 96, pp. 228, 231.

[33a] *Archaeologia* 96, p. 234.

[34] *Archaeologia* 40 (Spence Bate, p. 500 ff); R. H. Worth, *Trans. Devonshire Association* XX, 1888, p. 129 ff. All are now destroyed; these are valuable records, therefore, of Continental contacts with south-western Devon.

[35] For these Cornish sites, the tin trade, and the relations with the Spanish peninsula, see E. T. Leeds, "Excavations at Chun Castle", *Archaeologia* 76: also H. O'N. Hencken, *Archaeology of Cornwall and Scilly*, ch. V, p. 158.

[36] W. F. Grimes, *Prehistory of Wales*, p. 227 and *Plate XVI*.

[37] See C. F. C. Hawkes, *Ant. Journ.*, 1940, pp. 115–21. The brooch is illustrated.

[38] *Arch. Camb.*, 1927, p. 9, and M. Fowler, *Arch. Journ.*, 1954, pp. 92–3: Hawkes and Jacobsthal, *Ant. Journ.*, 1945, pp. 123–4.

[39] See Dr. F. J. North's report, *Arch. Camb.*, 1927, p. 81f.

[40] For Gaul, see Déchelette, *Manuel, Second Age du Fer*, p. 1247 ff. (numerous references); for Switzerland, Viollier, *Les Sepultures du Second Age du Fer sur le plateau Suisse,* 1916; for Germany, R. Beltz, *Zeitschrift für Ethnologie*, 43 (1911), p. 664 ff. There is a good collection of Gaulish examples from the Marne region in the British Museum.

[41] The illustrations and comment in this section are based on Cyril Fox, *Arch. Camb.*, 1927, pp. 67–112; Margaret Fowler, *Arch. Journ.* CX, 1953, pp. 88–105; C. F. C. Hawkes in *Ant. Journ.*, 1940, pp. 115–21, 276–9.

[42] C. C. Dunning, *Arch. Journ.* 91, 1934, p. 278: distribution map, Figure 6, p. 281. Also *Archaeologia* 67, p. 155, Figure 18.

[43] Joffroy, *Le Trésor de Vix*, Plate XXXII.

CHAPTER III. BRITISH SCHOOLS OF CELTIC ART:
THE FIRST PHASE *(commencing c. 230 B.C.)*

The "early group" of seven major works of British Celtic art we are now to examine—weapons and warlike trappings—reach a remarkably high standard of art and craftsmanship. Five of the pieces come from two rivers, the lower Thames and the Witham; two, from Torrs in south-western Scotland, may, from their condition, be assumed to have come from a morass. All then were lost, or deposited, in water, and recovered by accident.

Dr. Jacobsthal would say they were cast into the water as dedicatory offerings to river gods. In favour of this view is their excellent state of preservation; none shows sword cuts. Another obvious possibility, in respect of the Thames finds, despite this lack of evidence for war-use, is that their owners, fighting up to their waists in water—as Caesar's men will have done in the crossing of the river—were knocked on the head and slipped under unconscious, their shields and swords sliding to the muddy bottom.

It should be said, as an aid to the appreciation of the problem of craftsmanship these works of art will present, that they do not form a linked series, but all will be seen to be related, in one feature or another.

The two examples allocated to Northern Schools will be taken first: the five assigned to Southern Schools second. Six of the pieces represent the British development from the "Waldalgesheim style", or the "Plastic sub-style", referred to above: the seventh represents Dr. Jacobsthal's "Sword sub-style" contemporary with the latter, not otherwise seen in Britain: it is the Witham scabbard mount. "Horn-caps" and daggers will also be mentioned.

NORTHERN SCHOOLS

(a) Pony-cap, Torrs, Kirkcudbrightshire

The photograph of this remarkable bronze object on *Plate 19a* shows it as a pony-cap, that is without the horns that were incorrectly affixed to it (in the torn and altered holes in the centre) when it became known to scholars in 1870. It is a shallow dome, elongated, of thin bronze decorated with relief ornament, and with two round holes at the sides: carefully wrought marginal binding completes the structure. *Plate 19b*—which comes, like the other, from a definitive study by Atkinson and Piggott[1]—shows a pony wearing the cap, with a plume occupying the damaged area. The situation and character of the ornament confirms the view taken by these authors of the purpose of the piece: the date assigned is the second half of III B.C.

The pattern (Figure 16) shows fold-over symmetry on the major axis; it "consists of two analogous units each having a *gamma*-shaped loop diverging on either side into 'tendril' themes linked by arched members over the ear-holes". The arrangement, it will be observed, pre-supposes the ornamental central feature already mentioned, and it achieves, as the authors of the study remark, "quadrilateral balance in a curvilinear composition", thanks to the angular elements flanking the centre.

This composition is enlivened by minor themes—lobes and coils superposed—*and colliding* (*Plate 19c*, right, and Figure 16, top right)—also by scrolls "coming to life" as duck-heads, on

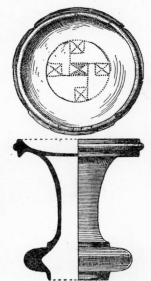

FIGURE 15.—"Horn-cap": Llyn Cerrig (Anglesey). (⅔)

22

the same plate.[2]   All these are early features which will—as we shall see—be discarded as our insular style develops: it is fascinating to study them on such a scale, so finely wrought.   Good as the design is, it does not wholly please when viewed on the flat, as

FIGURE 16.—Pony-cap, Torrs (Kirkcudbrights.): lay-out. (See *Plate 19*.)

in the drawing; the style of the front is more "open" than that on the back.   This criticism is, however, misplaced; the craftsman always had in mind, as the study of dozens of Celtic works convinces me, the appearance of the piece *in use*.   At the back sufficient interest must be concentrated for the owner's pleasure; he is standing in his chariot behind and above it. The design of the front, sloping down and away from him, will be foreshortened to *his* eyes; looking, that is, as "tight" as the back. The emphasis here is on the owner's share in inspiration and development. This is not nonsense: the creation throughout the occupied areas of Britain, a barbarous island, of an independent Celtic art of high quality, maintained for three centuries, implies a deep and competent interest in the subject, and in the techniques of the craftsmen tempted into Britain, by chieftains in the early days of the settlement. The debt of the designer to the Waldalgesheim style as illustrated in Britain by the Brentford horncap is manifest, but the known relations of its more individual features are scanty; a flask illustrated by Dr. Jacobsthal from Celtic (northern) Italy,[3] which also shows "lobes colliding" with other elements of a pattern, is the only clue I can find to one striking aspect of our piece: it has already been remarked that Celtic craftsmen travelled far. In Britain a related object is the Standlake scabbard, since it also has a *gamma*-shaped loop in relief (p. 13 above). As for the bronze-smithy concerned: it is in my view to be sought in east Yorkshire (though the authors place this region second, with Galloway as a first choice[4]). Hereabouts also, I would say, the Standlake sword was made—but not in the same shop.

No incised ornament decorates the surface of the major pattern of the cap, as in many works of the period, but minor repairs showing this technique suggest that the craftsman of the horns was working in the same centre.

(b) Drinking-horn mounts, Torrs

We turn then to these horns of thin metal, which terminate in castings—billed duck-heads with sockets for (coral?) eyes, recognized as the Shoveler Duck (*Spatula clypeata*. L.). The Shoveler—probably also represented on the cap—is a widespread species, summer-resident and winter visitor in Britain. The incised ornament is elaborate; both patterns are illustrated

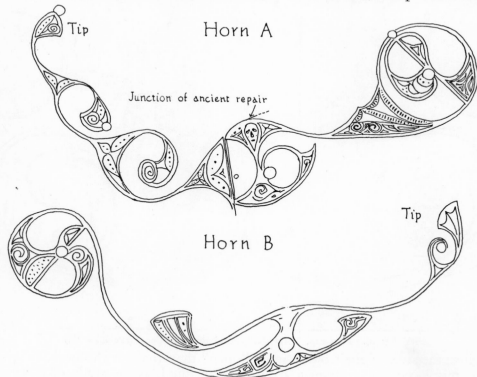

FIGURE 17.—Horns A and B: Torrs. Incised patterns. (¼) (See *Plate 20*.)

in *Plate 20* and Figure 17 from the same source.[5]   The Plate shows the quality of the work—the perfect curve and gradation of size of the horns, with the duck-head proportionate: the Figure provides a complete picture of the patterns.   Each pattern starts with a circular motif based on a *yin-yang* motif, and ends in a fan-shaped tip; the central feature of the larger, A, is a complex oval in which a human mask is incorporated, that of B a "hollow triangle" supporting the extended, double-ended, curved bar.   This is a fair description: but the interested student will observe that the central designs are very similar in concept.   The circles of A and B are each divided centrally by a straight bar which gives distinction to the design (Figure 82, E40): the oval centre of A is similarly, but eccentrically, divided.   Now the only large-scale and therefore comparable ornament we have to this forthright feature of the bar is on a Lincolnshire sword-scabbard to be dealt with in the next chapter; here, also, the device (in "B") of two elements joined by a narrow neck is repeated (Figure 83, J78).   The parallels and facts set out in this section, I submit, render the manufacture of both cap and horns in north-eastern Britain more likely than in Galloway.   It is, anyway, the better working hypothesis.

SOUTHERN SCHOOLS

(i) Asymmetric Patterns

(a) Scabbard "locket" (with sword), from the river Witham,[6] near Lincoln

This famous piece, now in the British Museum, is illustrated in *Plate 22b*.   The earliest of works of the "Southern Schools" to be studied here, it represents the "Sword sub-style" of Jacobsthal, and must be dated in the second half of III b.c.[7]

The bronze locket (partly parallel-sided, partly shaped) is embossed in a pattern extending (and receding) down the scabbard in two linked groups of subtle curves similar in character.   The mouth is boldly scrolled, the outline tapers *diagonally* towards the left in two phases, related to the ribbed spine of the relief which by an inward curvature restrains this leftward movement: the design has thus a certain tenseness.   The shape and significance of the relief work is emphasized by incised patterns[8]: the major swell in each phase of the design is dominated by bold palmette forms with broad rounded tips facing left, the minor by similar designs with sharply hollowed tips facing right (Figure 82, E34–35). Dr. Jacobsthal's remark that the incised motives heighten the rhythm of the frame is true,[9] but needs expansion: the two hollow-ended incised forms, boldly inscribed on the secondary swell in each sector, represent a rhythm of opposites—the receding, as well as the breaking, wave.   The style of the piece is different from the northern work we have studied; the diagonal lay-out, moreover, is only seen elsewhere on one British piece, but occurs on scabbards from Hungary, Austria, and Switzerland, illustrated in Jacobsthal's *corpus*.

The writer has long held the view that such patterns as these, on scabbards, are illustrated in our handbooks the wrong way up; they are intended to be appreciated by the owner as he looks down his hip—hence my choice of phrases—and they are thus reproduced here.

(b) (c) Two shield-bosses, from the Wandsworth reach of the river Thames

"The early settlers"—it is said in the introduction to the "Roman London" volume of the Royal Commission on Historic Monuments (1928)—"coming up the river highway, had no special reason for staying their progress at the future site of London.   Rather had they found their way upstream to the more friendly reaches . . . where long stretches of gravel flank the comparatively narrow waterway on both sides."   It is widely held that such a settlement, beside a ford, and in touch with the Continent, is represented by the important finds of works of art of several periods dredged up in the Wandsworth reach of the river seven miles above "London Bridge",[10] but the writer cannot find sufficient evidence of Iron "B" riverside settlement to support this thesis (p. 144 below).

25

The round shield-boss. The first piece to be considered is the round shield-boss (*Plate 13*), well known from the drawing by J. M. Kemble in *Horae Ferales*. The boldly-designed relief ornament on the "flat" surrounding the boss consists of scrolls and coils with leaves attached: these have softly-rounded outlines and hollow centres. There are also two duck-heads (?) with curved bills, having wing-like attachments in the same mode, and lightly-poised crests, all decorated with beautiful incised patterns, one with "bat-wings", that is, indented like some of those on the Witham scabbard mount (Figure 82, E37–38). The boss—separately illustrated on *Plate 13b*—is largely covered with similar incised patterns (Figure 82, E39) and is framed by a moulded ring with wavy crest. The main design, considered as a whole, is such as we shall often see in Celtic art: balanced, a scheme of opposites. The photograph shows the correct position on the shield, as indicated by a rivet-head of, and holes for, the (lost) grip. If the boss, thus set, is halved on a slightly irregular line from A to B as indicated on the photograph, every element on the one side has its counterpart on the other, but reversed, looking-glass fashion. *Enrichment* is limited to the middle portion of each of these halves, and the centre: that is, it occupies a diagonal zone of the design. The decoration in relief is bold and simple, the workmanship curiously soft and velvety, the relation of voids to solids carefully considered. The secondary (incised) ornament, taken as a whole, does not closely resemble that of the Witham sword scabbard.

The oval shield-boss. The second boss from the Wandsworth reach, being oval not circular, must, in my opinion, belong to a different tradition: the work of another *atelier*.

This boss-with-extensions, 14¾ in. long, was also published in *Horae Ferales*.[11] I illustrate it (*Plate 14b*) from this drawing, and from a photograph; the latter reproduces the quality, the former the incised detail. Some of the rivets remain and show that the shield itself (no doubt of lime-wood) was ⅜ in. thick; the shallow curve of the upper end of the piece points to a lost terminal (expanded, but not circular), while the greater length of the lower (broken) rib shows that the grip was above the centre of the shield. This is usual in long shields designed for service: the body cannot otherwise be properly protected. The upper ornament is a stylized human face in relief—no doubt repeated at the lower end—with incised tight spirals on the nose, similar to those on the boss.

The shield-boss itself, 6 in. from tip to tip by 3⅞ in. wide, is structurally elaborate—an S-coil with stylized bossy bird-head (?) terminal at either end, the relief being clearly defined, sometimes with a "sharp" ridge. A wavy crest draws attention to the thickened centre of the coil, and emphasizes the diagonal axis of the design. Two snaky twists with secondary bosses fill the elongated spaces: their pointed tips are emphasized by tight spirals and marginal serrations (Figure 82, E41). The bosses which all survive in part are of snail-shell form as seen on *Plate 9, e, f*; the hammering necessary to produce them from the flat made the metal so thin that it has largely perished.

(d) *Shield, river Witham, near Lincoln*

The magnificent shield found in the river Witham "adjacent to" Lincoln (*Plate 15*) gives some idea of the lay-out of the second Thames shield when it was complete, and I suggest that it comes from the same *atelier*, being a more developed and richer example of the craftsmanship of this school of armourers—who no doubt worked for chieftains all over eastern Britain, the area of primary settlement, as we have seen in Chapter II. It is regarded by Saxl and Wittkower as superior in technique to any contemporary work of continental Celtic art.[12]

Kemble's drawing of the shield is here reproduced (*Plate 15a*) because it shows clearly a feature much admired today, the stylized "boar-totem" of the primary owner, now surviving only as a stain on the bronze defined by numerous tiny rivet holes. The elaborate terminals differ slightly in size, the lower being the larger—possibly to give a more balanced perspective as the owner glances downwards—and the central boss is (as in the other piece) placed well above the half-way line. This boss (*Plate 15b*) is a pointed oval with a design in relief fundamentally similar to, but more elaborate than, that on the Thames oval boss. The reader will, in this connection, note the pointed narrow terminals that link the boss with the spine—which is indeed structurally part of it—and the presence of "snailshell" motifs in the large "comma leaves" (Figure 83, J70); also that the design on either side of an imaginary diagonal median line is again identical (and reversed). Studs of red glass, of which three survive, enhance the dominance of this central feature.

The spine expands at its junction with the terminal roundels (*frontispiece, a* and *b*) and has features (the face motif, here animal not human, with broad, rounded snout) which emphasize the relationship to the Wandsworth boss. The flower-forms (modified palmettes) in relief on either side are notable, as are the "eyes" and nostrils (Figure 82, 2, 3). Secondary (wholly incised) ornament in this magnificent piece is concentrated at the upper and lower ends: there is an elaborately wrought flat band occupying three-quarters of a circle in each roundel, detailed in Figure 82, E36. As the fine British Museum photographs show, the incised tight spirals (as in the Wandsworth oval boss) associated with palmette "leaves" are here set out in "S" and "C" shaped patterns, very varied in their freehand detail, many being in outline similar to the adjacent "comma leaves" with coils.[13] They are worthy of careful study by the student, and the scale of the photographs makes this possible. Precursors, on the throat of the Lorraine flagon (*Plate 1b*), should be noted.

The bold moulding which encloses the large "comma leaves" adjacent to the "face" is part of the main circular frame of each terminal; it has a sharp wavy crest (Figure 83, K88), identical with that crossing the Wandsworth shield-boss. Lastly, the upper and lower terminals are at first glance of the same design, but when closely studied the incised scroll patterns are seen to be different—a difference apparently related to the upright and inverted positions they respectively occupy. This underlines the originality and imaginative craftsmanship of a noble work; the artist's aim was *visual* perfection. Recent study shows that this artist cut down and decorated the early, plain, boar-totem shield.[14]

(ii) Symmetric Pattern

(e) *Shield, river Thames, Battersea*

The closely linked series of works of art we have discussed, from the two rivers, Thames and Witham, ends—*after a considerable gap*—with the famous Battersea shield in the British Museum, the design of which shows "fold-over symmetry"—being the same on either side of an imaginary line down the middle from top to bottom.[15] It is, of course, a classical mode, frequent in the pattern-making of the Graeco–Roman world.

The Battersea shield, then, is the latest piece on the grand scale in direct descent from, and in close relationship to, the beginnings of British art: its date will be about 75 B.C.

The surpassing virtuosity of the design of the shield should have encouraged many students to attempt a detailed description, but none such is in print, to my knowledge. *Plate 14a* shows the whole pattern, photographed diagonally to bring out the relief: *Plate 16* the boss and roundel: *Plate 17* the lower roundel. The piece is symmetrical on the horizontal axis as well as the vertical, the grip and boss being central, not above the middle line as in the Witham shield. This suggests that it was designed for parade rather than war.

Apart from its symmetry, and certain refinements which establish its uniqueness—at its own stage of development, of course—very little is brought into the pattern that is not, on the evidence of other works, already part of the Gallo–British tradition. The scrolls incorporating hollow-sided "triangles" are related to those on Gallic helmets (e.g. Amfreville,

Jacobsthal, *Plate 78*) and seen also in many British works; the "closed" palmettes from which they emerge are also traditional (Figure 82, A4, B9, 10); the snaily coils, comma forms, and leaf terminals associated with these are seen on the Torrs horns and cap, the paired coils on the axes of the lesser circles are based on the lateral features of the decoration of the Witham shield-boss: and so on.

The most remarkable and novel details, perhaps, are those which enliven the narrow bands in high relief which adorn the two lesser circles. The bands are dual, as it were two keels in intimate contact; one rises to form the dominant knife-edge while the other slides down the slope to become the bounding line of a terminal "leaf"-form, or to broaden the base of the frame-work of the pattern—which it formerly controlled. The sharp-pointed curved ends of this frame-work, and its stippled expansions, add to the distinction of the design. The writer had long regarded this lovely, exciting, and highly intellectual develop-ment of sharp relief, begun on the Wandsworth shield-boss, as having ended—so far as our knowledge could go—with the Battersea piece; but re-examination of the Seven Sisters hoard suggests survival in Dobunian workshops—and indeed development. Consider the tankard hold-fast in *Plate 66*, and its carefully-completed reproduction—the ridges of the interwoven coils on the "arch" meeting and dying into the central feature: from what other artistic source in Britain could the astonishing structure here, poised to a sharp crest like two unbroken waves that have collided beside a sea-wall, have been derived ?[16]

I return to the shield: duality, like that mentioned above, is also present in the major, central pattern, but accentuation of relief is here undesirable; the shield-boss must be dominant. Colour, however, can be massed with advantage, so there are twice as many discs of red glass[17] in the central boss, as in the others—with eight more, in two clusters, touching its frame-work on the axis. (See also Figure 82, B11, 12.)

Extending from these two clusters outward is the spine of the shield, reduced almost to nothing. In each, two domed rivet-heads flank a nose-like structure. I suggest that this is based on the face (also flanked by rivet-heads), eyed and nostrilled, on the Witham spine (frontispiece). The forehead remains, but conjoined discs of red glass replace the beady eyes.

Thus we have a *new* adaptation of a living creature for ornamental purposes: the "Duck" is replaced by Man.

A striking feature remains to be dealt with—the swastikas (Figure 83, G55). This symbol has a long history in Europe, and its varied forms are discussed in the "Llyn Cerrig Report".[18] The Battersea type of swastika, a Celtic innovation, in which the arms of the cross extend from diagonally opposite sides of a central rectangle (Figure 83, F44), is seen also on the horn-cap from Llyn Cerrig (Figure 15).

GENERAL COMMENT. In a previous chapter we noted the Iron "B" character, and approxi-mate range of date, of the Yorkshire Wolds and other settlements and have, on the evidence of works of art not of Continental character in the graves, concluded that the Marnian intruders brought their craftsmen with them, or tempted craftsmen from the Continent so soon as they were economically secure. This conclusion was extended to cover similar finds from graves and presumed settlement sites, elsewhere.

We now come to the isolated finds mostly from riverbeds with which this commentary is concerned. Can we be sure that these superb works also were made in this island by Celtic craftsmen?

Dr. Jacobsthal had in recent years attacked this problem with special relation to the eastern schools and with full knowledge of the Continental background, artistic and historical. In 1939[19] he pointed out that the decoration of the Witham scabbard had "its roots not in France but in Hungary and Switzerland", and that its style represented "renewed contact of Celtic craftsmen with classic, now Roman, art". In 1948 he dated the intrusion "at about the middle of the third century B.C.", and summarized his views on a broader basis, remarking that Celtic art "was introduced into the British Isles by artists who came from all the Celtic lands in the Continent. The immigrant artizans soon broke away from the continental patterns and created a new peculiar Celtic style". Such a development of insular individuality, which all the greater "early" pieces possess, must have taken time, and it is reasonable to regard the first of them as dating about 230 B.C. The time-range, from the Torrs cap and the Witham sword-locket to the Battersea shield, may be of the order of 150 years.

We can now consider the difficult problem presented by their variety. One feature (incised patterns) is present as the only decoration on one of the north-eastern pieces (the horns), and as secondary enrichment on four out of five of the south-eastern pieces. The "north-eastern group" is distinct from the "south-eastern": in the former—as we have seen (p. 24)—decisive cross-bars, at right-angles to the axis of these incised designs, occur: in the latter these are absent. There appears to be only one school of this minor art in the south-eastern series; the fact led Dr. Jacobsthal, I venture to think wrongly, to regard the Witham sword scabbard as closely related to the Wandsworth circular shield-boss[20]; I would indeed regard the former as (*structurally*) the work of an artist not elsewhere represented, at present, in the British series.

I now turn to the Witham shield. Such a stage of originality as it presents cannot in the nature of things be reached quickly in a new country, and we are fortunate in being able —as I hold—to compare a closely related earlier work (the Thames oval shield-boss) with it, to note the new use made of the "wavy" crest ornament, and the avoidance of crudities in the human mask, without altering the general pattern. The number and placing of the rivets of the boss, it may be added, is identical in the two pieces.

Again, the fold-over symmetry to which the Group as a whole approaches, present in the earliest piece—the Torrs cap, *c.* 220 B.C., and in the latest—the Battersea shield, *c.* 75 B.C., illustrates the powerful but intermittent influence of the classic civilization. We shall see that our craftsmen are, over and over again, led to employ that mode, only to slip back into an asymmetry more agreeable to their *ethos*.

How are we to explain the close relationship which exists between the Witham, and the Wandsworth and Battersea shields? It seems likely that *local* chieftains had their own armourers and other metal-workers, for there is much second-rate decorative metal-work in our museums. But the great achievements will, from the late III century onwards, have come from workshops established under the protection of leaders and rulers of the new British states or grouped communities, created by metal-workers with a fund of technical experience, here maintained and increased. Petty feuds, inter-tribal war, may have been endemic, but would not put out the fires in their smithies, or silence the clang of their hammers; the emergent victor needed the creative skill they possessed or controlled as much as, or more than, the leaders he supplanted.[21]

Two such armourers' workshops, the evidence suggests, were present somewhere in the Thames valley at the beginning of the II century.

The first has already been alluded to: it produced successively the Thames oval shield-boss, and the wholly bronze Witham shield. The second produced the circular "Thames" shield-boss with its integrated, formalized tendril-and-leaf ornament.[22] The finest and latest craftsmanship of these armourers, moreover, the Battersea shield, shows elements of both these schools: that of the Witham shield to a slight extent, mainly that of the Wandsworth circular boss. It also has its own, recently demonstrated, unique features (p. 28 above). The latter Wandsworth piece differs from all other early works in the importance attached to the sunk lobe or leaf. Now these sunk lobes of Wandsworth are seen, paired (and pecked), in four places within the terminal circles of the Battersea design. This also has four tight "snaily" coils in the hollow-sided junctions of the major pattern, indicative of the continental basis of the tradition, as in the case of Witham. It is difficult, however, to justify an earlier date than *c.* 75 B.C. for so formal a piece.

We are not yet at the end of our problems. This commentary shows that the quality of the Continental achievement at the presumed time of the Iron "B" invasion and the probable availability of Continental metal-workers to serve the newly established chieftains would account for highly-competent British-made works of art and use; it does not, to me at least, explain how such perfection of technique, such elaborate and exciting design, such originality as is shown in the *earlier* of the works here discussed, was procurable in newly settled regions of our country. We may note, moreover, that these qualities are particularly unexpected in an island where such sophistication in art, so far as our evidence goes, had never been practised before.[23] There was no high Iron "A" workshop-competence such as existed on the Continent to be trained in a more advanced technique.

The only reason I can suggest for this creativeness is that the younger, more energetic and experimental artists in the Continental shops were likely to have been tempted across the seas.

It would, however, be wrong to suggest that all the creative art discovered in Britain, and belonging to an early phase, was of native origin, or that all links with craftsmen on the western seaboard of Gaul ended (except here and there in the south-western peninsula) with the III-century invasion. Some evidence to the contrary follows.

Interposed: *Short swords and daggers of late II B.C., with anthropomorphic hilts*

A few short swords or daggers and their sheaths, varied in character but stemming from the III–II century type with loop-chapes, have been found in eastern Britain.

(*a*) The dagger illustrated in *Plate 10 f*, from Hertford Warren near Bury St. Edmunds, is lengthy, and the grip is elaborately designed in an anthropomorphic manner: above, three branches (arms and head) each with their knob form a pommel, while below are two branches (legs) linked to the blade-head by bronze knobs. The chape is broken off, but a tight loop is certain. The only parallel known, from the Netherlands province of Drenthe, is so closely similar as to suggest that both pieces were made by the same craftsman, probably Marnian. This has a ring-chape, undamaged.[24]

(*b*) *Sword, North Grimston.* Another work of the finest quality, which also is recognized as an import, is the completely anthropoid-hilted short sword (24¾ in.) from North Grimston (East Riding, Yorkshire) in a warrior's grave associated with a sword of the usual length—an early example with an iron scabbard; this burial is dated in the second half of II B.C. The hilt of cast bronze is illustrated, back and front, in *Plate 18*, and its place in the series, Continental and British, is shown on Figure 23, No. 6, after Clarke and Hawkes. The finely-detailed grip claims attention first: there is a succession of boldly-contoured mouldings closed at the upper and lower ends by a beaded one; each of the knob-ended limbs also has a hollow moulding and a bead. These limbs are four-sided in section to provide a firm grip; the head is sunk between the arms. The facial expression is harsh and dissatisfied, as is not uncommon in Early Celtic art. Special interest attaches to the hair-do, since it is so clearly defined; there is a fringe of curls on the forehead, the hair being combed straight down to the back of the neck. In so far as it is a natural and not merely a traditional treatment, it suggests that the Celts in this century oiled and curled their hair.[25]

A similar piece in the British Museum, said to be from Yorkshire, is less finely wrought, but more advanced in character, and *may* have been made in an east Yorkshire workshop. Close parallels found in Ireland (Donegal) and France (Haute Marne) are illustrated in a recent article in which the Continental origin of the group, with its British offshoots, are studied in detail.[26]

NOTES TO CHAPTER III

[1] *Archaeologia 96*, 1955, pp. 197–235.

[2] A bronze duck-head found at the Hengistbury, Hants., harbour settlement, associated with early (III century at latest) pottery is of the same character; in such a situation this may well be an import. *Excavations at Hengistbury Head*, J. P. Bushe-Fox (Soc. Antiq., 1915, p. 61) and *Plate XXIX,6*.

[3] *Early Celtic Art*, Plate *201, 1*.

[4] There is no reason why settlers looking for good land should not move from the north-east coast into the north-west—long treks are well known to history; but it leaves the undoubtedly close relationship of the northern Irish art to Torrs, illustrated by Atkinson and Piggott, still more puzzling.

[5] Atkinson and Piggott, *Archaeologia 96*, 1955, p. 219.

[6] The find-spot is unknown, but it was certainly on the eastern side of Lincoln Edge, probably at Tattershall Ferry. See footnote 14 below.

[7] I agree with Stuart Piggott as to its date within its early group: *Proc. Prehist. Soc.*, 1950, pp. 3–4—but see Jacobsthal, *Burlington Magazine*, Vol. 75, pp. 28–31.

[8] These incised patterns here and elsewhere are very evenly and smoothly wrought, but can hardly have been produced other than by chisel and mallet. A hair-line has been detected at points where the master's free-hand sketch was not exactly followed, in many works of art discussed in this book.

[9] *Burlington Magazine*, Vol. 75, 1939, p. 28: a very luminous appreciation. Parallels to the diagonal layout of the ornament "in Hungary and Switzerland" are referred to. See also *Early Celtic Art*, Plates *115–16* (Hungary and Austria).

[10] An opinion of Mr. G. Lawrence, given near the end of his life, was that the Roman (and earlier) crossing of the Thames above the city was at Wandsworth, not Brentford. See C. E. Stevens in *Antiquity*, 1947, p. 6.

[11] This nineteenth-century drawing shows, more clearly than any photograph, these secondary incised patterns, particularly the winged-duck motif, concentrated on the central boss. The bizarre forms are recorded, I find, with a high degree of accuracy.

[12] *British Art and the Mediterranean*: text to *Plate 4*.

[13] A common Continental detail.

[14] Mr. R. J. C. Atkinson and Professor Piggott made this interesting discovery.

When the beauty and importance of these R. Witham bronzes (scabbard and shield) is considered, the lack of information, in Lincoln, as to where in the river they were dredged up is surprising. (In the case of the river Thames finds the name of the reach is preserved.) I am told locally that most of the nineteenth-century finds came from the longitude of Fiskerton—a village on the northern bank, 5 miles east of Lincoln, which has an ancient ferry, "Tattershall", still nominally existent. ("Keels"—the local sailing barges—came up river to a basin at Lincoln, hence the nineteenth-century dredging.) This ferry was a link between strings of Saxon villages north and south of the river flanking the upland (Lincoln Edge). (Early traffic along the Edge is likely to have used the southern foot of the escarpment, above the springline, not the crest whereon the Romans built their city and highway.)

[15] Except for two minor elements of the design, the swastikas in the red roundels, and the leafy ornament in the "hollow" triangles: these cannot present fold-over symmetry.

[16] This hoard is again referred to on pp. 127–8 below.

[17] My friend J. W. Brailsford points out in a paper read in 1954 to the Prehistoric Congress at Madrid that the red material is "glass cut to shape and secured with a black bituminous cement in a true cloisonné technique". Dr. Plenderleith and Mr. Maryon demonstrated this, and showed also that the shield was "originally decorated by mercury gilding".

[18] *A Find . . . from Llyn Cerrig Bach, Anglesey*, 1946, p. 18, Figure 9, shows the structural range of the type.

[19] 1939: *Burlington Magazine*, No. 75, p. 2; see also Saxl and Wittkower, *British Art and the Mediterranean*, 1948.

[20] I think this arose in conversation: I cannot validate it.

[21] It seems indeed likely that the Germanic tradition of valuable gift-giving from princes to lesser chieftains on suitable occasions has a long history behind it, and that the ablest craftsmen in the Celtic world were continuously employed for that reason.

[22] Isolated by E. T. Leeds in *Celtic Ornament* as founding a distinctive style (p. 6), but I cannot wholly agree with the relationships there set out (the shield boss associated on the plate is incorrectly provenanced).

[23] Compare, with the harness ornaments we shall study, the drab series of Hallstatt bronzes of similar purpose obviously made for a chieftain, contained in the Parc-y-meirch, Abergele, hoard from Denbighshire already referred to; A. S. Sheppard, *Arch. Camb.*, 1941, pp. 1–10, and Piggott, *Proc. Soc. Ant. Scot.*, 1954.

[24] Figured by Mortimer, *Forty Years . . .*, p. 355. See Stuart Piggott in *Proc. Prehist. Soc.*, 1950, p. 26.

[25] Jacobsthal illustrates an "anthropoid" sword handle with a hair-do of exactly the same character as ours but less finely wrought, from Dinnyes, Hungary: *Early Celtic Art*, No. 884, *Plate 55*.

[26] This brief note is based on an exhaustive survey of the whole field, Continental and British, of these anthropoid-hilted weapons, an advance copy of which was kindly sent to me: R. R. Clarke and C. F. C. Hawkes, "An Anthropoid Sword from . . . Norfolk, with related Continental and British Weapons", *Proc. Prehist. Soc.*, 1956, No. 21.

CHAPTER IV. BRITISH SCHOOLS OF CELTIC ART
SECONDARY PHASES : c. 100–1 B.C.

It is now possible, thanks to the research of two generations of scholars in Britain, to begin to define schools of metal-workers deriving their impetus, methods, and ideas from the creative art of the primary phases which we have studied. Sometimes the pieces are individual, unique survivals : sometimes they occur in close-knit groups. Survival is a matter of chance ; and no work of art of individual character can be regarded as necessarily unique. The "shops" of workers in metal—practically everything of artistic quality that survives is of bronze or iron or (rarely) gold—each had traditions and techniques, rapidly modified in the time of a creative master, ticking over when an "old hand" was in charge, but always, it may be suspected, conforming to the *spirit* of the shop. This is the way, in such communities, new styles slowly arise ; and why the examples one studies seem always to our eyes, mature, though they are really links in a chain of evolution either of pattern or form, or both. The Celtic workshop rarely died, I think; individuals came in, and others passed out, but something more than the technique was preserved.

This chapter, then, analyses a progressive and varied phase of insular art, arising in both north-east and south Britain. The reader will see, in the Contents table, that several overlapping groups or schools are involved :

North-Eastern and Central	..	..	*c.*	100–50 B.C.
Southern	..	..	*c.*	75–40 B.C.
Central and North-Eastern	..	..	*c.*	60–30 B.C.
East-Central	..	..	*c.*	40–20 B.C.
The Thames Schools	..	..	*c.*	30–10 B.C.
Western	..	..	*c.*	70–1 B.C.

Llyn Cerrig, an Anglesey site, has *imported* objects judged to be from two or three groups, mostly from the north-eastern region.

We shall deal with relief and incised work, well represented in previous chapters, also with "matted" work, a technique in which the surface of the metal is in places roughened, to give a different reaction to light from that of the smooth metal and so giving solidity to an outlined pattern (or, sometimes, background). The find-sites are shown on Map B.

NORTH-EASTERN AND CENTRAL SCHOOLS *c.* 100–50 B.C.

(i) INCISED ORNAMENT (*c.* 100 B.C.)

The Sutton (Lincs.) scabbard

Incised ornament is the only decoration on a sword-scabbard (represented by its scabbard-plate), as it is on the Torrs drinking-horns. This plate is nearly 2 ft. long, and was dredged from the gravelly bed of the river Trent between Sutton and Cromwell Lock, Newark;[1] it is reproduced in three sections on *Plate 21*.[2]

The ornament begins at the scabbard-mouth on both sides of the central rib, thereafter alternating ; the units of the pattern diminish in size as the scabbard tip is approached and the penultimate one opens with a horizontal bar. Since this ornament has been dusted with chalk for photographic purposes, it here unduly dominates the object decorated ; the "blank" spaces are not wholly void, being roughened by parallel, just visible incisions of the utmost delicacy—25 to the inch—unlike anything else in the design.

The pattern is a repetition of simple forms (Figure 83, J77–79), defined by clean-cut, flat-floored lines constant in dimension, producing by their accurate and beautiful curves an appearance of effortless perfection. The enclosed figures are made by cutting back the bronze to define, within, circular spots of varying sizes and shapes. The units of the design differ in detail, giving liveliness to the pattern in general, but the repetitive features point to the piece being late in its class, as does a daintiness so extreme as to be, surely, the prelude to extinction of the technique. The double horizontal bar at the mouth represents a normal definition of this highly decorated part of the scabbard; but the single bars of the pattern near the tip of the scabbard are of particular interest. Such bars, surely, are survivals of the great period of the northern schools (cf. the Torrs horns), revealing the origin of the decoration: this parallel has not been appreciated. The date of our piece can hardly be earlier than 100 B.C.; the extent and quality of the lost second-century work in this mode in Britain can only be guessed at.

(ii) Relief Ornament, based on "Trumpet" Scrolls and Lobes

(a) The Llyn Cerrig Plaque, Anglesey[3] c. 70 B.C.

Seldom has it fallen to the lot of a student of Early Celtic art in Britain to discover a piece of such dynamic character and artistic significance as the Llyn Cerrig bronze "crescentic" plaque (*Plate 23a*). It is approximately circular, and a similarly shaped hole gives it a crescentic form; the broadest portion of the plaque carries the decoration. In the centre is a roundel enclosing a triquetra based on "trumpet" scrolls with lobed stems and domed mouths, three of which terminate on one side in a tendril curled round a boss (Figure 82, D24–28); a striking feature is the asymmetry of the design. The three voids though apparently dissimilar, are alike in that each is bounded by three curves, one of which is "S"-shaped (Figure 83, L98–100); to create them trumpets and lobes are linked or extended as required, by relief on a lower plane. Two large lobes flank the triquetral circle on each side: their thick ends touch each other: their tapering ends join their opposites at top and bottom forming an ovoid frame to the circle: from the point of contact of each pair a different but similar-sized lobe leads the eye upward and outward to the undecorated portion of the plaque (a unit is shown on Figure 83, J76). The work is freehand, no two elements being exactly the same size. The more the plaque has been studied during the last eight years the more extended have the repetitions and ramifications of its circular design in relief been seen to be: translated into a two-dimensional pattern it dominates the great series of bronze mirrors which, as we shall see, provide an unexampled concentration of fine craftsmanship, art, and ingenuity. That in it a three-way pattern had sufficient eccentricity of lay-out to satisfy the taste of its age is certain; but why did the age set such store by such a pattern?

This question must remain rhetorical; we have other business in hand. It is the flanking lobes best seen in Figure 18, not the circle-with-triquetra, which must first be stressed, for they indicate origins, being those characteristic of the Torrs school (Figure 16 and *Plate 19c*). Once this is noted, the congruity of the lobed stems of the triquetral element of the design is evident. We see, moreover, a massive development of the "dome with knob" present at Torrs (Figure 82, C20). Lastly, the voids of the pattern, isolated in Figure 31 below, have great influence in later art.

(b) Burial Group, Grimthorpe, East Riding (Yorks): *roundel, shield-boss and sword c. 70–50 B.C.*

The same eccentricity as the plaque presents is seen on the contemporary Grimthorpe (Yorks) bronze roundel (*Plate 23b*) associated with a burial, and apparently an ornament from the major axis of a long shield.[4] Elements of the design (Figure 19), moreover, closely resemble the larger lobe pattern of the plaque. Furthermore, the roundel introduces a wayward informal character to the lobed patterns which emerged in such impressive fold-over symmetry at Torrs. Torrs, as we have seen, is not to a modern mind rational in

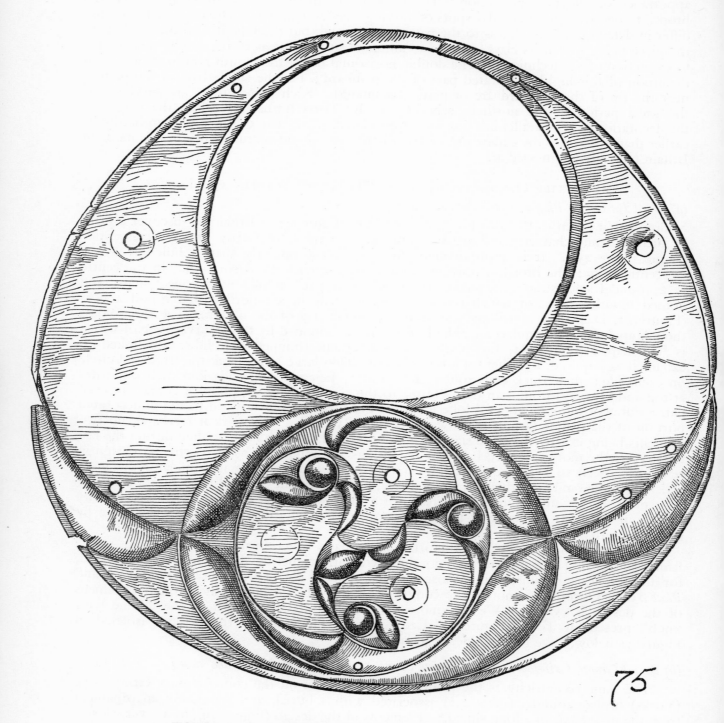

FIGURE 18.—Plaque, crescentic: Llyn Cerrig (Anglesey ⅓). See *Plate 23a*: detail.

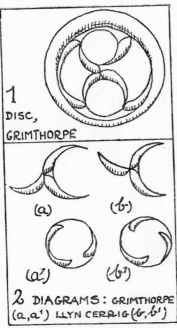

FIGURE 19.—Bronze disc:
Grimthorpe (East Riding, Yorks.).

detail: coils and lobes are imposed on larger swellings without congruity. This tiny roundel, anyway, goes further, presenting a complete, calculated irrationality, such as, it seems, may appear at any phase of Celtic art history: this is, to some students of the period, one of its attractions.[5]

We have hitherto endeavoured to follow the development of certain styles, or at least to group the known examples. The Grimthorpe roundel comes in without question; but its associates in the grave, a shield-boss and a scabbarded sword offers an opportunity, *en passant,* for considering the variety that ornament in the first half of I B.C. may present. The shield-boss (on the same plate (*23c*)) has a rigid, two-dimensional formal pattern (mainly geometric) in matted technique (83, 42–3); a classic piece in the strict sense. The sword is, on the other hand, "baroque"; there is a heavy bronze hilt-guard steeply arched, and the scabbard-chape (Figure 20) is equally massive. It shows the beginnings of the "lips" ornament (p. 41 below), and is therefore later (*c.* 50 B.C.).

From all this, it is clear that the Celtic craftsmen in the north now had a very varied and complex inheritance of ideas and motifs on which to employ mind and hand.

(c) Bridle-bit: Ulceby (Lincs.)

Closely associated in style with the plaque roundel, again, is the fragmentary bronze bridle-bit from Ulceby (in Lindsey, near the Humber mouth). It is of "Arras"[6] type, dating in mid-I B.C. and shows the Llyn Cerrig "trumpets" in relief adapted to a spherical surface — namely, the knob through which the bit-ring passes. The photographs kindly supplied by the Director of the Liverpool Museum (*Plate 24*) bring out the essential features of both parts of the piece. The material is iron cased in bronze, like so much of the early Northern metal-work, and the partial decay of the structure is due to oxidation and expansion of the core which has split the ring. The frilled seam of the casing is seen in "C", developed

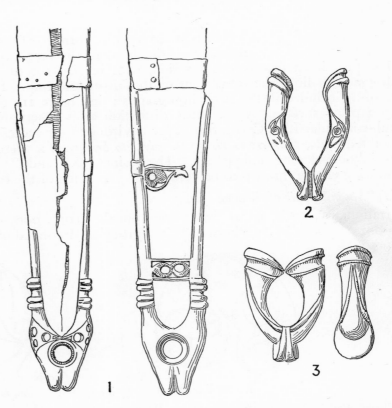

FIGURE 20.—Scabbard chapes. 1. Grimthorpe (Yorks.); 2. Glencotho (Peebles); 3. Hounslow, Westruther (Berwicks.) (½).

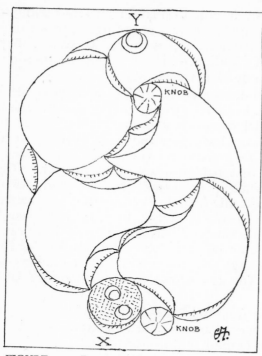

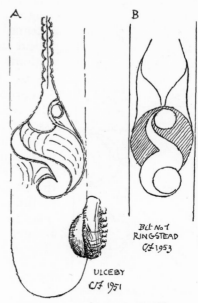

FIGURE 21a.—Pattern on Horse-bit: Ulceby (Lincs.).
(See *Plate 24*.)

FIGURE 21b.—Bits: Ulceby, and
Ringstead (Norf.). Detail.

below into a pattern of incised three-sided forms. These also are, in places, the background to the relief ornament on the knob of the bit; two are seen in both "A" and "B". The prominent discs on either side, with berried rosette ornament (Figure 83, G56), are designed to limit the movement of the bit on the ring. Practically all the pattern on the knob is included in the two photographs: in Figure 21a the whole design is translated on to a plane surface, with as little distortion as is practicable. The smooth voids, mostly sub-triangular Llyn Cerrig forms, are environed by a succession of tiny rounded ridges with pointed ends, *their crests rising sharply into bold relief*: these are characteristic features of a rapidly-developing unique art. The points "X" and "Y" marked on photograph and drawing enable the two to be compared. A sketch of the casing is added (Figure 21b).

(d) "Spoons", pair of, Weston (Som.)

Irrationality, such as we have seen on the Torrs pony-cap, occurs on one of a pair of bronze "spoons"—an otherwise "late" group of decorated objects discussed on p. 111 below

S.P. 1955 *(Drawn by Stuart Piggott)*

FIGURE 22.—Pattern on bronze spoons: Weston, near Bath (Som.) (⅔).

whose use is uncertain—found at Weston, Somersetshire (near Bath) on the line of the Jurassic Way. These patterns have been kindly drawn for me at the Scottish National

Museum by my friend Stuart Piggott (Figure 22). He remarks *apropos* of the difficulties he encountered, that the patterns are "in very low relief, and the spoons have been much handled; there is a quite incalculable quality of design that prevents one from anticipating what the curve will do next." The left-hand sequence, a double loop blossoming into a succession of lobes and triangles with curved sides and scrolled tips (Figure 82, C21) is rational and offers no problem, but the right-hand spoon presents a formless jumble, with the tips and sides of separate elements "colliding."[7]

Thus the development in this British art is precisely that from repetitive, ordered control to freedom which, though extreme, may have seemed exciting to the craftsman: it is fascinating to see the two stages side by side, obviously the work of one individual, working, it is likely, at the northern end of the Jurassic Zone.

Another point arises: had these two pieces been found separately, their presumed dates might well have been a generation (some thirty years) apart! Pairs, in these objects, are normal.

(e) Torcs in precious metals

The earliest gold torc of Celtic character, the magnificent piece from Needwood Forest in the Trent valley (Notts), is illustrated on *Plate 25*.

It is composed of six rope-like units, each of three strands of gold wire: its loop terminal shows simple incised and relief ornament in a minor key, the most interesting element being the wavy lines in relief (Figure 83, K87) which represent an *earlier* welding of torc-strands to a loop. Compare the functional jointing in *Plate 24c* (Ulceby). Its simple ornament indicates a date not later than the beginning of I B.C., and its provenance suggests that goldsmiths may then have been working in or near the middle Trent valley (p. 56).

A pair of torcs, of electrum (a gold and silver alloy) was found with the Ulceby bit just described, and should derive from the same region. One is rope-like, of two strands, with double-loop terminals, the other a fourfold plait with broader, four-strand, loops. Examples of this simple form occur, later, in the Snettisham (Norfolk) treasure (p. 45 below).

Comment. A variety of works of art has been discussed in this section. They cover a wide area: Grimthorpe in Yorkshire, and Sutton in Lincolnshire represent a creative region; Weston in Somersetshire is on the Jurassic Way leading from the middle Trent to the Mendips, and the Llyn Cerrig plaque has long been accepted as a product of north-eastern artificers. The Sutton and Weston pieces carry on the northern Marnian tradition, the former in incised, the latter in low-relief work. That this descent, in a transitional stage, is so inadequately represented in surviving bronzes is grievous: but the uniqueness in Britain of another work, the Grimthorpe shield-boss with geometric ornament, reminds us that many unknown styles of creative art may well be hidden in our soil.

The Llyn Cerrig plaque, the Grimthorpe disc, and the Ulceby bit, covering a period of perhaps twenty-five years, combine to show a pattern of lobes in relief, first on a flat, then on a curved surface which, initiated about 70 B.C., dominates the Celtic art of the following hundred years and more, as later chapters will show.

The gold and electrum torcs are of the highest importance. The Needwood Forest specimen (the earliest, *c.* 100 B.C.) comes from the upper Trent region, west of Burton; the others from Lindsey (Ulceby is in that region, bounded on the west and north by the lower Trent and the Humber estuary). Now the source of gold for Iron "B" people will have been either in the near west (Caernarvonshire)[8] or more probably further away, in Ireland (the Wicklow Mountains), but no route from the Clwyd estuary, rich in gold finds (Map B), a possible base for such traffic across Britain, by the Peak to the Jurassic Way, can yet be discerned in the find-pattern of our art. Neither the Mersey estuary, nor the Aire gap in the Pennine Chain, offer any focus of Celtic finds as yet, for an alternative route. Nevertheless, the probability is that the goldsmiths of the period were active in a "central" area—somewhere between Needwood Forest and Lindsey, at this period; the Wolds of east Lincolnshire indeed seem, for them (and other craftsmen), a likely settlement and "industrial" area.

SOUTHERN SCHOOLS c. 75–40 B.C.

A fresh art style arises in our southern region early in I B.C. It is expressed in incised work and in relief: the former is of the utmost delicacy.

(a) *Anthropoid-hilted dagger and scabbard*: *river Witham*

The earliest piece thus ornamented is the sheath of the anthropoid-hilted dagger which, like earlier works of the highest quality, had been deposited in the Tattershall Reach of the river Witham. Though, unfortunately, this has disappeared, its character and its grip are familiar to students of our art through the finely-detailed Victorian drawing in *Horae Ferales,* reproduced in *Plate 10 e.* It belongs to the series illustrated in Figure 23; the latest scholar

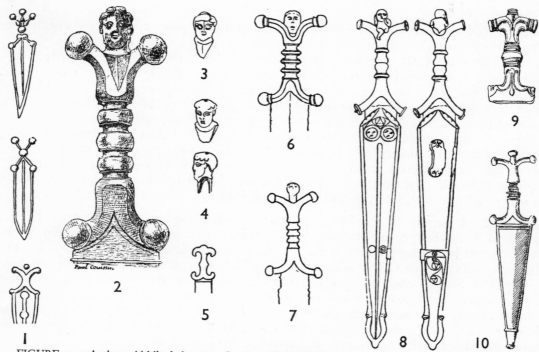

FIGURE 23.—Anthropoid-hilted daggers: Continental and British. No. 6, North Grimston (Yorks.) (⅓); No. 8, River Witham (Lincs.); No. 10, Ham Hill (Som.). (No. 8 is ⅕ scale.)

to be enchanted by its originality and quality, C. F. C. Hawkes, describes it[9] as "the final flourish of the whole story of the human hilt" since "the humanity has escaped from the typological prison of the grip and limbs and squats free upon it". The imp-like figure at the top of the grip, thus made respectable, is too Victorian to be entirely accurate, and a nineteenth-century record "Figure very barbarously executed" confirms this opinion. With this correction, we may accept the piece as genuine, for the careful drawing of the sheath, though unique, is recognizably Celtic, and British rather than Continental. The chape has a slight thickening at the tip, and the usual delicate mouldings at the sides: two rings at the mouth of the sheath show pin-heads for coloured bosses of enamel or glass. The distinctive British feature referred to is delicate incised ornament at the top of the chape making novel use of a form just coming to life in our art: two hollow-sided "triangles" within circles

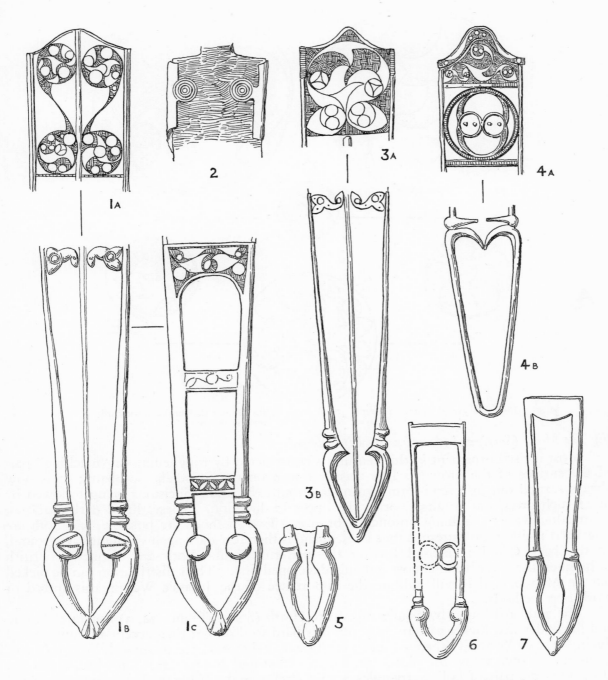

FIGURE 24.—Scabbards: 1, 2—Hunsbury (Northants.); 3—Meare (Som.); 4—Amerden (Bucks.); 5—Wood Eaton (Oxon.); 6, 7—Spettisbury (Dorset) (½).

(as Figure 82, C23) are enmeshed in "trumpet-coils", the "frame" of this complex being asymmetric. The character of this incised art points to manufacture in the Thames valley region.

Similar, more elaborate southern patterns and their technique, will now be examined.

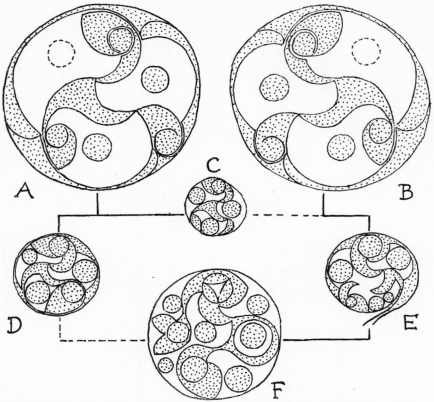

FIGURE 25.—Triquetral patterns. A, B. Llyn Cerrig plaque; C. Hunsbury scabbard;
D, E. "Mayer" mirror; F. St. Keverne mirror.

(b) The Meare (Som.) and Amerden (Bucks) scabbards

Most incised ornament in this century is constructed by roughening or "hatching" part of the surface of the bronze. This was first seen on the Standlake scabbard; it is now always carried out in a semi-formal manner, groups of parallel incisions being followed by other such groups at an angle, or in the opposite direction. These throw dark shadows, contrasting with the shining untouched bronze. Two methods are possible, and both are now used : either the pattern is thus incised, and is therefore dark against a light background, or the background is incised leaving the pattern bright. Both are distinctive British techniques, the latter being almost certainly developed first. Their distribution can be picked out on Map B, and it will indicate the importance of the Jurassic Way in this spread of workshop methods.

The scabbard found by chance on Meare Heath (Som.) (Figure 24, 3) has an elaborate and finely detailed locket pattern in which it is hard to do other than accept an "unresolved duality"; two "matted" shapes confront a lighter design outlined in smooth bronze (above them, as the owner saw the piece), greater in extent and complexity. This bronze shows, also, the same pair of hollow triangles within circles as the Witham sheath, one associated with a "trumpet" form (Figure 83, L98).

When the Amerden (Bucks) scabbard, on the same figure, is examined, no doubt arises as to the character of the two-dimensional pattern on the locket; it is a three-way coil of shining bronze, with a heavily matted background.[10] There are roundels with double circles in the structure, with trumpet shapes as at Meare, and the matted background is structurally similar. We are dealing with a single art-group, very delicate and refined, southern in its distribution.

40

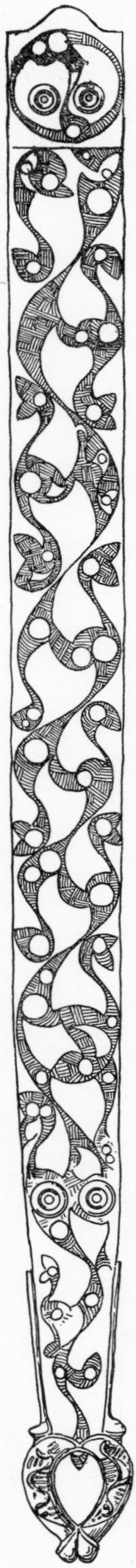

We are now to describe the beginnings of the two-dimensional art of the "Llyn Cerrig" school, under southern influence.

(a) Scabbard, Hunsbury (Northants)

This scabbard (Figure 24) has the beginnings of "lips" to the chape, and so is somewhat more advanced than the southern examples we have just considered; it is contemporary with the Grimthorpe scabbard (p. 35). The find-spot is near the Jurassic Way, and its maker could have been in touch with both the northern and southern workshops.

On the locket is a pair of opposed "S"-curves terminating in large roundels with complex designs; the upper has examples of the Llyn Cerrig triquetra in bright bronze (Figure 25), lacking the rigid, controlled excellence of the original —one also shows an incorrect copy of the "southern" hollow-sided "triangle" within a circle as a central feature. The lower presents a pair of trilobed figures with curled tips, one "moving" clockwise, the other in reverse; in both pairs the matted background is dotted with discs of bright bronze. The whole design on one side of the central rib of the scabbard being similar to its opposite, the piece provides in this field of creative art an approach to the canon of fold-over symmetry. Three-way figures are also seen at the head of the chape structure: that on the front in relief, on the back in matted technique. The latter is structurally identical with the ornament on the Amerden scabbard, but reversed and simplified; the art developed in the south-east has, in short, established itself, *with a difference,* in our central (Jurassic) region.

(b) Scabbard, Bugthorpe (Yorks.)

The earliest piece of importance in Britain on which incised "shaded" pattern is extensively employed is probably the handsome scabbard from Bugthorpe (East Riding, Yorks.). No two of the long rhythmic scroll-forms on the scabbard are exactly alike; this illustrates the free-hand character of Celtic incised art at the northern end of the Jurassic Zone at this stage. Figure 26 is a beautiful drawing by Professor Stuart Piggott of a very complex and intriguing pattern,[11] distinctively insular. (One element, the *yin-yang* circle at the mouth, is reproduced in the "Grammar"—Figure 83, G57.) Though northern, its connection with the Sutton (river Trent) scabbard—art is only in the rhythmic treatment—sweeping curves as a major theme, and with "T"-shaped laterals depending therefrom.

The heavy chape of the Yorkshire scabbard is of advanced character, being parted at the tip, with two full "lips", and having elaborate ornament in relief (*Plate 53*). Study of this delicate work in the British Museum shows that the wandering, knobbed coils seen in the photograph are a succession of tiny "Llyn Cerrig" trumpet-forms with "tails",

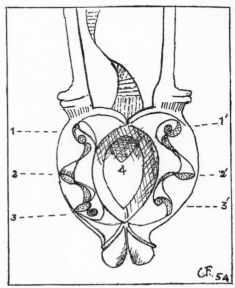

FIGURE 27.—Scabbard-tip: Bugthorpe. Detail. (⅓)

FIGURE 26. Scabbard: Bugthorpe (Yorks.) (⅓).

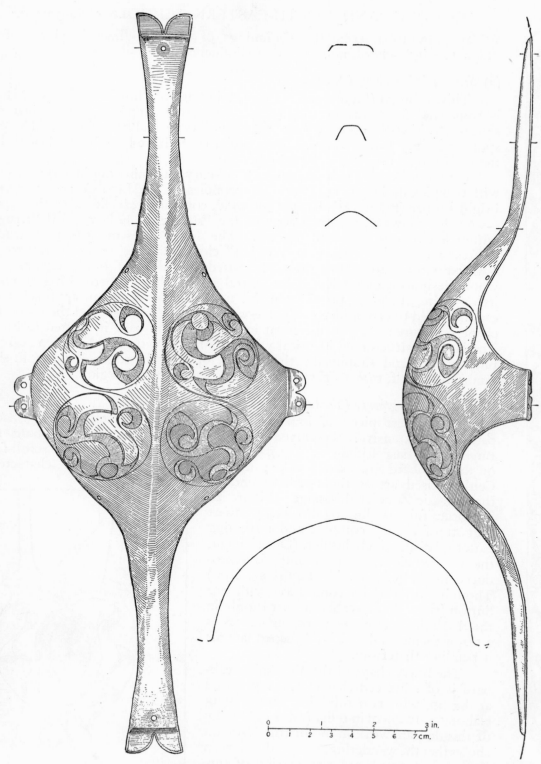

FIGURE 28.—Shield-boss, Llyn Cerrig (Anglesey).

widely spaced but carefully wrought: four have a terminal knob to the trumpet-head like the crescentic Plaque (but of course cast, not hammered up from the back). These are sketched on Figure 27; the trumpets with knobs are numbered 1 and 3 on each side: those without, 2. The two patterns are not identical. The tongue numbered 4 is the tip of the scabbard decoration. The date of this fine piece will be about 50 B.C.

This loose-jointed, tenuous art of the chape is distinctly northern; we shall in due course study examples from Norfolk, and chronicle an extension to the Thames valley (p. 49).

The relation of Bugthorpe to northern Irish art of the later I B.C. is close, and therefore worth recording here. A Lisnacroghera, Antrim, piece, illustrated on *Plate 73b*, shows this clearly; but it retains "Marnian" motifs,[12] which British art has now lost. We do not know how the Irish folk could have picked up the new design, but must assume a certain amount of cross-channel traffic, and a flourishing British settlement in Galloway, retaining early traditions for which the only known evidence are the Torrs pony-cap and horns.[13]

Lastly, the florid style reflects a richness in the northern art of the time, as a whole, in this phase: the bronze mount with pinned-on domes of red enamel, on *Plate 11c*, was associated with the sword.

(c) Shield-boss, Llyn Cerrig (*Anglesey*)

The next piece with incised ornament we should look at is the shield-boss from Llyn Cerrig (Anglesey), which has triskeles in pairs on either side of the central rib, capped with scrolls in the north-eastern tradition, but with coiled terminals, and therefore later. It is very difficult to reproduce direct, and a museum drawing is therefore substituted (Figure 28). The pattern is beautiful, and the quality of movement it possesses adds to its interest. Furthermore, as Figure 29 shows more clearly, it has, as I noted in 1945, a character new to us, tenseness: an expression in abstract art of force held in leash. Look at the top left-hand roundel, its clockwise movement is manifest; look again, and you perceive that this movement is countered by the

Tooling enlarged 3/1

FIGURE 29.—Shield-boss: Llyn Cerrig. Detail of roundels. (¾)

"broken scroll", taut, rigid, angular, curved like a scimitar in the opposite direction, whose point is held in place by the bounding-line of the roundel—which proceeds on its way to create similar tension in the next unit. The key-note of the design then is unstable

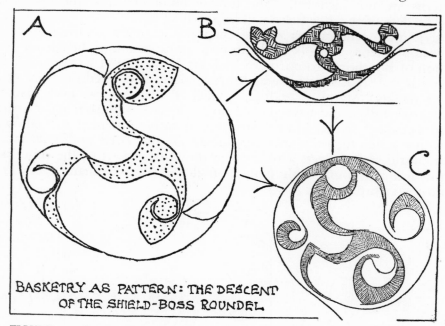

FIGURE 30.—Details of: A. Plaque 75; B. Bugthorpe scabbard; C. Shield-boss 98.

equilibrium, balance not permanent but temporary and precarious, exciting, like that achieved by a man on a tight-rope.

This shield is an import into Anglesey, as is nearly all the metal-work found at Llyn Cerrig. Figure 30 shows its relation to the Bugthorpe pattern; it is obviously later.[14] The voids on the shield boss, as on the plaque (Figure 31), are recurrent in the art of the period (e.g. Figure 83, L101). The plaque forms are the more important, in our art history.

Comment. The elaborate stylized ornament on these pieces inspires much of the decorative metal-work—mainly two-dimensional—of the next half-century, as we shall see in the following section of the survey.

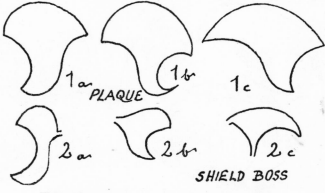

FIGURE 31.—Shapes of voids: Llyn Cerrig.

EAST-CENTRAL SCHOOLS *c.* 40–20 B.C.

(*a*) *Horse-bits, Ringstead (Norfolk)*

The north-eastern (Ulceby) school (p. 35 above) is represented at this stage by horse-bits in the Ringstead (Norfolk) hoard;[15] these are in the same technique, and have the same berried knobs. But a comparison of the relief on the Ulceby piece with theirs (as seen on *Plate 28*) shows that the integration of detail is less orderly; these designs seem here to have reached an almost formless stage. I include, on Figure 21b, a sketch of my own, of the ornament

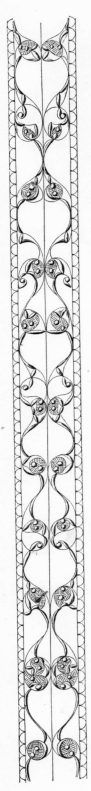

at the end of the casing—in the same tradition as, but later than, that at Ulceby: note the scroll, knobbed at either end, in each. A date about 40 B.C. and manufacture in the east-central region—middle Trent and upper Witham basins—are likely.

(b) (c) *Gold bracelet and electrum torc, Hoard E, Snettisham (Norfolk)*

We should bring in, at this stage, one of the famous finds from a small area on Ken Hill, Snettisham (Norfolk); "Hoard E", now in the British Museum.[16] The two pieces in this find well illustrate the view that the principal centre or centres of goldsmithery in eastern Britain from mid-I B.C. onwards worked in the modified "Llyn Cerrig style" exemplified on the Ulceby (Lincs.) bridle-bit.

Ken Hill is a prominent landmark—especially from the sea (the Wash)—and is close to the north end of the Icknield Way (Map B). Early Celtic finds of metal-work are concentrated hereabouts—at Bardsey, Ringstead, and North Creake, as well as our site—and there may have been a little harbour at the end of the Way, just beyond Ringstead, providing means of access to the Lincolnshire coast, or further, to the Humber estuary. Ken Hill yields Iron Age "A" pottery; it is not clear whether the site was inhabited when the gold ornaments and gold fragments (Hoards A to E, as they are termed) were buried, but the work was carried out with care, that is, with intent to recover.

The pieces here referred to are a small gold bracelet and a large torc with ring terminals, of electrum.

The pattern of the former piece is finely illustrated in my Figure 32, from R. Rainbird Clarke's paper. It shows the elongated, pointed, curved ridges of the style, with one "steep" side, linking the concentrations: these are modified "Llyn Cerrig" trumpet coils sometimes with terminal knobs and, important for relative dating, matted surfaces—circular, "trumpet-shaped", or like a "fat" comma, each with two pin-heads. The voids of the pattern, along the axis, are large, heart-shaped and onion-shaped, with half-units of similar character at the sides. In technique the ornament resembles that on the Broighter (Co. Derry, Ireland)[17] torc which, whether made there or in Britain, is certainly by an "east-central" goldsmith, as understood in this section.

I now turn to the great torc from Hoard E which is obviously from a different workshop. Mr. Alan Sorrell, R.W.S., whose sensitive handling of works of art is well known, was invited by the National Museum to make the drawings reproduced on Figures 33 and 34, which fully bring out its quality. The massive rope-like twist and the ring terminals with their bold and varied enrichment show a magnificence surely associated only with Icenian royalty on state occasions, or with Druidic religion.[18] The piece lacks the repose of noble art; but high rank or national ritual requires, on occasion, extravagant display. It is interesting to note that the delicate sinuous "joint" pattern of the Needwood torc (*Plate 25*) is here an ornament defining, on either side, the junction of the neck with the loop and with the rope-like twist.

FIGURE 32. Ornament on gold bracelet: Snettisham (Norf.) (⅝).

Figure 33 shows the piece from two aspects. The type is known as a ring- or loop-terminal torc; the "hoop" is of eight strands each of eight twisted wires; the rings are hollow.

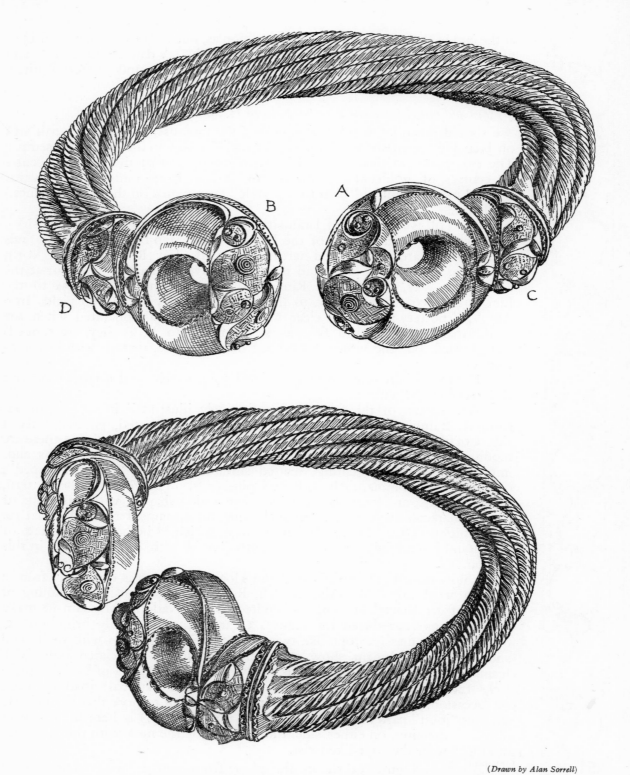

FIGURE 33.—Torc, electrum: Hoard E, Snettisham (Norfolk) (⅓).

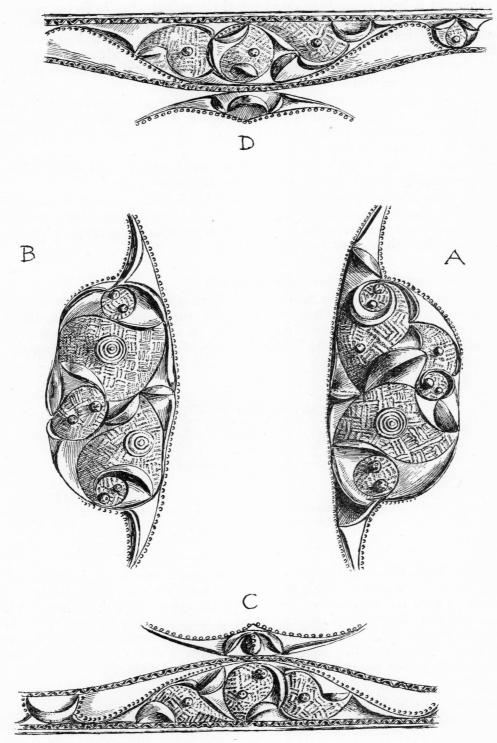

FIGURE 34.—Torc, electrum: Snettisham. Details as lettered on Figure 33. ($\frac{2}{1}$)

47

The ornament is bold enough to dominate the terminals, but in fact it is restricted on each side to two panels, one on the front of the outer face of the ring, the other encircling the neck—but most concentrated, of course, on the outside. Cross-hatched units, some shaped like Llyn Cerrig-plaque backgrounds (*Plate 23a*), and with pin-heads wrought as though they fastened the relief to the ring, are very effective; for their place in the designs we must turn to the copies set out on a plane surface (Figure 34).

A, on the right-hand ring, shows a medley of sub-triangular and circular cross-hatched patterns with one or more decorated or plain pin-heads, and plain domed units, one shaped like a cornucopia; much of the work is in high relief. The interested reader can easily isolate similar shapes on the opposite ring.

The ornament on the necks is also set out on this Figure (C and D): it shows closely related patterns, mostly within narrow sinuous borders also in relief.

As for the date of these pieces: they are both latish in the century, because the single "pinhead" which characterized *functional* studs, is on bracelet and torc represented by a variety of decorative projections, often two on the same stud. Function is here forgotten; torc and bracelet, then, should not be earlier than, say, 20 B.C.

(d) Electrum tubular torc, Hoard A, Snettisham (Norfolk)

The only other ornament from Snettisham requiring consideration here is one of three tubular torcs in Hoard A (No. 1, Rainbird Clarke): the metal is electrum, the structural character, again, that of the Broighter, Ireland, torc. It is the largest and best preserved of the group and, as *Plate 32b* shows, the "heavy rear moulding" survives undamaged. A band

FIGURE 35.—Torc, electrum, tubular: Hoard A, Snettisham. Detail. (⅔)
(After R. Rainbird Clarke, *P.P.S.*, 1954, p. 37.)

of three double-lobe-and-boss patterns in relief, the largest in the centre, is framed by delicate herring-bone incised ornament. Each boss is composed of four lobes (Figure 83, J71): the centre one is seen to be "moving" in a direction opposite to the others. The larger lobes swing outwards, the sense of movement being heightened by the curved "shading" of the background (Figure 35). These lobes have a curved line incised along their mass which shows that they derive from the Llyn Cerrig "trumpet": that the piece was made in an east-central workshop, like the other, has thus considerable backing.

(e) Torc, Cairnmuir (Peeblesshire)

To this east-central school of Snettisham torc "A" belongs the well-known gold torc-terminal found at Cairnmuir, Peebles (*Plate 29a*); it is here regarded as an export to the North. The high relief of the ornament in this style, and its character, is well shown in the photograph: it well illustrates the rich, glittering quality of the Snettisham gold-work.[19]

48

(a) *The Horned Helmet* : *river Thames at Waterloo Bridge*

The famous "Horned helmet" in the British Museum is one of the best-known Early Celtic works of art in Britain. Unique in character, it was dredged from the bed of the Thames at Waterloo Bridge, below, one would suppose, any possible early ford of the river. It measures $16\frac{1}{2}$ in. from tip to tip of the horns, and is a work of a "Thames Valley" school already referred to (p. 43), dating about 25 B.C. (It has seemed to me necessary, theoretically, to move the creative centres of this southern art further inland than the lower Thames, closer to sources of metal (Mendips ?) and to the Jurassic traffic route to and from the northern settlements.) Many photographs of the helmet have been published ; one, showing the softly-rounded character of the detail is here reproduced (*Plate 27b*). This piece also was considered very suitable for Mr. Sorrell to exercise his perceptive artistry on, and there are, as in the case of the gold torc, two pages of drawings. One (Figure 36a) shows the helmet from two points of view, so that the reader can judge the character of the piece and the effect of the relief work on front and back. The other (Figure 36b) is a finely detailed drawing of the two ornamental patterns. In front is an inverted "V" figure, consisting of complex units at three salient points linked by two tenuous bands. Three applied studs, enamelled, with knobby central rivet-heads, reinforce the triple theme. The rim of the helmet above the forehead of the warrior was, I consider, unornamented. This was an artistically sound decision, remarkable at such a time ; for the return of the piece to the workshop—either for repair, or deepened to fit another owner, let in a band of ornament which, though clearly by the same craftsman, was unrelated structurally to the work above it.

The back, wholly original, but damaged, has an eccentric design similar in character, with the point of the "V" at the bottom. Studied on a colleague's head at the Museum, it seems right thus to emphasize the vertical axis (spine) of the human body, and so to spread the ornament outwards and upwards ; this axial theme, moreover, was restated as a feathery crest between the horns. Turning to detail : the ornament consists of narrow curved stalks thickening here and there and expanding into "trumpets", or rising into higher relief to display half-circle, lobed, or other forms (e.g. Figure 83, J72–3). The bold S-curved pair of lobes on the outer coils at the back is in the Torc style; the patterns each present, it will be noted, a close approximation to fold-over symmetry. Lastly, the constructional joints of the helmet are, as can be seen, decoratively rendered. What an astonishing new life in the "Thames" workshop the piece represents ! The nearly contemporary Battersea shield technique with its meticulous formalism is put aside : a *renewed* creative urge, stimulated by the northern achievements—renewed since it incorporates early southern technical skill—is triumphant. The character of the relief work, more soft and rounded than the northern pieces, strongly reminds one of the technique of the much earlier Wandsworth round shield boss (*Plate 13a*) and I suggest it may come from the same *atelier*.

(b) *Spearhead, river Thames at Datchet* (*Berks.*)

The linear decoration in a southern mode (*Plate 39*), stimulated by the Meare and Amerden craftsmanship, on an iron spearhead, say *c.* 30 B.C., from the "Thames near Datchet" is remarkable. The shape and placing of the ornament, on the other hand, are strongly reminiscent of the much earlier mount on the Witham scabbard (*Plate 22* above) which—I am now suggesting—may also have come from a workshop on the Thames. The spearhead should indeed be regarded, in my view, as an expression of a continuous tradition in the (middle ?) Thames region (sustained no doubt by ancient patterns hung on grimy walls) of the way an ornamental panel of the sort should be shaped. I say shaped, advisedly ; for the patterns the forms enclose, separated by centuries, are quite different.

FIGURE 36a.—Horned helmet: River Thames at Waterloo Bridge ($\frac{1}{2}$). A, front (with later strip);
B, back (slightly damaged).

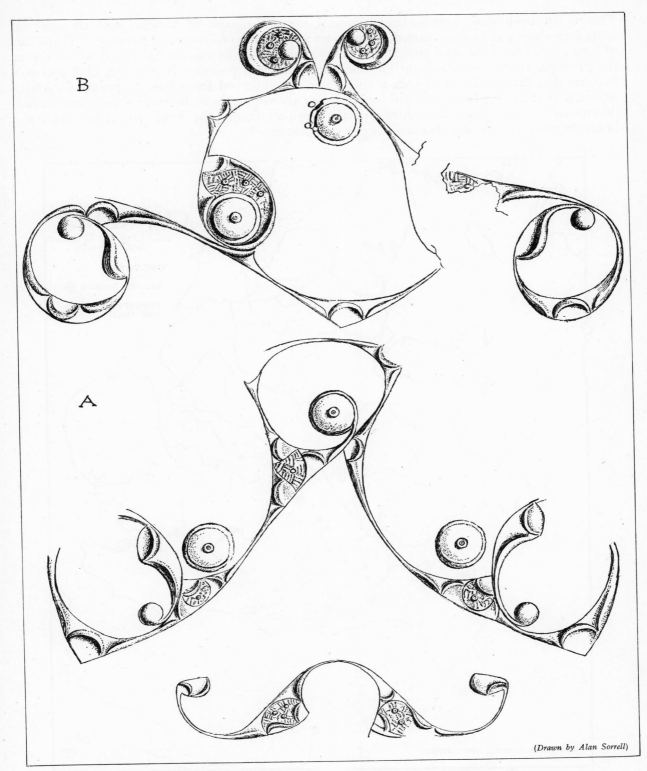

B

A

(Drawn by Alan Sorrell)

FIGURE 36b.—Horned helmet: detail ($\frac{1}{1}$). A, front (with repair-work); B, back.

This is an up-to-date asymmetric, balanced, applied design in bronze, and though the bounding shapes are subtly varied, there is an approach to fold-over symmetry. Three out of four elements of the dual pattern, however, face the same way (to the right) which forces the principal motifs, scrolled and knobbed, into different postures (Figure 82, D28 and 29). Incidentally, the parallelism (since a spear *must* be observed from base to point) illustrates my view that the Witham scabbard locket (p. 25 above) ought to be studied from the mouth downwards. The piece also shows in the outlines facing the blade on either side, the beginnings of the "broken-backed" curve in Celtic art.[20]

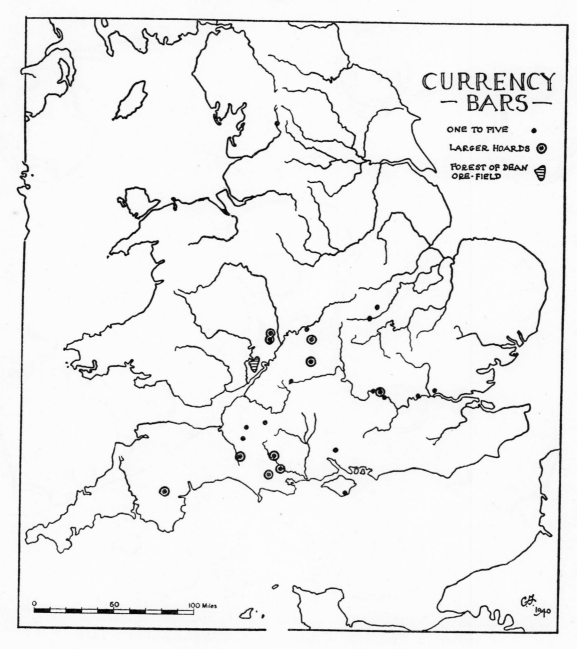

FIGURE 37.—Currency bars: distribution map.

Particular attention should be drawn to the three-way figure in the right-hand band of ornament, at the base of the spear-blade; it is a fresh integration of a familiar scroll-form, and will be seen to influence the later development of pattern-making in Britain.

(c) Bronze Cap, Wood Eaton (Oxon)

For example, it is the only decoration, laid out as a three-armed whirligig in low relief, on the Wood Eaton (Oxon), bronze cap, with central hole for attachment; this is illustrated on *Plate 12c* and sketched on Figure 9a: see also Figure 82, D30. Each arm is of different thickness: two have terminal knobs, the third dies into the edge of the button; the whole is finely modelled, well-balanced, and achieves elegance. The button represents an early decorative tradition, that of the "Marnian 3-way motif" (Figure 6a), bringing the refinement of a "Silver Age"—which this period surely was—into it.

WESTERN SCHOOLS : c. 70–1 B.C.

The Western (Iron) currency

Dobunic, Durotrigan, and Dumnonian territory is covered by the term "Western." The development by the Dobuni (occupying parts of Gloucestershire, upper Thames valley and Somerset) and possibly associated with the Durotriges of Dorset, of a distinctive currency marks a cultural advance, correlated as we shall see with some slight indications of a distinctive art.

The currency was of thin iron bars, each with one end hammered out and bent: a convenient medium for their trade, since they controlled[21] the rich iron-ore deposits of the Forest of Dean. (It precedes, of course, their coinage (*Plate 80*), which appears later than in east Britain). Figure 37 shows the distribution of these bars; it extends into south coastal areas, Durotrigan and Dumnonian (Map C) as well as parts of Hampshire and Isle of Wight, and the Thames valley: two finds on the Jurassic ridge near Northampton suggest connexions with the Hunsbury settlers. Too much must not be made of this wide extension, for my Figure 38 shows that the currency was mainly for home use; the large numbers represented by the *tall* lines on the Figure were found within forty miles of the ore-field: it is a Malvern-Cotswold concentration.

That a currency arose here at all at this time was probably due to the contacts with Brittany, referred to on p. xxv, where a famous means-of-exchange (gold coins imitating staters of Philip II of Macedon) will have been in use from the end of II B.C. Like it, this Dobunian currency had intrinsic value, but it was very much less!

We shall now consider a few works of art from west and south Britain, likely to be of Dobunian or Durotrigan origin.

(a) Torc, Clevedon (Som.)

The buffer terminal of a gold torc of three twists from Clevedon (Som.) (*Plate 25b*)[22] shows a triangular whirligig (Figure 82, D32) and a series of palmettes in low relief. This has always seemed to me a perfect piece of minor Celtic art, in character and site, for the student. Structurally it has a long history behind it; decoratively we have the classical closed palmette, Celticized, on the swell of the terminal, and a distinctive insular pattern on the face, of horned-helmet style: debased "trumpets" with knobbed tips and matted circles (Figure 83, K80). It should date in the second half of I B.C. Lastly, its find site is in a region, the Dobunic-Durotrigan territory, subject to continental as well as insular influences. It is then likely to have been made in a centre of goldsmiths' work other than the east-central one we have predicated; possibly in Dorset.

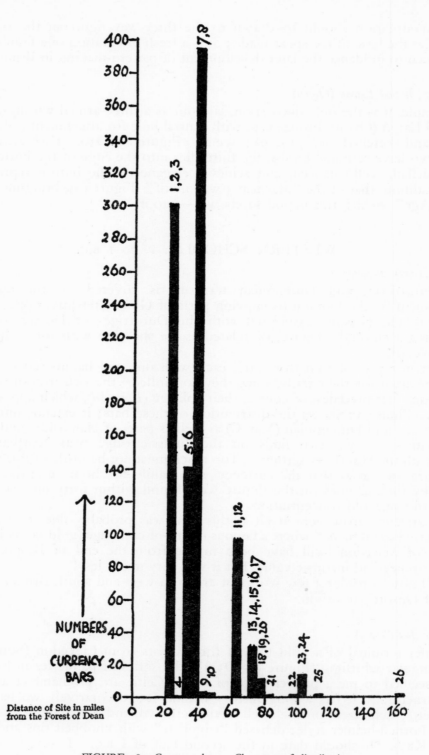

FIGURE 38.—Currency bars. Character of distribution.

(b) Bridle-bit, Llyn Cerrig (Anglesey)

A bronze bit of elaborate design, from Llyn Cerrig, is seen in *Plate 5b* and Figure 39; one knob remains and the holes of others are visible. The bit has a mount—for a lost stud of red (?) enamel—showing an incised border-pattern of loops with the free ends facing outwards. Each pony of the pair in the chariot would have had one, on the outer side, of course. The "reel ornament" on the shafts of the side-links is the feature indicating late date (Figure 83, 75): its evolution is set out in Figure 15 of the "Llyn Cerrig" Report. All this Anglesey material was imported, and this piece was almost certainly made in the south-west, and (I now consider) not earlier than *c.* 25 B.C.

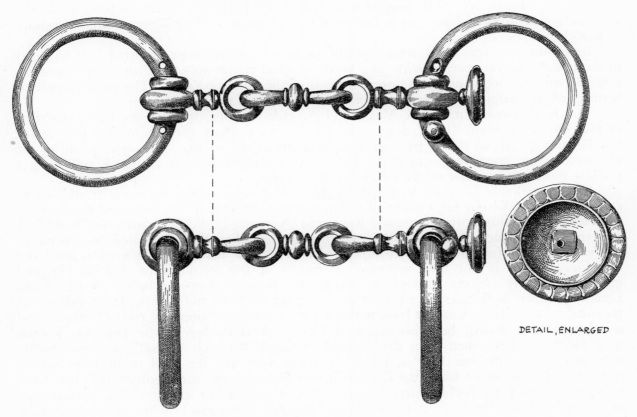

DETAIL, ENLARGED

FIGURE 39.—Bridle-bit 51, Llyn Cerrig (Anglesey). (½)

(c) Brooch: Datchet (Berks.)

We have studied brooches at some length, but an unusual example, transitional to the "Belgic" phase (in which the bow extends from hinge to tip in straight alignment), from the bed of the river Thames at Datchet (Berks.) deserves illustration here as, I think, a Western product (*Plate 41a*). Such a find-spot accounts for the perfection of its preservation; the pinned-on globes of coloured glass (so seldom surviving) enrich a finely proportioned design characteristic of its place in the evolutionary series. It should be dated about 40 B.C.

(d) Decorated pottery (Dumnonian and Durotrigan): a note

Pottery of the "B" culture, with linear decoration of character or quality, is best illustrated in the south-west—where it originated. A coastal site, suggesting that the impulse for the making in Britain of such wares came from the Continent (Brittany) to the Dumnonians in early I B.C., is Castle Dore, a small hill-fort near Fowey (Cornwall). Similar wares have been found at the Milber Down hill-fort near Torquay, and at Hengistbury Head (Dorset).[23] One of the Hengistbury types, Bushe-Fox's Class B, was shown by (Sir) Mortimer Wheeler to have been imported from Manche, Brittany.[24] The bowls and pots are well-shaped, and the curvilinear ornament (when it occurs) bold and decorative. The range of date for these wares will be *c.* 70–1 B.C. The classic site for developed styles made mainly in western Britain, beginning at the close of this century, is the Glastonbury "lake village"; wares from here, from the adjacent lake-side settlement at Meare, and from Hunsbury (Northants) will be discussed later, in the section entitled "Peasant Art".

GENERAL COMMENT. The vigour and variety of fresh art forms in Britain are the outstanding features of I B.C., as is indicated by the number of groupings found necessary in this chapter.

Interesting aspects are the refinement of the new southern work—centred (as I suggest) in the middle Thames region with (as I hold) its great traditions of craftsmanship—and the rich baroque developments at the northern end of the Jurassic Zone. The most surprising features are the magnificence and bulk of the gold-work of the period.

The linear ornament on the Meare and Amerden scabbards (with the minor addition of that on the Witham "Imp" dagger) is, I hold, the primary expression of a new style: the Thames spearhead shows its later developments in the south. The style spread to the already creative north-east, where the Llyn Cerrig shield-boss was designed, providing a prelude to the mirror-style of the following generation.

The remarkable freedom in three-dimensional design, shown by these north-eastern craftsmen on the Ulceby bit, continued to flourish and develop, in the middle of the century, as is seen on the Bugthorpe chape and Ringstead (Norfolk) bridle-bit. Such scroll-and-lobe patterns also became gold-workers' chosen themes, magnificently represented on two pieces of the Snettisham (north-west Norfolk) hoards. The view that this gold-work is local and therefore Icenian is not here accepted; a centre of the manufacture of Irish (?) gold into these lovely objects somewhere beside the Jurassic Way—probably on the south Lincolnshire wolds (Kesteven) adjacent to the upper Witham and middle Trent valleys—is regarded as probable. Contact *could* perhaps have been maintained by river (Witham) and sea (across the Wash), but this seems unlikely. A track across the Fenland—known geologically to have then been dry ground—through Wisbech "island", an area thickly populated in the Bronze Age, is, I hold, a likely route for the gold traffic into Icenian territory. On the other hand, the Cairnmuir torc (made by the same goldsmith!) may have been transported to Peeblesshire, by sea, from the Humber estuary. The presence in northern Ireland of the Broighter gold tubular torc (the ornament of which is fundamentally British, and of the period we are discussing) is another indication of widespread trade in our native gold work.[25] The concentration of Celtic art works in or near the Clwyd valley (Map B) suggests that the control of gold imports from Wicklow was centred here: the Mold "corslet" of the Hallstatt period, found hereabouts, is the heaviest piece of precious metal known in Britain.

The economic situation that made barter for, or purchase of, gold objects possible to the Iceni is a proper subject for enquiry, but we have little to go upon. "Norfolk" may then have bred a fine pony-type in great demand by landed men elsewhere in Britain, but the purchase of gold-work of such quality, in such volume as the Snettisham finds, casually deposited, suggest, could hardly have been organized by other than a kingly family or a priestly (Druidic?) corporation—probably centred at the predecessor of the Roman town *Venta Icenorum*.[26] The influence of this advanced northern and midland art, in bronze and gold, later extended to the south, where a master of the Thames valley school (as the writer holds) operating in the "round shield-boss" tradition, produced the attractive horned helmet, whereon wandering scroll-work of a softer character than its exemplars is never out of control: and a goldsmith in the same southern region, under continental (classical) influence, wrought the Clevedon torc.

Lastly, the creation, in this century, of an iron currency in the west is a notable advance —stimulated, no doubt, by knowledge of the Gallic and Roman use of metals (coinage) to facilitate trade.

NOTES TO CHAPTER IV

[1] C. W. Phillips, *Arch. Journ.* XCI, 1934, p. 105 ff.

[2] By the courtesy of Mr. J. B. Fay, whose photographs were obtained at the Mortimer Museum.

[3] Cyril Fox, *A Find of the Early Iron Age at Llyn Cerrig, Anglesey*, 1946, *Plate XXXIII* and pp. 46 ff.

[4] All illustrated in *Archaeologia* 43, p. 483 (Figures 179–80): discussed in *Llyn Cerrig*, p. 50 and Figure 26.

[5] Compare the Old Warden, Beds., mirror, p. 94 below.

[6] Llyn Cerrig Report, pp. 30–3 and p. 7 of this work.

[7] A late example of these "spoons" from Penbryn, Cardiganshire, is illustrated (*Plate 70*), and the type discussed on p. 111 below.

[8] Mr. C. N. Bromehead, F.G.S., dealing with the metals in ancient Britain in *Proc. Geol. Assoc.* LVIII, 1947, pp. 345–67, says that no traces of pre-Roman gold workings exist in *Britain*. They would be alluvial, either on a small scale or incidental to stream-works for tin (p. 365). Consequently, evidence is unprocurable.

[9] R. R. Clarke and C. F. C. Hawkes, *Proc. Prehist. Soc.*, 1955, pp. 215–6.

[10] Piggott, *Proc. Prehist. Soc.*, 1950, Fig. 3, p. 8, Nos. 3 and 4.

[11] *Proc. Prehist. Soc.*, 1950, p. 7, Figure 2.

[12] Cyril Fox in *Arch. Camb.*, 1945, *Plate V*, where the two are placed side by side. Stuart Piggott in *Proc. Prehist. Soc.*, 1950, Figures 2, 5, 8; also *Plate III* which brings out the richness of the British style.

[13] Independent contact of Ireland with Brittany by the western sea-route must, anyway, be recognized. The monumental sculptured stones, such as that at Turoe, Galway, unrepresented in Britain, can have no other explanation. For Brito-Irish contacts, see Stuart Piggott, *Archaeologia* 96, 1955, pp. 230–1.

[14] For the discussion of this important piece, see Fox, *Arch. Camb.*, 1945, p. 199 ff.; also *A Find . . . at Llyn Cerrig, Anglesey*, p. 53.

[15] R. Rainbird Clarke, *Proc. Prehist. Soc.*, 1951, pp. 214–25. For Ulceby detail, see J. Ward Perkins, *Proc. Prehist. Soc.*, 1939, p. 181, Figure 6.

[16] R. Rainbird Clarke, *Proc. Prehist. Soc.*, 1954, pp. 27–86.

[17] R. Rainbird Clarke, *Proc. Prehist. Soc.*, loc. cit., 1954, *Plate IV*. Also Stuart Piggott, *Proc. Prehist. Soc.*, 1950, p. 15, Figure 8c.

[18] Probably both. Consider Dio's account of the Boudiccan revolt in A.D. 61 (Book LXII 2). Boudicca is speaking to her army, around her neck a large golden necklace . . . After employing a species of divination, Boudicca, raising her hands towards heaven, said: I thank thee, Andraste, and call upon thee as woman speaking to woman. (Cary's *trans.*)

[19] R. R. Clarke, *Proc. Prehist. Soc.*, 1954, p. 64, and *Plate XVII, 1*. The piece has "tooling identical with that of the Bugthorpe scabbard", which confirms its source in an eastern *atelier*. *Inf.*, Professor S. Piggott.

[20] E. T. Leeds, *Celtic Ornament*, pp. 52, 53, and p. 107 below.

[21] The Forest of Dean miners then (as now) seem to have been a law unto themselves. No works of Celtic art have come from the area, Dobunic or other.

[22] R. A. Smith characterized it as "of Gaulish derivation", *B.M. Guide, Early Iron Age*, 1925, pp. 150–1. It is well photographed on *Plate XVII, Proc. Prehist. Soc.*, 1954.

[23] and [24] Castle Dore was excavated by C. A. Ralegh Radford: the construction of the fort is dated to II B.C. *J. Roy. Inst. Cornwall*, N.S. I, Appendix, 1951, p. 79 ff. For Milber Down, Devon, see A. Fox and others, *Proc. Devon Arch. Expl. Soc.* IV, 1949–50, pp. 48–9 and *Plates 7–9*: for Hengistbury, *Excavations at Hengistbury*, J. P. Bushe-Fox, 1915 (*Soc. Ant. London*), p. 39 and *Plate XX*. For Hengistbury "type B" see R. E. M. Wheeler in *Antiquity*, 1939, pp. 78–9. Another site yielding decorated pottery is Porthmeor, Cornwall (*J. Roy. Inst. Cornwall*, Vol. XXIV, 1937, p. 73 and Figure 6).

[25] See R. Rainbird Clarke, 1954, loc. cit., p. 42. The raw material is probably Irish.

[26] Caister-next-Norwich: well away from the southern influences illustrated by finds in the Lakenheath district.

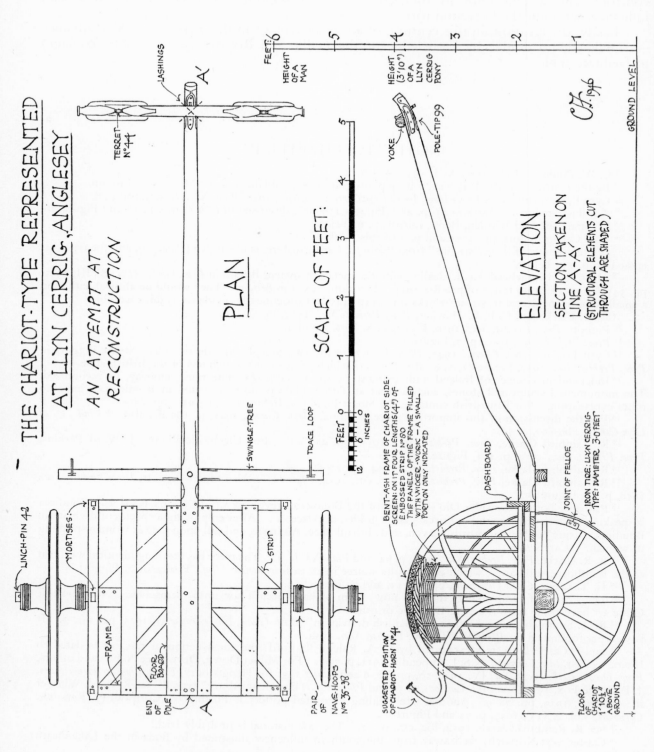

THE CHARIOT-TYPE REPRESENTED AT LLYN CERRIG, ANGLESEY

AN ATTEMPT AT RECONSTRUCTION

PLAN

LASHINGS

TERRET N° 44

SWINGLE-TREE

TRACE LOOP

A'

A'

LINCH-PIN 42

MORTISES:

FRAME

FLOOR BOARD

STRUT

END OF POLE

PAIR OF NAVE-HOOPS N°S 36-38

A

SCALE OF FEET:

FEET 0   1   2   3   4   5

6 INCHES
12

ELEVATION

SECTION TAKEN ON LINE A-A'
(STRUCTURAL ELEMENTS CUT THROUGH ARE SHADED)

YOKE

POLE-TIP 99

HEIGHT OF A MAN

HEIGHT (3'10") OF A LLYN CERRIG PONY

FEET: 6   5   4   3   2   1

GROUND LEVEL

C·F· 1946

BENT-ASH FRAME OF CHARIOT SIDE-SCREEN: ON IT FOUR LENGTHS (4'1") OF EMBOSSED STRIP N°60 THE PANELS OF THE FRAME FILLED WITH WICKER-WORK — A SMALL PORTION ONLY INDICATED

DASH BOARD

JOINT OF FELLOE

IRON TYRE: LLYN CERRIG-TYPE: DIAMETER 3·0 FEET

SUGGESTED POSITION OF CHARIOT-HORN N° 4

FLOOR OF CHARIOT 1'10¼" ABOVE GROUND

FIGURE 40.—The Celtic chariot. (See also *Plate 6*.)

CHAPTER V. HISTORICAL INTERLUDE

(i) THE BEGINNINGS OF BRITISH HISTORY, AND THE BELGIC INVASION

In the first chapter of this book imported bronzes held to date in III B.C. were discussed, and the probability of the invasion of Britain by Celtic chieftains and their followers from central Gaul (the Marne region in particular) in the same century emphasized. Early Celtic art, primarily of Marnian character, practised in Britain down to the close of I B.C. has been discussed, the sequence of surviving works being largely a linked succession of the initial decorative forms and patterns. We must now retrace our later steps to deal with historic events in the first half of this first century.[1]

About 75 B.C., certain tribes of the Belgae, a people of mixed Germanic and Celtic origin, pushed across the Straits into the Thames estuary, occupying east Kent and feeling their way from the lower Thames valley into the hinterland of present-day Hertfordshire.[2] They were agriculturists, bringing with them a type of plough with heavy coulter adapted to clayey soils, and therefore suitable for that countryside.

Now Julius Caesar makes it clear in his commentaries that all the fighting, in the course of his raids, took place in Belgic territory; before, then, we study the art of these Belgae, it will be well to remind ourselves of the beginnings of British history in which they played a part.

Julius Caesar in Britain, 55 and 54 B.C.

In the fourth decade of I B.C. Caesar had brought the greater part of all Gaul—Aquitanians, Celts, and Belgians—into subjection, and had shown the Germans his power and the technical skill of his legions by bridging the Rhine and raiding beyond it. Towards the close of the campaigning season of 55 B.C. then, he made preparations for an invasion of Britain: his reasons scarcely seem adequate to such an adventure at such a time, but it was as characteristic of the man as that crossing of the Rhine.[3] His purpose became widely known, and representatives of several states in Britain came overseas to promise submission; in his turn he sent Commius, an Atrebatian chief whom he trusted and who had British contacts, to announce his speedy advent.[4] Whatever the reason for the assault, we are his debtors; the "ablest Roman of them all" wrote a famous account of the military adventure—and its repetition in the next summer, 54 B.C. It is very likely that the several states, referred to above, were those threatened by Belgic expansion: certainly one named tribe, the Trinovantes of Essex, was in this category. In the fighting which ensued, Caesar was intrigued by the technique of chariot warfare: its flexibility and close integration with the Belgic cavalry arm are specifically mentioned. This collaboration of the earlier Iron "B" people with the Belgae is interesting: it is unlikely that equines large enough to carry men were in Britain before the newcomers brought them from Gaul.

We are fortunate to possess at the closing phase of its history, to be counted in millennia,[5] this appreciative description by a master of the art of war of the highly trained team, warrior, charioteer, and ponies in concerted action,[6] involving close fighting on foot at favourable points, and rapid disengagement.

Such good fortune is heightened for the archaeologist of today by the recovery at Llyn Cerrig of chariot fittings sufficient for detailed reconstruction of the British vehicle (Figure 40), aided by finds in Yorkshire and in Champagne,[7] and by its representation on coins.[8] It was very light and small: the wheels were only 3 ft. in diameter and the chariot body less than 18 in. from the ground. We can then see how the tactic described by Caesar, of galloping

59

the teams down steep slopes, checking and turning in a moment, was possible. Craftsmanship among the descendants of the Marnian Celts was as competent as their art : the iron tyres are seen to have been heated to redness and shrunk on to the wheels—a technique never reached thereafter, I believe, until the late eighteenth century.[9]

Caesar does not mention, but the reader can perhaps imagine, the beauty associated with such rapid and (since it was a fighting manoeuvre) violent action, from my illustrations of helmets, shields, sword scabbards—and even spears, if the river Thames example (*Plate 39*) were a common type; pony trappings of bright bronze will have added to the flashing brilliance of the scene.

The leader in the defence of south-eastern Britain in the second year's fighting—a campaign, not a reconnaissance—was the Belgic King Cassivellaunus, chosen by all the threatened tribes, who forgot their deep-seated feuds in the urgency of the occasion. He brought into play other war techniques than those already mentioned, as Caesar was moving west north-west from his east Kentish base towards an unnamed ford on the lower Thames.   There were woodland fortifications banked and ditched, feeble by comparison with our great Iron "A" and later earth-works in open country, but associated with felled-tree barricades difficult to pierce ; the woods moreover were used for guerilla warfare by chariots-with-cavalry.   As C. E. Stevens rightly remarks, the Germanic element in the Belgic make-up is here manifest.[10]   Caesar found the military counter to this, by giving the attacking chariotry no chance to switch over to their favourite practice—close-fighting on foot—when "favourable conditions" (temporary disorder in the front ranks of the infantry, no doubt) had been created by the rush and swirl of their onset.

The ford of the Thames which Caesar used and which his men forced against opposition, wading up to their necks, was probably at Wandsworth, not at Brentford—Wandsworth, where such important weapons—possible indications of earlier clashes—have been recovered.[11] The capture of Cassivellaunus's stronghold with its great store of cattle (almost certainly the existing "*oppidum*" in woodland country near Wheathampstead in Hertfordshire)[12] was followed by his request for peace and offer of hostages.   Thus Caesar's operations ended ; the year was moving on apace, and "circumstances made it necessary" that he should winter in Gaul.

Caesar's comments on the country and its inhabitants, much briefer than the war record, are familiar.   A brief reminder of the more important of these may prove useful : his "travellers tales" are omitted.

The limitations of Caesar's direct knowledge of Britain are severe.   He was impressed by the agricultural prosperity of Belgic Kent ; the population was large, the farm buildings close together and very like those in Gaul.   He refers to British currency : gold and silver coinage and tallies—bars—of iron.   The distribution of the former (Map C and p. 136 below) was widespread in the south and east ; iron currency (Figure 37) was confined to the Dobuni of Gloucestershire and their fellow traders, the Durotriges, as we have seen.   Caesar learned something of the western sea route up the Irish Channel, but *not* at its south British or west Gaulish terminals.   The Veneti who controlled the western sea traffic to Britain had been destroyed by his legions in 53 B.C. and the Morini and other seafaring tribes who made their living by the island trade would not talk.   If they had, Caesar might have landed in Christchurch harbour : his galleys would not have suffered damage as they did on the open beaches near Deal, and the raids could have become a conquest, ninety-seven years before this was actually achieved.   The victor at Alesia and Uxellodunum could have taken Maiden Castle, Hod Hill, and Hambledon Hill fortresses, that would thus have faced him, in his stride.

The information Caesar received about the inland tribes—that they were indigenous and lived on milk and flesh, clothing themselves in skins, is remarkable.   If Map B, the distribution of Celtic and Belgic works of art, be examined, it will be seen that most of the finds lie to the east of a diagonal line from the Exe estuary in Devon, and the Severn estuary, to the plain of York. His "inland" area, uncivilized, then, is almost certainly the country to the north-west of our Jurassic Way.

This west-central countryside drained by Severn, Avon, and upper Trent is the Midland Plain of the geographers, comparatively infertile and largely forest : areas where, in Caesar's time, tribes and groups of hunters and keepers of sheep, cattle, or pigs, may well have been the principal inhabitants. They will have been in either the Iron "A" (like the Wiltshire folk), or the late Bronze Age, stage of culture. It will be recalled that the Parisi of east Yorkshire (a much better land!) seem to have been mainly pastoralists themselves, and to have brought into subjection a local Iron "A" peasantry.

On the other hand, it is recognized that when, after the partial conquest by Claudius in A.D. 43, the country up to the Pennines (Wales as well as England) comes under observation *as a whole,* it was Celticized; the known names of tribes, anyway, both in the west-central region of the lowland and in the "highland zone" were Celtic.

The Brigantes of the north who come under close scrutiny by the Romans in the second half of I A.D. include tribes—such as the Setantii on the Ribble estuary—which whether Irish or British also have Celtic names.

Northern Ireland (as we have noted, p. xxvi) was probably celticized by invaders coming direct from the Continent by St. George's Channel—the western sea-route; they are likely to have helped, by cross-channel trade, to Celticize west Britain. The Silures of the South Wales coastal plain, fronting the Bristol Channel, it should here be said, seem to have come into the comparatively civilized Celtic network of southern Britain—Iron Age "B"—late in our period (p. 127 below).

Furthermore, we have seen that not only in Anglesey, whence came the Llyn Cerrig material, and the Clwyd—probably Deceanglian territory, and an entrepôt of the gold trade—but here and there in western Britain, works of British Celtic art of high quality are known[13]; chieftains on the west coast of Wales, for example, were able to acquire expensive things from the workshops of an accessible higher culture, as the forefathers of the British Celts themselves had done, long before, on the continent.

Little has as yet been said here about the south-western peninsula : it is indeed curious how little there is to say. We share, to a large extent, Caesar's apparent lack of knowledge of its culture. Cornwall and Devon were certainly settled to some extent, long before his time, by Iron "B" folk, probably, since they made pottery with curvilinear ornament, from western Gaul as well as from the Seine (Marnian) region—an intrusion referred to on p. 15 above.

It might be expected that tin-producing Cornwall in particular, though geologically in the Highland Zone, would in his time have shared in the culture of the Lowlands, as illustrated in our bronzes, but evidence for this is slight. A hoard of Gaulish coins of the Bellovaci comes from Carn Brea, Camborne ; Chun, near Penzance, is a strong dry-walled fort where tin-smelting was carried out.[14] We recall the Spanish brooch-type found on Cornish sites (p. xxv above) and so have reason to hold that the wealth of the country was exploited by merchants and traders from overseas. Aileen Fox, in a study of "hill-slope" forts[15]—a type with wide interspaces between the outer and inner defences, peculiar to South Wales and our peninsula, concluded that these must have served a constant need of the Iron "B" population in the south-west, and that this need was economic—the main occupation of the builders was cattle keeping. Good examples are Tregear Rounds, St. Kew (Cornwall) which produced south-western "B" pottery, and Milber Down (Devon). Wide-spaced defences giving protection for herds in case of need, are also found in plateau forts, such as Clovelly Dykes (Devon).

(ii) A Second Belgic Invasion : the Dual Centres of Belgic Influence

From about 30 B.C. onwards (Introduction, p. xxiv) a second entry of Belgic folk (Atrebates and others) influenced the older Celtic culture (Iron "A") in the Hants, Berks, and Wilts. region: but works of art are uncommon in the area, as Map B shows. Its significance is chiefly political; there were now two controlling centres in the much-widened area of Belgic influence, that of the Catuvellauni at Verulamium, who (under Tasciovanus, successor to Cassivellaunus) had by now gained complete control of Trinovantian territory[16] and the Atrebates at Calleva (Silchester, Berks) under the new "Commian" dynasty. These new-comers may have introduced the art of coinage.

This second intrusion of Belgic tribes has an historical background. Caesar's one-time friend, Commius the Atrebatian, who was evidently, as we say, a "character", parted company with him, and led insurrections in Gaul, becoming such a nuisance that Caesar felt justified in compassing his death. He escaped the dagger of a hired assassin, and when later (51 B.C.) he became a Roman prisoner and was banished from Gaul, asked to be sent where he would never meet a Roman face to face. We next come across him in the above-mentioned territory wherein no *specific* Belgic culture is known to have developed; cremation is rare and the "bead-rim bowl", characteristic of the inhumation culture of south Britain hereabouts, seems to have been adopted by the newcomers. Extensive territory to the south (adjacent to the Durotriges of Dorset) was also occupied by Belgae, in another (unrecorded) exodus from Gaul. The latter were collected—for fiscal convenience, no doubt—into a canton thus entitled, after the Claudian conquest in A.D. 43 with a capital town, Venta Belgarum (Winchester).

NOTES TO CHAPTER V

[1] Collingwood and Myres, *Roman Britain and the English Settlements,* Oxford, 1936, chapters II–VI, can be read with advantage at this stage.

[2] C. A. Ralegh Radford, "The Tribes of Southern Britain", *Proc. Prehist. Soc.,* 1954, p. 3, has a map showing the territory these tribes occupied in Gaul.

[3] See C. E. Stevens's comments, 55 B.C. and 54 B.C.: *Antiquity,* 1947, pp. 3–10.

[4] See *The Belgae of Gaul and Britain,* Hawkes and Dunning, 1931, *passim*: *Verulamium,* R. E. M. and T. V. Wheeler, 1936, Introduction.

[5] Chariotry was in West Asia and in Europe the primary arm for open fighting, usually with *ponies* as the tractive power. As the *horse* becomes available and horse-breeding a normal activity, cavalry tends to replace chariotry. The change, in our Aryan history, moves from east to west. It was very slow in Britain: Boudicca (Queen of the Iceni, a tribe never Belgicized) had chariots in A.D. 60; chariot-furniture of about A.D. 50 comes from Brigantian lands (Stanwick), and Galgacus (in North Britain) used them in A.D. 83. The last stronghold of the technique in the European area was Ireland in the Dark Ages; the latest description of a chariot-using society, the Cuchullain (Ulster) Saga.

[6] *Gallic War,* Book IV, p. 33. The Loeb Library translation, by H. J. Edwards, is recommended.

[7] e.g. Déchellette, *Manuel, Second Age du Fer,* Figures 424 and 425.

[8] Stuart Piggott, "Celtic Chariots on Roman Coins", *Antiquity,* 1952, p. 87.

[9] Mr. F. G. Payne, F.S.A., an authority on these matters, commends the *Ency. Brit.* article on such traction.

[10] *Antiquity,* 1947, pp. 3–9.

[11] The principal crossing of the tidal reaches of the Thames at low water in prehistoric times is, as we have seen, important. The opinion of Mr. G. Lawrence—the collector of antiquities from the river—given near the end of his life, was that it was at Wandsworth, not Brentford. See C. E. Stevens, *Antiquity,* 1947, p. 6.

[12] R. E. M. and T. V. Wheeler, *Verulamium,* p. 19.

[13] e.g. Trawsfynydd tankard (p. 109), Llandysul collar (p. 106).

[14] E. T. Leeds, *Archaeologia* 76, p. 205 ff: G. C. Brooke, "Gaulish and British Coins in Britain", *Antiquity,* 1933, p. 268 ff.

[15] *Arch. Journ.* CIX, 1952, pp. 1–22.

[16] Caesar had enjoined Cassivellaunus not to interfere with Mandubracius, king of that tribe. Their territory, and Camulodun, their chief town, yield much Belgic pottery: it became the capital of Belgic Britain in I A.D.

CHAPTER VI. BELGIC (IRON "C") ART AND CRAFT
c. 75–1 B.C.

The Belgae came into south-eastern Britain, it would appear, with much the same social structure as the pure Celtic tribesmen they dispossessed, but with a higher—more sophisticated—culture among their leading families. This is to be expected: the Roman conquest of Gaul was but the violent last act of an extended process of diffusion of southern culture and manners throughout the country, including most of the Belgic tribes in the north-east.

This ready acceptance of elements of the higher Mediterranean civilization is illustrated in Britain, perhaps by their adoption of cremation, certainly by their competent use of the potter's wheel, and (more particularly) by many richly furnished burials, which throw light on the manners and customs of the ruling class, as well as on their standard of culture.

(i) WHEEL-MADE POTTERY

The pottery will first be illustrated. The invaders had two principal wheel-made types: the "pedestal urn", so-called from its shape—which is elegant—and frequent use for the ashes of the dead in burial, and the *tazza* or bowl-with-foot, also common in graves: the latter is based on a metal original. The colour is usually grey or black, but warmer tones are sometimes present. Early examples of each, from Essex, are illustrated on *Plate 30*; this pedestal urn has a "dice-box foot", and the *tazza* is cordoned; a third piece, a bowl-with-cover, is of the same quality and fine proportions as the others.[1] The east Kentish settlement is illustrated by a less distinguished *tazza* from Aylesford (*Plate 26*): the various types are shown also in section, in Figure 41. The distribution pattern of the commoner form, the pedestal urn, is interesting; it is that of Belgic occupation and control after the absorption of the Trinovantes of Essex (Figure 42) in late I B.C.[2] The beauty and refinement of these and other shapes in pottery, maintained throughout the whole period of Belgic ascendancy, is notably illustrated by Bushe-Fox in his study of the urn-field at Swarling (Kent), 1925.[3] A *tazza* of Kimmeridge shale, turned on a wheel, is illustrated on *Plate 45*.

(ii) BURIALS

We may now turn to the richer burials. These represent a feast of the dead noble with a chosen companion, the associated objects being set out on an excavated floor—representing a room—which may be some 15 ft. by 12 ft. in area, and 4 ft. below ground level.

(a) At Welwyn (Herts) and Stanfordbury (Beds)

Two such burials, in Hertfordshire—a primary centre of Belgic settlement in Britain, as we have seen—found by chance in 1906 at Welwyn, were ill-preserved; they fortunately came to the notice of an able scholar, Reginald Smith, and are as well recorded as was possible. Their setting was evocatively presented by Mortimer Wheeler in his "Belgic Cities of Britain".[3a]

Each included urns and other pottery, of types already described; imports, Mediterranean *amphorae*—the Greek type with cylindrical body—containing wine or olive oil, bronze vessels, and iron fire-dogs.

The more important of the two had in addition a massive iron frame—possibly a sacrificial table—with which the bronze jug (*oinochöe*) and pan (*patella*) would have been associated. There were also silver vessels—a lovely pair of full-bodied wine cups with delicate incised patterns on the moulded rim, shoulder and foot, of which one is illustrated on *Plate 54*, and the remains of elegant silver "kylixes" (to modernize the Greek name)

63

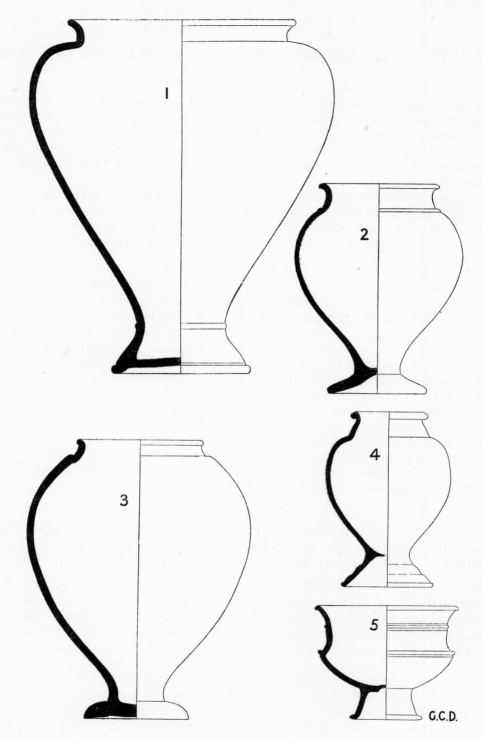

FIGURE 41.—Pedestal urns and tazza: Belgic. 1 and 2. Aylesford (Kent); 3. Newnham (Beds.); 4. Strood (Kent); 5. Woodcuts (Dorset) ($\frac{1}{4}$).

shallow, with widespread handles.   These were all of Italo-Greek manufacture and probably from Campania.

The fire-dogs, on the other hand, are characteristically Celtic, each with two ox-head terminals; they were badly decayed (p. 75).   Dr. I. C. Peate has shown that in early times this double-ended type was placed across the hearth; thus *two* in a grave—as here—is part of the evidence for a guest in this *simulacrum* of a feast, and shows that each was considered to need a fire.

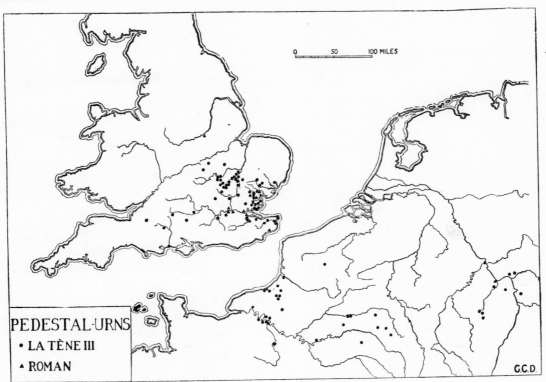

FIGURE 42.—Pedestal urns: distribution map.

Other objects of interest are three cast-bronze masks of mustachioed Celts (*Plate 33b* and p. 72) and a tankard, vertical-sided, made of wooden staves and with ornamental cast-bronze grips, of British workmanship.   The type is discussed on p. 108 f below: here only the grips survive.

Well-provided burials of this character of mid-I A.D. date were discovered at Stanfordbury (Beds.).[3b]   Two "rooms" were found; the richer contained two fire-dogs, a tall iron tripod with six hooks for spits, a skillet, six *amphorae*, two urns with burnt bones, Samian (Gaulish) red-ware, and a glass: gaming counters and a bone flute for after-dinner entertainment. *Plate 32* shows an amphora, with hearth furniture, from this collection.   Was the companion of the nobleman killed ritually, to accompany him to the other world?

(b) At Mount Bures (Essex)

Another burial of similar character and interest is that found at Mount Bures on the river Stour (Essex).[4]   There were two groups of *amphorae* each with their necks resting on a similar fire-dog: there were bronze knobs on the oxhorn terminals of the latter, possibly a reflection of current practice in the farm,[5] foreshadowing our modern practice of dehorning. A casket (for the ashes?), plates, and cups of "earthenware" (certainly wheel-made) are also recorded.

Smith's record, which summarizes this culture, is an archaeological classic; it has been left to a later writer[6] to point out the parallels these burials present to the rich chieftain's graves of early La Tène date (V and IV B.C.) on the middle Rhine, wherein a drinking party for two is indicated by cups and other movables in pairs, twin hearths for prince and guest, and three amphorae each.

From a continental Celtic source then, the Belgic chieftains (of mixed blood, we recall) will have derived the custom; by the time they entered Britain its practice had been modified in some particulars by fresh Mediterranean (now Roman) contacts.

(iii) BROOCHES, 50–1 B.C.

The Belgae introduced and acclimatized a distinctive brooch-type which largely replaced the "B" types throughout the country. The earliest form was called after the cemetery site in the Medway valley (Kent), where it was first studied technically, the "Aylesford" brooch.[7] An example from Arundel Park (Sussex) illustrated in Figure 43 shows the specific characters and is closely dated by association to mid-I B.C.[8] It has a trumpet-like expansion of the bow-head (to keep the *internally-placed* chord of the 4-coil spring in position), a moulding with a hook-like projection high up on the bow, and a triangular catch-plate with pierced ("openwork") ornament. The moulding is a vestige of the foot-attachment of the earlier

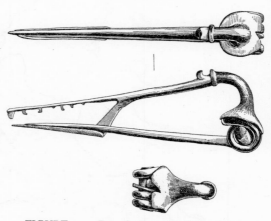

FIGURE 43.—Brooch, Arundel (Sussex). (⅓)

(La Tène II) brooch type (p. 18). An open-work catch-plate (here damaged) is usual in such brooches—and helps to bring them within the range of an art-form.

The type with internal chord almost died out, for the older bow with external chord was preferred to it.[9] The fretted plate was, however, retained and few Celtic ladies would have noticed the difference: this is shown by a British Museum example (*Plate 40a*) in which the basal expansion of the bow is diminished, and the ornament an elaboration of that on the Arundel example. The perfect lay-out at this evolutionary stage is shown in *Plate 40b* —a pair of silver brooches, with attached rings and chain, from a burial in Brambleshot field, Great Chesterford (Essex), now in the Museum at Cambridge. There was a vein of austerity in the brooch-designers of the period, manifest in the lovely proportions and limitation of ornament of this masterpiece. Consider the enlargement on the same Plate showing the detail of the undamaged bow: the fretted plate is diminished to a decorative link strengthening the pin-catch.

In the next stage the bow, slightly curved, presents an unbroken line from spring to foot; examples from an urnfield at Deal (Kent) are illustrated on (Figure 44).[10]

Torc from the Medway, near Aylesford (*Kent*)

This buffer torc, 5 ft. 7 in. in diameter, illustrated on *Plate 26b*, is a southern type without the classicism, and may be a Thames valley product. The hoop is square-sectioned set diagonally, and the expanding terminals have a beaded moulding.

(iv) GANG-CHAINS

We now turn to a purely technical achievement, the iron gang-chain, here illustrated by the example in the Museum from Llyn Cerrig (*Plate 38*). It is likely that the sale into slavery of men and women from the non-Belgic areas of Britain was mainly organized by the Catuvellauni, the evidence being the distribution of gang-chains within their territory

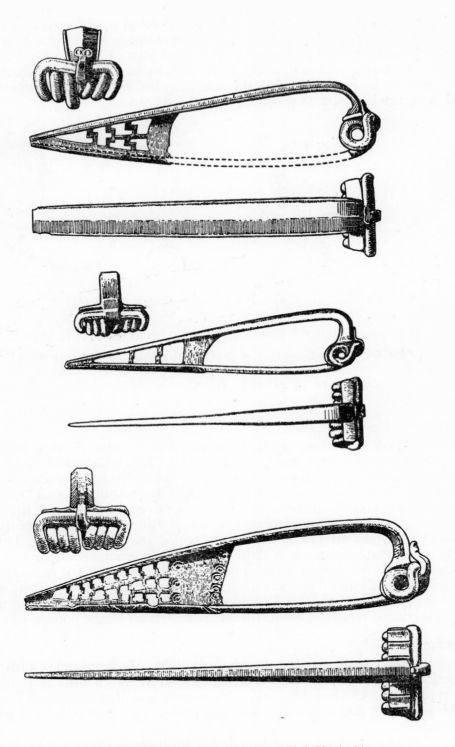

FIGURE 44.—Brooches, "C" type: Deal (Kent). (⅓)

(or area of influence) and the discovery of this one, identical in character and technique, far outside it. We are concerned in this book with craftsmanship as well as art, and the quality of these chains is outstanding; the photographs show part of a chain for six captives; in the upper one a neck-ring is closed, in the lower it is open. The whole chain beyond this ring had of course to be passed through the oval loop before the next victim of this odious traffic could be secured: Figure 45 shows captives on the march.[11]

FIGURE 45.—Captives in a gang-chain. (See also *Plate 38*.)

(v) STAVE-BUILT VESSELS IN BELGIC BURIALS: IMPORTED

In two deposits, one a known, the other a presumed Belgic burial in southern Britain, the important work of art was stave-built, like the Welwyn tankard. These are almost certainly imports, but are too suggestive of possible religious aspects of Belgic life and culture in Britain to be omitted.

(a) Bucket, Aylesford (Kent)

The famous handled bucket, 10 in. in height and breadth, from a Belgic cemetery at Aylesford, Kent, has been frequently illustrated.[12] The well-known "human" faces in cast bronze, crested, which mask the slots into which the ends of the handles are fitted—one is seen in profile in *Plate 33a*—are described by Sir Thomas Kendrick as an "example of that terrifying formal distortion whereby the Celt knew how to create a vision of the super real."[13] The Plate shows a band of repoussé ornament round the rim consisting of typical Celtic "comma-leaves" variously arrayed in curves and coils, and two creatures, horse-like, but beaked and horned, double-tailed, with shoulders touching, heads reverted.

These creatures, as Sir Arthur Evans pointed out,[14] are paralleled on coins of a Gallic tribe, the Remi; we shall find them, in this developed form, elsewhere in Britain. The date of the bucket is probably *c.* 50 B.C.; in it were cremated bones; a bronze jug and pan (the Mediterranean sacrificial types already mentioned) and typical Belgic pottery were associated.

(b) Vat, Marlborough (Wilts)

The second stave-built vessel of this sort, the Marlborough (Wilts) "vat"—as I would describe it—is later; it was found in 1807 at Collingbourne near to that town, and is preserved in the Devizes Museum. "Skeletons and Roman pottery" are recorded "in its neighbourhood", and it had no doubt been used like the other, as a receptacle for cremated bones.[15]

The general character of the great vessel, $21\frac{1}{2}$ in. high and nearly 2 ft. in diameter, is shown in two drawings made some four years after its discovery, at the instance of Colt Hoare, for his well-known book, *Ancient Wiltshire*. The owner sent him a letter (preserved in Devizes Museum) with all the bronze fragments, telling him that the vessel had fallen to pieces on removal, but that a sketch existed of its character before it was touched; this his draughtsman could study. As now repaired and set up in the Museum, some of the decorative bronze work is manifestly out-of-order, but an examination of Colt Hoare's drawings shows that these also are wrong in some respects, as well as incomplete! I reproduce them on *Plate 34a* and *b*, however, as the best early evidence of the arrangement we have. The three bands of bronze reliefs, with delicately moulded edges, are from $3\frac{3}{4}$ to $4\frac{1}{2}$ in. in height; between the bands are hoops of iron which kept the staves (now renewed) in place; the base cannot be examined.[16]

The vat (it will be seen) was lifted by loop-handles of iron, finely wrought; the rings to which they are secured have moulded basal flanges. The square iron bar at the top, hollow and light, was secured to the bronze casing outside and inside the "ears" of the vessel, and seems to have sustained nothing more than two half-covers of wood. The vat, then, will doubtless have contained beer or mead for feasts which, judging by the reliefs, will have been of a religious or ritual character.

To selected examples of these reliefs, much damaged (no doubt by the collapse of the vessel) we will now turn.[17]

The pair of heads on each "ear" of the vat (extensions upwards of two of the staves, *Plate 34, a* to *d*) are closely similar, in so far as they survive. The rope of hair curling outwards on *d*, left, may have been matched on *d*, right, but it is not likely to have been a feature of the design of the other pair: the knobby curls survive too far down the napes. The faces are naturalistic: "such modelling is inconceivable without the strongest classical influence".[18] *Plate 35a* presents the head of a Celtic warrior (hero?) on a large scale; the moustache and the modelling of the nostril are notable details, as are the swept-back locks of hair with curled tips. These latter are a feature of male types on Armorican coinage.[19] The warrior was facing his fellow, now fragmentary.

The full-face heads on *Plate 36* are inferior artistically; the upper one with swept-back hair is photographed from the side (*a*) and full-face (*b*); it is clearly related to the Welwyn masks. The lanky-haired one (*c*) a female (?) has a horse on her right and facing right; this was almost certainly on the middle register, *34b*, but omitted by Colt Hoare's draughtsman. These beings will have had coral or enamel eyes, which may differentiate them from the side-face personages, and entitle them to be called Gods—in the case of the long-haired one, Goddess. The puffiness below the eyes, particularly of the latter, is an interesting aspect of the representation. Lambrechts[20] notes that for the Celt, the human head sufficed to symbolize a person or personality.

We turn now to the animals. The horse facing the God-head in *Plate 36a* in an attitude of adoration (key *34a*, second register) deserves to be considered first: the face is (for the period) marvellously modelled—and yet the forepart of the body has a conventional framework! *Plate 36c*, below, shows a slim body, with short tail turned back onto the rump; the bronze lips-up at the curve on the right making a close fit with the Goddess's portion of the frieze. Turn to the creature on *Plate 35c*: the mane is rope-like, the tail fleshy and upturned, and the thigh-muscle has a prominent Celtic coil. How like Scythian art is the tense stretched pose! There must surely be a link with the Near East (later than that postulated by Jacobsthal in his Survey, probably by a north-of-the-Alps route) to account for this.

We now come to the sea-horse (hippocamp) designs, wherein Celtic fantasy reigns. They are dual, with muzzles opposed and with Celtic lobes, scrolls or palmettes (honeysuckle) as dominant centre-pieces. The bold sweep of the left-hand body, on *Plate 35b*, with a terminal coil (tail) is attractive, and the bent forelegs of both creatures (a classic pose) should be noted. The descendant-lobes are well placed between the broad muzzles.

69

The variety of craftsmanship on the vat (mentioned above) is here seen in the broad triangular frame of the neck of the right-hand creature, represented by a narrow hollow on that of its fellow.

Turning to the much less naturalistic "land horses" of the third register, and *Plate 34e*, we note the formal sub-angular ridge of metal which frames the bodies of these creatures and which unites to form their limbs. This represents a stylistic variant, showing that more than one artist was engaged in making the reliefs on the vat. The tenseness of the tortured bodies is remarkable, as is the termination of this angular structure at the ears ; the creatures' heads—with muzzles extended to form descending coils (? trunks)—are rounded and "softly" modelled.[21] They show their family relationship to the other "land horses" by their short up-turned tails.[22]

The vat, then, will have been an imported piece of religious art (work of the Veneti ?)[23] dating about 50 B.C. It deserves the detailed monograph for which it has waited a century and a half in vain, for the unanswered questions it offers are manifold. Why should the creature, for one, turn its back upon the God ? And who are these figures from a Celtic pantheon ?

A significant parallel to these bronze reliefs of divine beings, and their worshippers (or heroes ?), on wooden vessels, is provided by the famous Celtic bronze bowl from Gundestrup, Jutland, in the National Museum at Copenhagen. By the courtesy of the Director, the writer obtained the photographs here reproduced (the entire bowl and one of the panels, *Plate 37ac*). The divine "heads" had inserted pupils of glass or paste in their bronze eyes like ours, and the human representations are, as on the vat, side-face.[24]

So much for the high-lights associated with the newly-introduced culture. The Armorican stock which this type of bucket-art probably represents may never have *effectively* occupied any part of southern Britain, though an intruding Breton chieftain must have surely done well, and become part of the Belgic community, to possess such a concentration of divinity. The hippogriff, however, on *Plate 37b*, from a disc-brooch found at Santon Downham is likely to be British, and shows familiarity with one aspect at least of contemporary continental religion.

A work related to, and probably contemporary with, this religious bucket-art in Britain, is the Uffington White Horse[25] (*Plate 42*), a familiar figure cut in the turf of the steep northern scarp of the Berkshire downs, which has an open "beak" and a tuft on the head, like the reverted heads on the Aylesford piece. This may be dated in late I B.C.

GENERAL COMMENT. In this chapter there have been shown examples of the art and craft of the Belgae in Britain, and continental imports such as bronze jugs and wine amphorae, the Aylesbury bucket, and the Marlborough vat. These illustrate the refinement of their pottery forms, the wealth of their chieftains, the elaboration of a religion (which they were, at least, acquainted with) and of their burials, and the organization of a slave-trade which may be a principal source of their evident purchasing power in Gaul. The influence they exerted on the earlier Celtic cultures was, as will be seen, profound. They initiated inscribed coinage in Britain (p. 136 below) and their superiority in the art of government is suggested by the extent of country they seem to have controlled at the time of the Roman conquest. Their manifest failure, culturally, to influence the Iceni—near neighbours—is remarkable, and had tragic consequences in I A.D. for these isolationists—the cultural links of this tribe, as we have seen, were with the north (Catuvellauni, and possibly Brigantes).

[1] These photographs of *early* types for Essex were kindly prepared for me by Mr. M. R. Hull, Curator, Colchester and Essex Museum.

[2] About 10 B.C.: Tasciovanus was then king of the Catuvellauni.   See Hawkes and Hull, *Camulodunum*, *Soc. Ant.*, 1947, p. 5.

[3] Research Report, Society of Antiquaries.

[3a] Reginald Smith, *Archaeologia* 63, pp. 1–30: (Sir) Mortimer Wheeler, *Antiquity*, 1933, pp. 30 ff.

[3b] *Archaeology of the Cambridge Region*, pp. 99–100.

[4] Roach Smith, *Collectanea Antiqua*, ii, p. 25.

[5] These knobs, in Lord Raglan's opinion, may have been placed on the horns of oxen destined for sacrifice, but support for either of these opinions seems to be lacking.

[6] Stuart Piggott, *Antiquity*, 1948, p. 21 ff.   See also Jacobsthal, *Early Celtic Art*, Introduction.

[7] Sir A. Evans, *Archaeologia* 52, p. 381, Figure 19.

[8] C. F. C. Hawkes, *Ant. Journ.*, 1940, p. 493.

[9] Hawkes and Hull, *Camulodunum*, pp. 309–11 and *Plate XC*.

[10] J. P. Bushe-Fox, *Swarling Report*, p. 61, *Plate XIII*; *Soc. Ant.*, 1925.

[11] The procedure is discussed at length in the Llyn Cerrig Report, p. 37.

[12] It was well published by Sir Arthur Evans in 1890; *Archaeologia* 52, p. 361 ff.

[13] *Anglo-Saxon Art*, *Plate II* and p. 7.   The knobs of the cresting represent (as was pointed out by Reginald Smith in 1925) the ends of the double-handles of earlier Continental buckets.

[14] *Archaeologia* 52, *Plate XIII*.

[15] C. Ralegh Radford, *Proc. Prehist. Soc.*, 1954, p. 9, suggests an Augustan date, and a settlement rather later than that of the Atrebates.

[16] Mr. Nicholas Thomas, Curator of the Museum, kindly gave every facility for the examination of the piece, and for taking the photographs here reproduced.

[17] All the knobs they show are, of course, modern brass nail-heads, and care must be taken not to mistake stiff brown paper backing for bronze (e.g. on *Plate 36c*, below hair).

[18] Paul Jacobsthal, *Early Celtic Art*, p. 20, apropos of a similar work.

[19] As (e.g.) in "Armorican Art", *Société Jersiase*, 1937, wherein a hundred coins are figured.

[20] *L'exaltation de la Tête dans . . . . l'art des Celtes*.

[21] These muzzles will be met with again in British work.

[22] Quite unnatural, for horses!

[23] *Arch. 52, Plate XIII*, p. 360 ff.

[24] This well-known piece is published in *Danmarks Oldtid* III by Dr. Brondsted, HON.F.S.A.   We are reminded of the most sacred cauldron of the Cimbri, sent to the Emperor Augustus as a propitiatory offering: Strabo, 7.2.1.   The Celts must have had stories about these gods, heroes, and monsters—like Beowulf and Grendel in the Germanic, later, tradition.   The piece was made in the Danube region, under Eastern influence.

[25] The best illustrations of, and comment on, this horse are by Stuart Piggott in *Antiquity*, 1931, p. 37 ff.

Part II

ASPECTS OF CELTIC AND BELGIC ART IN BRITAIN
c. 20 B.C.—A.D. 80

As we move down the stream of time in this survey, there comes a point when the study of groups of art-works of similar character is more important than consideration of regional contributions to, and regional differences in, the creative work of British artists and craftsmen. From the close of I B.C. onwards, for example, British mirrors have a certain unity whether they come from Dobunic or Belgic territory; that point, then, is reached, and the question "was the mirror made in the region where it was found?" is secondary to a determination of its place in the series.

In the rest of the book, then, groups of kindred art-works will be studied, section by section, without much reference to the tribal or racial divisions in Britain, but including, of course, any evidence of source that aids understanding of a particular group or individual piece. There is one reservation: Brigantian art takes on towards the close, special importance, and is treated accordingly. Summaries will be brief: the organization of the material, it is hoped, makes such largely unnecessary. We begin, then, with

CHAPTER VII. THE REPRESENTATION OF MAN AND ANIMALS

No aspect of Celtic art needs more careful consideration if we are to appreciate the craftsman's outlook than the representation of living beings. It is not consistent: the fundamental tendency of the Celt is towards pattern-making based on a creature's individuality, but this is now overlaid, except in the north, with representational art, mainly Belgic, resulting from close contact with Roman civilization. Even so, the essential *character* of the creature portrayed is sought—as indeed it was in the imported bronzes discussed in the last chapter—rather than superficial likeness.

(i) MAN

Few representations of Man in the last eighty years or so of Celtic or Belgic art in Britain extend beyond the head or face. The most carefully detailed are the three cast bronze heads from a metal bowl (fragmentary, about $4\frac{1}{2}$ in. in diameter) in the Welwyn (Herts.), burial (*Plate 33b*). These may usefully be compared with the earlier (imported) representation of a head on *Plate 18*. They are certainly less unhappy-looking; eyelids and hair show a beaded formal roughening of the bronze, but the heavy moustaches are modelled naturally. The eyes are unduly large, like the Grimston head; the pupils of two are "drilled". The third mask shows hair parted in the middle, and a head-band. Chins show curved incised lines. Since the beaded treatment referred to is seen near the terminal knobs on the "legs and arms" of the earlier piece, we are perhaps dealing with one stream of tradition in this branch of art. Gods or heroes may be depicted: we recall Lambrechts' dictum that to the Celt the head *is* the essential being, and remember the gods on the Gundestrup bowl, portrayed down to the breast only, whereas the humans are seen full-length (*Plate 37*).[1]

Other representations are fearsome creatures, demons rather than human beings.   Such are the two masks in a well-known collection of bronzes from Stanwick (N.R., Yorks.), with features built up of scroll and other shapes in high relief. `With eyes of coloured glass or enamel and golden pupils formed by the bronze pinheads, they will have been striking objects; ornamenting (and protecting?) a chariot-body or a wooden house (*Plate 43b*). These came, it should be noted, from the now less advanced north-east of Britain.   Another mask (ill-preserved) from this Brigantian area (Aldborough, Yorks.) forming part of a terret moulded to the curve of a pony's yoke, is certainly intended to be fearsome, and is to our eyes repellent (*Plate 43a*).   The artist's design includes part of the (now broken) functional rein-ring, and so the god or demon illustrated may have been horned, like *Cernunnos*.[1a] The dual sweep of the ornamental pattern, from breast to shoulders, coiled round glass or enamel bosses, will have completed a brilliant concept: facing the enemy, not the charioteer. A remarkable feature of the piece is its "leaf-crowns"; these are associated with divine heads on the Continent.[2]   The edges of two "leaves", extending outwards from the centre, and throwing a shadow on to the curve of the terret ring, are seen above the full-face photograph; a second pair, expanding down the back of the head on to the shoulder, is also illustrated. The creature, side-face, in the third photograph, looks almost human and slightly pathetic; perhaps because his dominant nose and fearsome red eyes are missing.

(ii) Animals

(a) Bovines

Among animals in our art, the Ox and Cow take first place: a wide range of head-types is seen mounted on buckets, or is known as survivals from lost vessels of this character—used, no doubt, as milk pails.   An attractive example, with associated handle, is the pair from Felmersham (Beds.) (*Plate 46* and Figure 46)[3] dating early in I A.D.   These Belgic heads, both of a cow, are naturalistic and suggest a countryman's appreciation of bovine character; but the influence of classical art is manifest.

A different artistic approach is seen in two Celtic studies of this animal.   The first is from the Iron Age fortress on Ham Hill (Som.) in which a rollicking humour is indicated by the large eyes, almond-shaped, and the sensitive nostrils (*Plate 48b*): elaborate pattern-making underlies the apparent freedom of treatment.   The edge of the lower eye-lid continues, as a faint ridge, over the skull and round the base of the horn on either side; again, there is a noticeable raised band crossing the nose, which forms a sensitive margin to the nostril and then "dies into it".   The knob on the bull's horn has the triangle-in-circle motif (elaborated in Figure 83, 54) incised—surely a reflection of Celtic practice, on the farms, for stud bulls?   This important piece comes from the rim of a bronze vessel, from which it was violently wrenched (a rivet under the chin being bent and part of the casting torn away); the shape of the vessel is, for this reason, not determinable.   Another such work, in a western idiom, from the great hill-fort of Dinorben (Denbs.) (*Plate 48c*) is a more sedate rendering of the theme.   It reduces the creature to a pattern, but with art.   Consider the diagonals of the structure—the horn, the eyes, the expanding muzzle—all "held" by the horizontals of the broad brow.   Repose, then, characterizes the tiny piece: one might almost say that a contemplative humanism had been imported into this study of a bovine.

Equally suggestive interpretation of animal character, but in a lighter vein, graces an important find of chariot-fittings in Bulbury, a very small hill-fort near Wareham (Dorset) overlooking Poole Harbour[4]; there were four bronzes in the set, two of animal form (*Plate 44*). These two are based on the ox, with bodies moulded in smooth sweeping planes, angular at the junctions and with broad-based horn-cones[5]; the fantasy controlling the representation reaches a climax in the tail-tips, which are transformed into flowers (Figure 83, G58).   Each little beast rode, it may be supposed, on the rounded crests of a wooden yoke of a noble

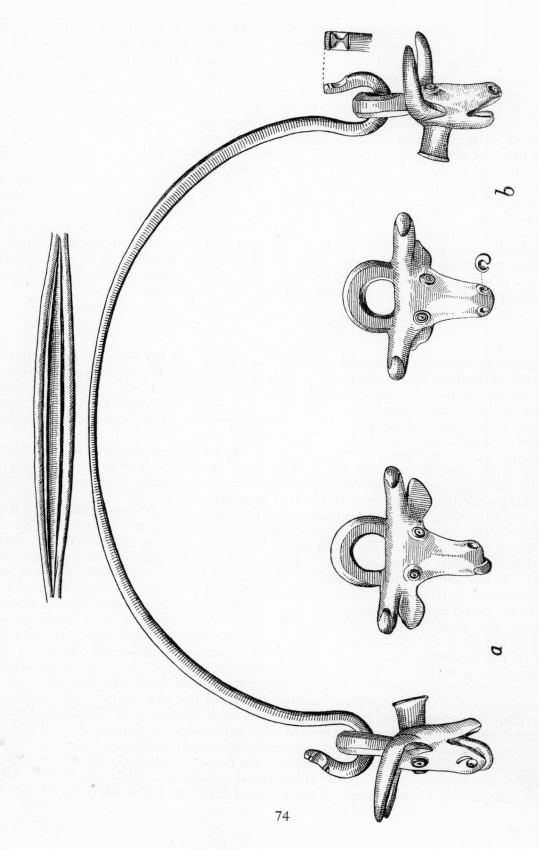

FIGURE 46.—Bucket-handle, with cow-heads: Felmersham-on-Ouse (Beds.). (¼).

74

lady's chariot used for social calls,[6] such as the one buried with its owner at Danes' Graves (p. 7 above). I suggest that these animal forms, framed so solidly, and with surfaces so smoothly wrought, arise because the metal moulds were shaped on wooden models. The two mounts, for the ends of the yoke on either side, could also have been designed in wood; they are of less interest. These bronzes, in Dorchester Museum, were illustrated in an early volume of *Archaeologia*; it is a pleasure to reproduce such admirable drawings.

It may here be noted that early Celtic wood-carving, as a likely basis for bronze-work, has long been recognized, the embossed triquetra from Moel Hiraddug (Flints.) (*Plate 45b* and Figure 82, D31), having obviously been hammered out on a metal mould cast from a wooden prototype.[7] It is analysed on p. 117 below.

The most frequent use of the ox-motif is for fire-dogs, and two types of this Early Iron Age hearth furniture occur in Britain. The more realistic (distinctively Iron "C", Belgic) has shafts with ox-head terminals and no other ornament; its best-known representatives are the Lords Bridge, Barton (Cambs.) example, the Stanfordbury (Beds.) pair, and the Mount Bures (Essex) pair, all from eastern Britain.[8]

The first-mentioned is illustrated on *Plate 47*: the technique of the heads, which have knobbed horns, is masterly, and the breadth of treatment notable. The nostrils have been indicated by two blows of a convex-faced hammer; the brow ridges and the eyes exhibit similar methods. Though exact realism is perhaps not the smith's aim, the essential bovine bony structure is admirably indicated; the curve of the horns and the broad brow, the plane of the cheek and the right eye, the angle of the jaw, and the droop of the lower lip :—the elongated delicacy of shape is, however, outside nature! The female of the Celtic breed, *Bos taurus longifrons*, is probably indicated. An attenuated example, only 11 in. high, without knobs on the horns, from the fortified Belgic settlement at Bigbury (Kent) is illustrated on *Plate 26*: the back half is lost, but this seems to matter little. The piece has a gay insouciance which marks the skilled craftsman: appreciation and understanding accompanied the hammer strokes which created it.[9]

A rarer, Iron "B", decorated western type is represented by the Capel Garmon fire-dog found in a peat bog in Denbighshire 700 ft. above O.D., in 1852, and now in the National Museum of Wales; *Plates 48* and *49* show the front and one end of the piece[10] which is some 2½ ft. in height. It is essentially barbaric, product of another world of art and craft. The two shafts are each bent over to form a neck, on to each of which are fastened the horned head of an ox with its crest or "mane"; the shafts stand on semicircular arched feet and are connected by a horizontal bar, thickened towards the middle, on or behind which the fire was built. These shafts are ornamented on each side by a broad ribbon of iron bent into semicircular loops, and with coils at the top and bottom; between the loops the ribbon is fixed to the shaft by rivets with heavy decorative knobs in the same "rococo" fashion as the coral, glass, or amber knobs of our early brooches and other works of art (p. 7 above). In short, the piece should have a long history behind it.

The crest or mane consists of a curved bar of iron terminating in a coil and decorated with knobs similar to those of the ribbon-loops, fixed to the neck by means of a thin iron plate in which there is a series of circular holes set parallel to the curve of the neck. Though more like a helmet-crest than a mane, its parentage from a true mane is well attested in contemporary Celtic art.[11]

This western, probably Dobunic, type is represented also—in a modified form—by the Welwyn (Herts.), fire-dogs. It is now recognized that the stubby serrated mane of this pair in an *Archaeologia* illustration of 1911[12] is an incorrect restoration, traces of a thin iron plate or *septum* being clearly visible in the decayed remnants; thus must surely have carried a crest of Capel Garmon type. Again, the Welwyn ox-heads are of a flattened form with wide mouths resembling the Capel Garmon heads, but less like the Lords Bridge and Stanfordbury heads (to name examples of the eastern type well known to me). Romilly Allen suggested for the Capel Garmon fire-dog a date within the century 50 B.C.–A.D. 50, but it seems that closer dating is now possible—25 B.C.–A.D. 25.[13]

To sum up: we have a remarkable range of treatment of the ox and cow in our "Celtic" art, illustrating the importance in everyday life in Britain of dairy farming. The sober Roman realism of the Lords Bridge ox-head[14] and the "baroque" gaiety of the Ham Hill mask well represent two of the newer elements in the outlook on life and art in south Britain from about 50 B.C. to A.D. 50; the Belgic, and the Armoric-trained, craftsmen each transmuting classical technique to his own ends. A third group, illustrated by the Dinorben head, represents an older, more truly British, pattern-making Iron "B" tradition: a fourth type is impressively barbaric.

A playful use of the ox theme, in a southern manner, may find mention here, at the close; it is a knife handle thus carved, from the Birdlip (Glos.) burial group of about A.D. 10.[15]

(b) Horse (pony)

The outline of the "White Horse" seems suited to small-scale Celtic relief work, but nothing of the sort is known until Romano-British times, when an "improved" example in bronze was made—and lost—in Calleva (Silchester, Berks.).[16] There is, however, a familiar example of the horse-head in Celtic art, the miniature mask (*Plate 52*) possibly (like the technically similar human masks) decorating a chariot, from Stanwick (North Riding, Yorks.); here a Brigantian craftsman evidently watched the older ponies at leisure in the stable yard. Using lyre-shaped scrolls for the bony structure of the face and the nostrils, and the "lip" motif for the eyes, this bronze-smith has marvellously given life to abstract forms; never was bland, smug, full-fed stable horsiness better delineated.[17]

(c) Pig (Boar)

The pig was an important food-animal among the Celts, as the "joints of pork" referred to in Chapter II (p. 5) indicate: but the art of the period suggests they were a lean and tough lot. In the beginnings the "boar-totem" on the Witham shield is, of course, outstanding, and in the later phases several bronzes of boars, more or less lifelike, are known. One of the two from Hounslow (Middx.) in the British Museum, designed as helmet crests, is here illustrated; it is rightly characterized by Sir Thomas Kendrick[18] as "a brilliant shorthand statement of the force and form of the animal" (*Plate 53a*).

A remarkable boars-head found at Deskford (Banffs.), 8½ in. long, is built up from sheet-bronze; the treatment of the eyelids shows its technical relationship to the Stanwick horse-head and therefore its possible source in the north-eastern, Brigantian, province of our later Celtic art. (We have other evidence suggesting a sea-trade in metal-work from south to north along the east coast of Britain.) The piece is held to have been part of a "military standard or ensign".[19]

(d) Sheep (Ram)

Representations of the heads only of rams are rare: the best is a pair in cast bronze, 3¼ in. in height, found in 1867 with objects indicative of a Belgic burial of early-I A.D., near Harpenden (Herts.) (*Plate 50*). These were a decayed bucket (bronze bands and wood), two heavy bronze rings, and two cordoned vessels of Kimmeridge shale. The original record is in Cussan's *History of Hertfordshire*[20]; the rings were illustrated in 1928 as hanging from the rams' skulls, and this was reproduced in Leeds's *Celtic Ornament*.[21]

The rams' heads are superbly sculptured, presenting close study of an old leader of the flock. The bony facial structure is emphasized by transverse scoring of the metal, and the horns are ribbed; the dignity of the pose when the mask is mounted in the position obviously intended, is most striking. The axial—back to front—swell of the skull rises to a narrow ridge-mane or crest; this is grooved cross-wise. There are traces of enamel—blue in the eye sockets, which may have had white pupils, red in the nostrils and in the corners of the mouth drawn back by muscular action; all will have provided strong contrast with the golden bronze of the casting. The masks, then, heighten our appreciation of the table service associated with feasts, secular or religious, in a Belgic nobleman's household of the period.

The writer studied these bronzes at the Wardown Park Museum at Luton[22] in 1954, and came to the conclusion that association of rams' heads and rings in the manner suggested was extremely unlikely.

The perfect ram-mask of the pair was mauled in the nineteenth century: hollows for enamel had been "cleaned up", as *Plate 50*, left, shows. Worse than this, the loop cast with the head, a vital element of the problem of attachment, has been worked over and

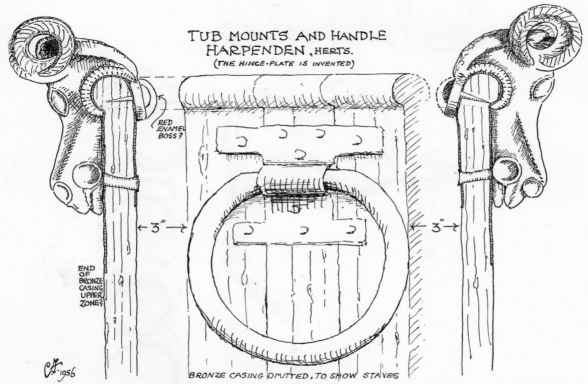

FIGURE 47.—Rams' heads and ring: Harpenden (Herts.). Mounted, in probable positions, on a tub. Cf. *Plate 50*.

bevelled as though for a steel screw (!). Nevertheless, the problem of masks and rings is not insoluble, and Figure 47 illustrates my views on the matter. The tub with staves ½ in. thick was ringed with bronze bands, the uppermost of which gave a secure hold for the rivets by which the rams-heads on each side were attached. The hollow curve below the ram's skull, ridged and ornamented, fitted the roll-rim of the tub. The plain loop carried a nail which, being driven into a stave, prevented the upper part of the mask from "rocking"— it also, I feel convinced, carried a large boss of red enamel, as outlined on the sketch. The 4-in. bronze rings (*Plate 27a*) were hung on opposite sides of the tub for lifting it—the masks being purely decorative. These rings are flattened at the top for a broad metal attachment-loop.[23]

A less likely reconstruction is that the loops behind the masks secured the hooked ends of a curved bronze handle—as on the continentally-derived Aylesford bucket (*Plate 33*):

less likely because it involves the transference of the associated rings to another vessel of which nothing else survives or is known.   The rings may look large, but a human hand could not grasp a smaller one, and a tub of 12 in. internal diameter full of beer is heavy.

Another remarkable bronze tub- or bucket-mount, from Hertford Museum, coming from one or other of the Belgic burials at Welwyn, shows heavy enamel bosses facing inward (as well as outward) and so tends to confirm my "repair-work" on the Harpenden mount. This will, I hope, excuse a diversion.   The fine drawing reproduced in my Figure 48[24] and

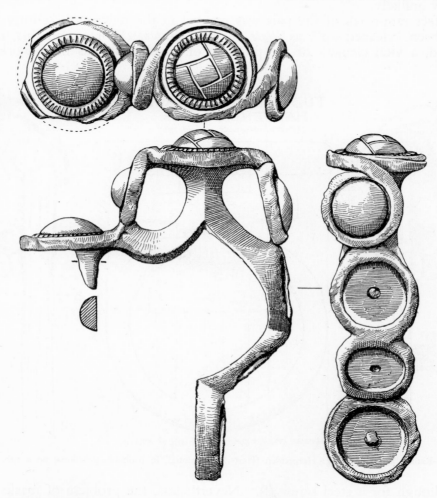

FIGURE 48.—Mount of wooden tub: Welwyn (Herts.).   Side, back, and top views. (¼)

used in Figure 83, F46, provides some hints for reconstruction of the vessel it adorned, but there are difficulties.   Professor Hawkes presented two or three tentative solutions in 1935, but none satisfied him, so they need not be discussed: I offer a fourth.

The vertical staves of the tub, plus its bronze bands, will have been 1 in. thick—this being the horizontal distance between the inner vertical face of the "peg" (shown also in section on the drawing) and the vertical face of the terminal knob of the decorative structure diagonally below it.   These staves—like the Harpenden ones—expanded at the top to form a broad rim which occupied the whole of the area thus framed by the bronze.   The rim, then, was concavo-convex in outline, and 2 in. broad.   I see no difficulty in the fact that this reconstruction leaves an enamelled boss projecting for $\frac{3}{4}$ in. into the body of the vessel on either side; it is *buttressed below* to look, and to be secure! The tub placed beside the master of the feast has to present as decorative a character as possible, *at the top*.

The piece can claim a place in its own right in a book on Celtic art: its design is original and bold with every element proportionate to its heavy duty, and its ornament—strapwork and enamel—effective and brilliant. The rectilinear pattern on one boss takes its place in my "Grammar" (Figure 83, F46).

I return to the Celtic motif of the ram's head: this was used to decorate a delicate bronze bowl with beaded rim, "spun", and therefore of high quality, found at Youlton, Treneglos (east Cornwall).[25] It was found beside the trackway which all early land-based traders or invaders of Cornwall will have followed, along the backbone of the peninsula, passing close by Tintagel. The grotesque addition to this bowl, cast and tooled, had, as the photograph (*Plate 51*) shows, a hole for a ring of bronze wire to seize the bowl by, between the ram's "eyes and mouth". That the ram's head should be upside down is at first sight strange; but an observation the writer made in 1939[26] on cauldrons of the late Bronze Age in another western region (Llyn Fawr (Glam.)) provides an acceptable explanation. Surface wear on minor projections of the flat bronze *rims* showed that these vessels were stored upside down, pulled forward and pushed back, no doubt, on a shelf in the rude, dusty-floored, but possibly spacious, "hall" of a western landed-man.

This mode of keeping showy and decorative "plate" in an Iron Age house deep in the south-western region is likely enough; we may then picture a set of these bowls on a shelf, just within reach, with their ram escutcheons right side up! The date of the finished piece may be late I century B.C.; the inverted horn motif, however, is seen on the well-known *situla* from Certosa, northern Italy, of the VI century B.C.[27]

The ram may have had a ritual significance among the Celts[28]; the famous Frasnes, Hainault, gold torc of *c.* 50 B.C., the detail of which is closely related to our Snettisham style (p. 46), has a magnificent head with curved horns, occupying a central position in the decoration.[29] The God of the Underworld is a serpent with ram's head (p. 81 below).

(e) Birds

Heads of the duck are common element of pattern on our Iron "B" bronzes, as preceding pages show; otherwise the representation of birds is not common in Celtic Britain. The find, during excavation in a rampart of Milber "hill-slope fort" in south Devon in 1950[30] of three bronzes—one a song-bird, the second a duck, and the third a reindeer—was therefore of great interest. The writer was invited to comment on them; the note on the birds is here quoted.

The "song-bird" shows clever naturalistic (classical) modelling—there is nothing Celtic about it—whereas the duck (*Plate 42b*) is "essential duckery" expressed in the simplest terms, of the same order of excellence as the Hounslow boar. The enchanting little creature represents a British–Celtic improvement on a known theme of west European art: it is not just "duck", it is a duck swimming, alert and expecting interference, because it has a griddle-cake in its bill. The horizontal recessed lines on the body are slightly broader in front and behind; the duck's movement creates a double bar of light and shade, stronger in front than on the side, and lapping up when, as here, the tail is lowered.

It seems likely that there were ducks kept on the sacred pools of the Celts such as that in which the *Aurum Tolosanum* was hidden, and fed by the priests; watched by craftsmen and others, as we watch the ducks in our parks. Such a creation as this, simplified in the Celtic manner, can only come about after long practice by a school of artists: the duck-with-cake-in-mouth was a subject of art on the Continent, as is shown by the photograph of the goddess (*Plate 42a*) in the sacred boat, set up in Roman times at the source of the Seine.[31]

Lastly, an attractive ring-brooch from a burial in a cave at Llanferres (Denbs.), with duck-head terminals, is illustrated on *Plate 41e*. The treatment of the heads is as sensitive as in the previous example, but gayer, more lighthearted.

(f) Fish

The only example of a fish—or rather fish-head—is the massive bronze found with the ox-and-cow masks (p. 73 above) and other objects at Felmersham-on-Ouse.[32] This strange creature, dated in early I A.D., is illustrated on *Plate 46*. It is by a Celtic artist very different in outlook from him who produced the bull escutcheons in the same collection of scrap metal; "the formal treatment of detail captures the realism of caricature, an essence of fishiness". W. Watson, who published the piece, emphasizes the "power of witty and concentrated statement" shown, and concludes that "classical naturalism has here undergone a change amounting to original creation, in which barbarian genius asserts itself". "Two details of style," he adds, "link it with other contemporary work. The first and most striking is the form of the eye. At this period the motif of a circle set . . . eccentrically within another which is peaked up at one or two points, appears to be an innovation in Celtic design . . . The originality of the piece lies just in the adoption of this unit of design, this use of geometrical abstraction, to interpret a natural form." I would add that the "snaily coil" so often seen in our earlier art had a part in its development, and that a tankard handle such as he has in mind, of mid-I A.D., is illustrated on *Plate 66*.

Watson visualizes the spout "fixed to a robust shallow vessel, rounded in plan, but not necessarily completing the circle, installed immovably at a . . . spring, and directing the water in a disciplined jet from the fish's mouth. Such an arrangement would reflect a classical idea".

FIGURE 49.—Fish-head spout, bronze: Felmersham-on-Ouse (Beds.) (¾).

I studied the Felmersham collection in 1954,[33] and only in minor points do I disagree with Mr. Watson; one is in respect of the angle at which the fish-head is set at the side of the vessel (Figure 49 is corrected). I am convinced, moreover, that the bowl it was fitted to was less bulgy,[34] and that the parallel lines on the piece were intended to be vertical, thus depressing the spout, and giving a purposeful fall of water. The fish-head was designed for a bowl ½ in. thick and 1¼ in. at the rim—clearly the whole structure had been thought out as a permanent and attractive feature of a precinct (close to the chieftain's dwelling, no doubt): how modern it all seems !

(g) Serpent

A remarkable and rich burial by cremation at Snailwell (Cambs.) of another Belgic dignitary yielded (in 1954) a bronze armlet (*Plate 53b*) of four coils, 40½ in. long and nearly 4 in. in diameter, of sub-triangular section with identical heads at each end, part serpent, part ram, the "backbone" having a delicately incised pattern of linked diamonds bounded by incised lines—a common late Belgic ornament. One side *only* of each zöomorph is finely detailed—another late feature; by accident this was placed *inside* in the final coiling process!

The nostrils are a single coil deeply cupped to a central point, and there is a well-defined bulge between them. The eyes are tiny circles within a frame of enamel and ribbed bronze; the eyebrows grow out of the eye-frame in Celtic fashion, they are scored cross-wise, and so is the "ruff" at the back—a snaky feature! The cheeks have a patch of stipple outlined in a curve; a zone of this stippling extends from the head along the back for 3 in.[35]

This is perhaps the only rich cremation burial of its class and date in Britain which has been carefully recorded, on discovery, by a competent archaeologist (Mr. T. C. Lethbridge). Thus we learn that the armlet did not pass through the fire with the owner, like most of the numerous objects in the grave: and that of those that were *not* burnt, it was the only object placed on the owner's couch with his burnt bones. It had then a special significance, which was clearly religious; Lambrechts notes that a serpent with ram's head was a Gaulish divinity equated with Mercury.[36]

(h) Winged griffin

A bronze plate-brooch of middle-I A.D. with a griffin in relief of the school of the Aylesford bucket and Marlborough vat[37] is in the hoard from Santon Downham (Suffolk) (*Plate 37b*). It has wings that have become Celticized (scrolls), a horn, and a beard-like projection which hangs from its lip. It resembles opposed animals on the Marlborough vat (*Plate 35*), and is closely akin in character and pose to the pair of griffins on the Gundestrup bowl (*Plate 37a*). These have no horns, but horned creatures are associated with them, as is seen on the left of the bowl (*Plate 37c*, background).

A variant of this mythical beast, incised on a chalk hill-slope, was mapped by percussion by Mr. T. C. Lethbridge in 1955–57 near Wandlebury hill-fort, Cambridge.[38] The creature also appears on a coin of Cunobelin (my *Plate 79*, No. 14, obverse) which confirms its eastern (Trinovantian) connexions.

GENERAL COMMENT. The differences of style and of technical and artistic approach in these representations of living creatures, held to have been produced in Britain during the last eighty years or so of freedom are remarkable. A borrowed naturalism is nobly rendered by a Belgic artist in the Lords Bridge fire-dogs, and humorously recorded in the Felmersham bull and cow. The Hounslow boar is a superb piece, unmatched among our works of art for forcefulness and individuality: the Ham Hill ox and the Bulbury oxen in their different ways show the keen and friendly interest taken in farm-animals of the village by Celtic bronze-smiths. The Milber duck shows character and movement recorded in the most simple terms possible, while the Harpenden rams' heads are a harsh and uncompromising record of animal toughness: as for the fish-head, its cold-bloodedness transcends nature. Every piece we have studied indeed demands an appreciative adjective—except the ram on the Youlton bowl; this shows that extreme barbarism in art can survive, or regain control, on the fringes of a stagnant or decaying Iron "B" culture. Lastly, the griffin on the Suffolk brooch, and the Snailwell ram-serpent, suggest that religious art in metal-work on the scale of the Gundestrup bowl may turn up some day in Britain.

NOTES TO CHAPTER VII

[1] *L'exaltation de la Tête dans . . . l'art des Celtes*, 1954, Chapitre II.

[1a] Native, though probably of early II A.D. From ISVRIVM BRIGANTVM, the Roman capital of the tribe. See I. A. Richmond, *Journ. Rom. Studies*, 1954, p. 49.

[2] See Jacobsthal, *Early Celtic Art*, pp. 15–16.

[3] After W. Watson, *Ant. Journ.*, 1949, p. 40, Figure 2. See C. F. C. Hawkes, "Cauldron and Bucket Animals", in *Aspects of Archaeology in Britain and Beyond*, 1951, pp. 172–99.

[4] Visited in 1952: situated on good farm land, without natural advantages for defence, and nearly ploughed out.

[5] The horns are probably immature, the bovine represented being a bull-calf.

[6] The Chatelaine had a mirror, and may have been entertaining an overseas trader; a Gallo-Roman type of anchor, with chain, was part of the find. All can be seen in Dorchester Museum.

[7] W. J. Hemp, *Arch. Camb.*, 1928, p. 283.

[8] After Fox, *Ant. Journ.* VI, pp. 317–18. Other examples are listed by Fox, *Ant. Journ.* XIX, 1939, p. 447. Handsome specimens of this type of ox-head are the pair on the Lydney bowl, *Soc. Ant. Report* IX, 1932, Figure 11.

[9] Well described by R. F. Jessup, *Arch. Journ.* 89, 1933, p. 110.

[10] After C. Fox in *Ant. Journ.*, 1939, p. 446 ff. This article contains references to the relevant literature.

[11] See *Archaeologia* 52, p. 370, *Plate xiii*, Nos. *1, 2, 3*.

[12] "On Late Keltic Antiquities at Welwyn, Herts.", *Archaeologia* lxiii, p. 1 ff.

[13] The analysis of the Welwyn finds was inconclusive in this respect; loc. cit., p. 29, lines 14 ff.

[14] In *Aspects of Archaeology* ([3] above), p. 192, Hawkes points out that the knobbed horns must represent current practice among Belgic and other farmers.

[15] *Archaeologia* 61, p. 332, Figure 2.

[16] Figured by Stuart Piggott, *Antiquity*, 1931, *Plate II*, Figure 5. This author suggests that it stems from the Marlborough vat style.

[17] A horse-mask brooch, in the Stanwick tradition, was found at Richborough, Thanet. Report IV, *Soc. Ant. Lond.*, 1949, *Plate XXVII, 29*.

[18] In *Anglo-Saxon Art*, p. 7.

[19] *Ancient British Art*, Piggott and Daniel, No. 61.

[20] Quoted in *Ant. Journ.*, 1928, p. 520.

[21] Leeds's description of the piece, p. 93, *Celtic Ornament*, is excellent.

[22] By courtesy of the Curator, Mr. C. E. Freeman, F.M.A.

[23] These heavy rings are 4 in. in outer diameter. Wear on one suggests that it was carried on a loop of metal half an inch wide. Such a loop from the site, bronze, of similar diameter with attachments, is preserved.

[24] After C. F. C. Hawkes, *Ant. Journ.*, 1935, p. 353.

[25] "Spun." The technique is described by W. Watson in *Ant. Journ.*, 1949, pp. 51–2. The bowl is highly skilled work, here probably Dobunic, and it suggests that the ornamental casting on it may have been added by a south-western bronze-smith, working in a worn-out Iron "B" tradition. It is important because we have so little art work from the region, the natives of which got little good out of their wealth in tin. Compare the bowls in the Birdlip Mirror grave.

[26] Fox, *Ant. Journ.* xix, p. 373.

[27] Thurlow Leeds, *Archaeologia* 80, 1930, p. 25. Hencken, discussing the piece, suggests that the ornament imitates classical "lion-heads": but rams-horns decorated Italian bronze buckets of the VII–VI centuries B.C., if Mediterranean parallels *must* be sought (*Cornwall and Scilly*, 1932, p. 111).

[28] The *data* collected by Olwen Brogan on religion in Roman Gaul confirm this: *Roman Gaul*, pp. 187–9.

[29] The piece is owned, and preserved, in New York.

[30] *Devon Arch. Exploration Soc.*, Vol. IV, 1950, p. 44.

[31] Reproduced from Olwen Brogan, *Roman Gaul*. *Note.*—The "stag" of golden bronze found in this Milber group (*Plate 42d*), 2½ in. overall, must be Roman, and an import. It may be a reindeer in the Hercynian

Forest; and is depicted as lassoed, and collapsing, the left *hoof* being shown inverted on the left side of the body, the right leg (broken off) being in front. The tense, tortured pose of outstretched head and neck is remarkable. The base is flat, the modelling being cut off abruptly. The whole is purely naturalistic, except that the ear ($\frac{1}{2}$ in.) is much too long.

[32] W. Watson, *Ant. Journ.* XXIX, p. 37 ff.

[33] By the kindness of Mr. Kuhlicke, Curator of Bedford Modern School Museum.

[34] A curve $\frac{1}{8}$ in. in 2 in., as I worked it out.

[35] T. C. Lethbridge, *Proc. Camb. Antiq. Soc.* XLVII, p. 25 ff. In this paper Mr. Lethbridge refers (p. 31) to late, and ornate, derivatives in Scotland.

[36] P. Lambrechts, *Contributions à l'étude des divinités Celtique,* Chapitre III, p. 45.

[37] Figured by C. Fox, *Arch. Camb. Reg.,* 1923, p. 106. It will be a generation later than these works, and is certainly British.

[38] I had the pleasure of referring Mr. Lethbridge to this representation as a contemporary local parallel, when I received his first outline of the creature, which then seemed incomprehensible.

CHAPTER VIII. PERSONAL DISPLAY, INDOORS

(i) MIRRORS AND THE MIRROR-STYLE

In the last quarter of I B.C. skilled metal-workers in south Britain (in the area of Dobunic influence, as I hold), began the manufacture of bronze mirrors, an activity which continued, here and elsewhere, until the Claudian conquest. They produced a variety of handle designs (as we shall see), but their realization of the possibilities of the mirror-backs for elaborate incised pattern-making is more significant. The ready market for such attractive vanities among the womenfolk of Celtic and Belgic chieftains is indicated by the number which survive, wholly or in part (many from graves); it is, then, remarkable that no parallels exist in Celtic Europe to the achievements this chapter will record.[1] Most of the decorated mirrors will be seen on *Plates 56a* and *56b*: the latter includes the early, plain, Arras mirror already mentioned (J), and four late undecorated mirrors (L, M, O, and Q), the handles of which have character.[2]

The fact that no decorated mirrors come from the region of the northern tribes—the Parisian and Brigantian area—shows how markedly the creative urge, notable here in the period of settlement, had swung to the richer central and southern countrysides in I B.C. The former will have remained pastoral; the latter will have developed a widespread agriculture.

The use of the incised technique and the "matting" of either pattern or background is well shown in the former Plate. In the upper row are two mirrors in which the background is matted—the early method; in all the others (which are later) it is the design that is matted.

The fact that A1 and A2 represent the same piece (the "Mayer" mirror) lighted differently, shows how complicated the study (as works of art) of patterns formed by roughening selected portions of a polished metal surface can be ! The dark parts of A2 and B are *background* from the point of view of the later history of mirror design; but it would be hard to deny that these could be treated as *pattern*. "Ambivalence of positive and negative forms" remarked Dr. Jacobsthal, "is a feature of Celtic art."

The matting of the surface in all these mirrors (and, it may be added, the scabbards already discussed) is carried out in the following manner: A chaser is used to make (sometimes with a rocking motion) tiny dents—parallel rows of short strokes filling, *or* framing, the design previously drafted by fine incision on the metal. In the best examples a regular chequer pattern was achieved by turning the chaser, and making blocks of strokes at right-angles to each other; hence the term "basketry ornament" for this technique. The variations are seen in Figure 83, K81–86.

Such mirror designs look very different one from another at first glance, but relationship is recognized when they are closely studied and when large-scale photographs are available. A, C, D, E, and F on *Plate 56a* are three-some patterns, and there are two more such on *Plate 56b*, K and the fragmentary P. This feature is best understood in F, wherein the triple structure is simple and the lost portions easily restored. On the other hand, G and H show what often happens to patterns—any patterns—which have an extended vogue, that is a break-up of the governing design, which in this case is illustrated by pattern F; it could be said that we are observing the replacement of a rational pattern by irrationality—but such a conclusion might be unwise (p. 94 below).

Mirrors, then, provide a series of related patterns which best illustrate the character of the later Celtic art in Britain; their evolutionary (or perhaps revolutionary) modifications help us to appreciate the mentality and the genius of the Celtic artist-craftsmen. This is why the writer has worked on them so intensively, and why they are discussed at length in this book.

The earliest of the mirrors is the unprovenanced "Mayer", made almost certainly in Dobunic territory, at the south end of the Jurassic zone. It is seen with its equals, on *Plate 56a*; the pattern in isolation on *Plate 55*. Here the superb technique of the craftsman can be studied; the freehand setting-out lines (scratched on the metal) are rarely visible, and the perfect thing we see must be, in the main, the sketched outline intensified. Such virtuosity is hardly credible.[3] The very remarkable design is built up of three roundels, a primary motif: the upper one is completely enclosed, the lower two have breaks in their circumference. The bounding-line of each of these leads upward, in matching curves, to end on the upper roundel, and another incised line derived from the *interior* of one lower roundel is carried in a sweeping curve to the top of the mirror and then downwards, ending within the other (Figure 50, 2)!

The minor patterns will now be described, beginning with the upper roundel. Two arms of the central, three-way pattern in smooth bronze, those to right and left, have each a filbert-shaped terminal the bounding-line of which coils inwards to define a circle at its base. The third arm, at the base of the figure, is sickle-shaped with no terminal. There are rounds within each of the three matted backgrounds (which are isolated); two of these matted fields have the Llyn Cerrig "trumpet" shapes, the third is a "triangular" figure with one domical and two incurved sides. The "entrant" line in the lower right roundel combines with the boundary line—which here runs close and parallel to it—to create the same sort of three-way pattern as we have just studied; it is here so arranged that *all* the matted backgrounds have the Llyn Cerrig shape with curled tips. There is great variety in the size of the circles in this pattern.

In the third (left-hand) roundel no such simple pattern is present: it is not unfair to describe it as a jumble of all the elements present in the other two with additional shapes both in smooth and matted bronze. For example, on the left-hand margin, a circle outlined in smooth bronze contains a matted "circle" which is itself overlaid, wholly or in part, by two plain, smaller, circles. One of the new forms, twice repeated, is tongue-shaped.

Though defying a full verbal analysis, the final word must be that the design of this roundel fits successfully into the major pattern, and the reader might say that it is not really different from its neighbours, though a little more complicated. In the Celtic art of Britain, such obscurity is, as we have seen, not unique: a Weston (Som.) spoon pattern (Figure 22) has been cited.[4]

The undoubted attractiveness of the style, then, is mainly due to a masterly and apparently effortless technique, shown particularly in the creation of curves of unusual beauty. Here and there in this and other such works the faint scratch of the setting-out is visible beside the finished line. Sometimes the former seems more "true", but not usually; the quality of such line-work in metal as "Mayer" illustrates seems, indeed, to reach the perfection of harmony between hand and eye. We must not leave this piece without emphasizing the quality of its matting.

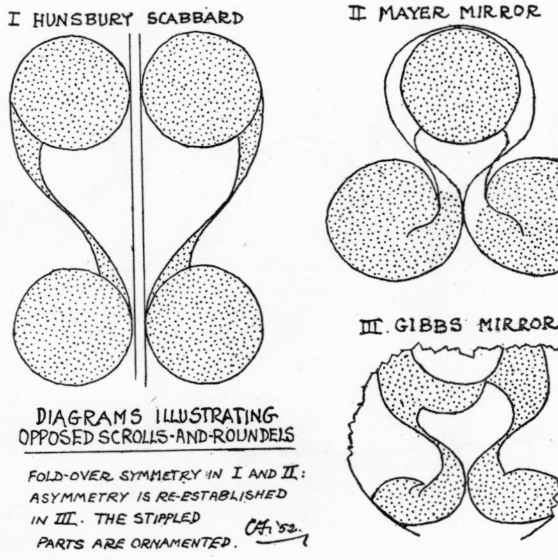

I HUNSBURY SCABBARD   II MAYER MIRROR

III GIBBS MIRROR

DIAGRAMS ILLUSTRATING OPPOSED SCROLLS-AND-ROUNDELS

FOLD-OVER SYMMETRY IN I AND II: ASYMMETRY IS RE-ESTABLISHED IN III. THE STIPPLED PARTS ARE ORNAMENTED. CF. '52.

FIGURE 50.—Diagrams.

FIGURE 51b.—Colchester mirror: the incised design, restored. (⅔)

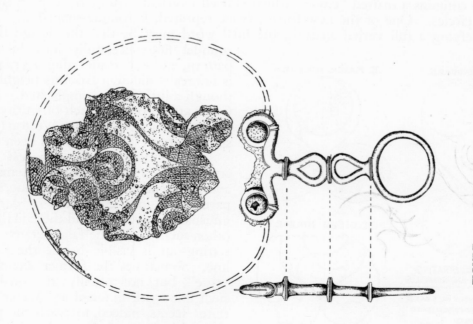

FIGURE 51a.—Colchester mirror: the surviving portions. (⅔)

86

This is usually regular in pattern (as Figure 83, K83), suggesting that a true weave was in the mind of the craftsman, but it changes character in confined spaces.

The source of the device "of opening the roundels" is the Hunsbury scabbard, whereon paired roundels, flanking the central rib, are thus linked (Figure 50) to create opposed scrolls. It is a delicate and attractive motif, and it initiated an outstanding achievement in decoration. This is seen, at a stage later than "Mayer", in the Colchester mirror (Figure 51); it is a damaged piece which has been restored with fair certainty.

The outstanding features, then, of the Colchester ornament are massive, opposed, hatched scrolls, adopting in their progress the Mayer form; their ends, partly preserved, face inward (above) and outward (below). In the central interspace is a familiar Celtic motif, a concave-sided triangle within a circle (Figure 82, B9); it is set in a semicircular frame. This frame is a Celtic version of the Greek palmette placed upside down: "the leaves have gone and a closed-up configuration remains";[5] the device is set on a stem, again a common feature. In Figure 52, two Continental examples are sketched, together with one on a Polden Hill (Som.) harness-mount, and another on a mirror-handle from Desborough (Northants.).

The circle in the Colchester piece is repeated, with a simplified internal structure, at each end of each scroll; three out of the four are wholly or in part preserved. They are notable features of the pattern; the "matted" or hatched almond shapes within them diverge from the base of each of the fans which complicate the scroll structure, and they each mask part of a negative comma-shape (Figure 56c).

The lower ends of the two scrolls on the fragment are ill-preserved, but there is surviving detail to indicate that they formed part of the build-up of lateral structures similar to the one we have described, but inverted.

1 WALDALGESHEIM 2 BRUNN AM STEINFELD

3 DESBOROUGH 4 POLDEN HILL

FIGURE 52.—Palmettes and tendrils.

In Figure 51 (b) the elements of the design known to us are completed on the assumption, then, that a fold-over symmetry, within the limits imposed by an approximately circular frame and by his freehand draughtsmanship, was the Celtic artist's intention. The palmettes are now seen to be related to the opposed scrolls in the same way, broadly speaking, as on the Waldalgesheim torc, the Brunn am Steinfeld bronze, and the Polden Hill enamel illustrated in Figure 52. The tightness of structure imposed by the limitations of the circular frame of the mirror gives these scrolls the character of lyres, and the ornament is thus a triple lyre-palmette, the principal (central) lyre being, of course, inverted.

"Lyres have their roots in spiral ornament" says Dr. Jacobsthal, "but they early entered into symbiosis with palmettes and flowers."[6] Designs from Umbria and Etruria (Figure 53) illustrate the evolution of the comparatively "barren" from the "flowery" lyre. Our design, regarded as a lyre form, finds a parallel in other British pieces; the closest to it is the fragment of a frieze from Great Tower Street, London, with tenuous scrolls and much simplified closed palmettes in relief. Purer lyre types, loops with head scrolls, are illustrated in the same figure from a noble harness-fitting found in Northamptonshire (see also p. 121 below) and from one of our unprovenanced mirror-handles. These three pieces are all to be dated within the first half of I A.D.; they have ancestors in the Cerrig-y-Drudion bowl and the Wisbech scabbard (Figure 54).

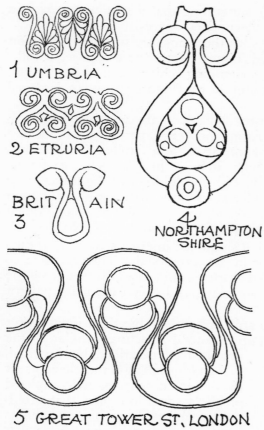

FIGURE 53.—Celtic lyre-designs in Britain, and
their origins.

1 UMBRIA

2 ETRURIA

BRITAIN
3

4 NORTHAMPTON
SHIRE

5 GREAT TOWER ST. LONDON

We may now sum up the artistic significance of the "Colchester" achievement. "Mayer" is a balanced design, but its triple roundels contain completely asymmetric patterns. As may fairly be held, asymmetry was outmoded in the chief centres of the bronze-worker's craft in southern Britain shortly before it was made[7]: classical (Roman) influence was great. The mirror-makers had to move with the times; and a unifying motif was needed which could provide symmetry for the circular field of the mirror-plate without sacrificing structural forms traditional in the craft. The grouped lyre-palmette pattern was the very thing; its major curves were those already in use—as Mayer shows; it provided a context in which Celtic motifs hitherto treated *eccentrically* could be placed *in formal opposition*.

We have not quite finished with our mirror-design, for the shape of the mirror itself has to be considered.

The lyre structure demands a "kidney" shape rather than a circle, as indeed does the grip of the mirror-handle. Thus framed, handle, mirror-outline, and incised ornament as set out in Figure 51 are in aesthetic accord—note the relation between the circles on the mirror and the bosses within the terminal scrolls of the handle: the whole piece presents a controlled and studied rhythm.[8]

The Birdlip (Glos.) and Desborough (Northants.) mirrors

In the three-roundel sequence of mirror-ornament, then, we place Colchester next to "Mayer"; and by good fortune we can study the use subsequent artists made, not necessarily of our mirror, but of the group of mirrors on which we may suppose the lyre-pattern was employed, of which Colchester is the sole surviving example. The principal designs available are those of the Birdlip and Desborough mirrors (*Plate 57*). As an aid to the analysis of these designs, their essential elements are outlined in Figure 55.

First, the Birdlip mirror; this has a generic resemblance to Colchester. The same triple structure is apparent, and the scroll-curves are similar, though they are undoubtedly disintegrating; Figure 56D is an illustration of the process. From a truer angle of view, one would say that new integrations are developing. This is certainly the case in respect of the inverted Y-forms of Colchester (noted on the drawing); the Birdlip artist inserted lovely coils which cut clean across them (the position of these coils is indicated by a curved line in my Figure, and they can be studied on the Plate). On the other hand, disliking the *inverted* upper palmette of Colchester, the Birdlip artist replaced it, not by something new, but by a small-scale replica of one of the lower nodes of this mirror.

Turning to Desborough, we see a further stage in the devolution of the lyre-palmette pattern; work of a master of greater sensibility, it may be thought, in another *atelier*. Desborough might seem to be stylistically nearer to Colchester than is Birdlip, because the upper "fans" (F) are larger; but these have, in fact, been completely assimilated, and their attendant circles so carefully preserved in Birdlip[9] have in Desborough vanished. The feeling for rhythm, again, is more strongly marked: there is a recovery of the Celtic spirit.

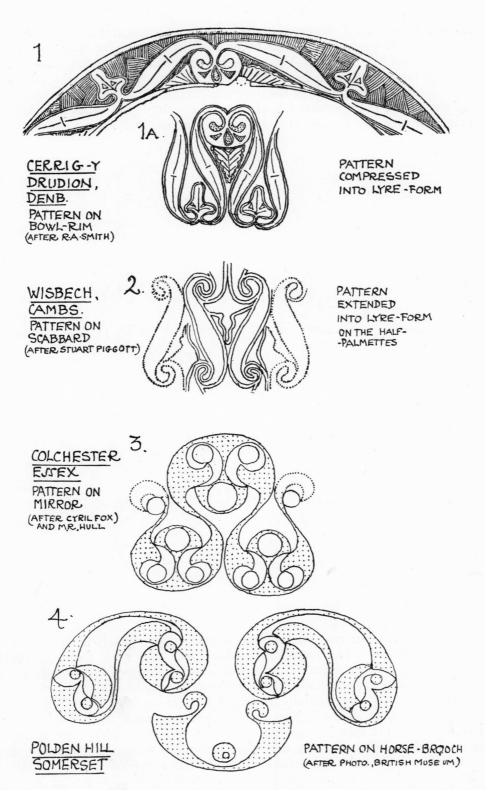

1

CERRIG-Y DRUDION, DENB.
PATTERN ON BOWL-RIM
(AFTER R·A·SMITH)

1A

PATTERN COMPRESSED INTO LYRE-FORM

2

WISBECH, CAMBS.
PATTERN ON SCABBARD
(AFTER STUART PIGGOTT)

PATTERN EXTENDED INTO LYRE-FORM ON THE HALF--PALMETTES

3

COLCHESTER ESSEX
PATTERN ON MIRROR
(AFTER CYRIL FOX) AND M.R.HULL

4

POLDEN HILL SOMERSET

PATTERN ON HORSE-BROOCH
(AFTER PHOTO., BRITISH MUSEUM)

FIGURE 54.—Ancestry of the Colchester mirror and Polden Hill brooch patterns,

89

The most important structural change is in the lower nodes; the inverted Y-form of Colchester is reduced in size and pushed into the outer margin, as can be seen by comparing, on Figure 55, the *inverted* Y2, Y3, and Y4. The lower scrolls, moreover, have vanished, and a design bearing no resemblance in outline to these symmetrical forms takes their place. We see, in fact, a minor resurgence of the asymmetric tradition; minor, because the fold-over symmetry of the whole is unimpaired, and there is continuity in other decorative elements, the "F" series, isolated on Figure 56. A fourth mirror, the unprovenanced "Gibbs", is

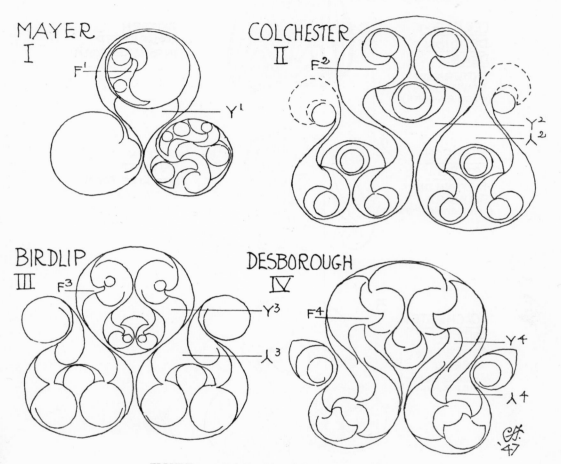

FIGURE 55.—Relationship of four mirror patterns.

included on *Plate 57* to illustrate an extreme development, which is in the asymmetrical tradition (see p. 96 below). The piece shows also a late "trumpet" form (Figure 83, K85).

One other aspect of the mirror series Colchester–Birdlip–Desborough is important. The duality of the Colchester scroll design is obvious: the positive element is so drawn as to need the carefully shaped and partially enclosed background or "field" for its complete comprehension. A new twist was given to this attractive trick in Birdlip, where complex negative forms are inextricably involved in the coils and roundels. The group of artists represented by Desborough saw that this gay, rotund treatment presented a new artistic possibility, and they invented a ribbony design, the structure of which was lightened by incorporating such negative patterns throughout. It is, indeed, a synthesis of glittering, aery, lace-like forms.

A word is needed on the technique of the matting on the Colchester mirror. Of the mirrors discussed, Birdlip and Desborough show the regular pattern which justifies the term "basketry filling",[10] while Mayer illustrates the phase in which this device was being evolved by the bronze-workers. Colchester shows little resemblance to either; its reticulated pattern is not elsewhere represented in the incised designs of the period in Britain. We must, then, provisionally assign the Colchester mirror to a workshop otherwise unknown.

Apropos of "matting", an interesting discovery, made in the course of recent repair work on the Birdlip mirror carried out in the Technical Department of the British Museum in 1953, is that the portion of the plate concealed in the slot of the handle "had been used" in Dr. H. J. Plenderleith's words, "as a trial piece for tooling by the craftsman before tackling the main subject in chased ornament".[11] A Museum photograph illustrating this newly discovered incised work is reproduced on *Plate 58a*. The technique is becoming looser: interlaced work is associated with broad bands of parallel lines.

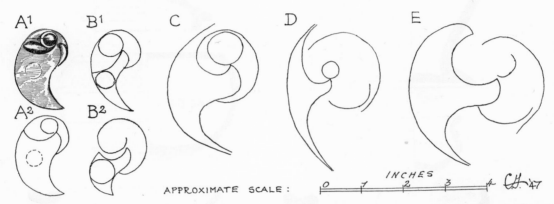

FIGURE 56.—Evolution of the fan, comma, and circle motif. A—Llyn Cerrig plaque; B—Mayer mirror; C, D, and E—Colchester, Birdlip, and Desborough mirrors.

Summary. To sum up this section of our mirror survey, it is held that the Colchester mirror ornament was designed as a variation on an original concept of three linked circles; its principal motif, the lyre-palmette pattern, is an intrusion which explains much that, on this three-circle theory, had hitherto been obscure in the magnificent designs of Birdlip and Desborough. Thus it illuminates and strengthens a synthesis sketched out prior to its discovery.[12] All these designs are efforts, in a creative age (of whose merit and, having regard to time and place, importance, the art world is perhaps not yet fully appreciative), to modify the three-circle motif in the direction of an ever-closer rhythmic integration involving fold-over symmetry.

Dating evidence for these mirrors

This small but important group can be approximately dated, on the basis of the sequence suggested: the Colchester mirror was part of a rich cremation burial including late Belgic pottery of exceptional quality illustrated in Figure 57, and the beautiful "spun-bronze" handled-cup on Figure 58. The cup is $2\frac{7}{8}$ in. high with rounded base and no footring; the metal very thin, with a thicker, finely-outlined rim, sloping inwards. The cast bronze handle has a hemispherical boss of red enamel (?) secured by a bronze pin. The technique is Iron "B", not Belgic.

Mr. M. R. Hull, who has detailed knowledge of the early history of Colchester, suggests that the pottery was made in the reign of Cunobelin (A.D. 10–43), the range of date considered

91

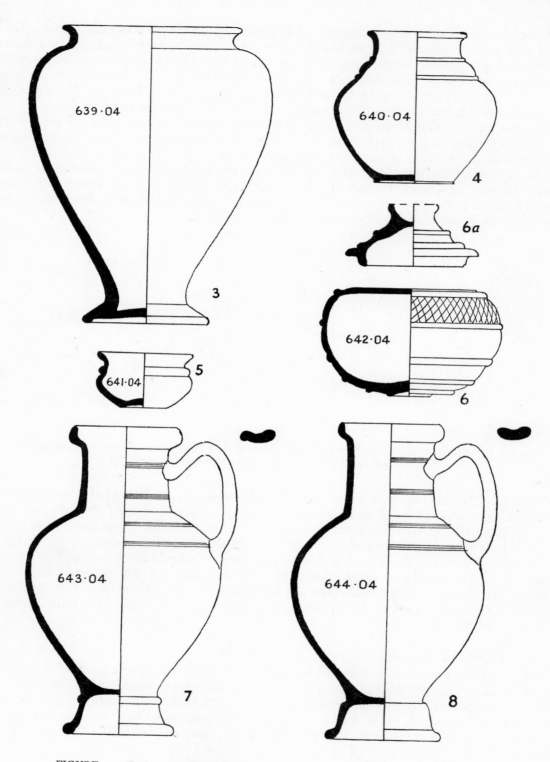

FIGURE 57.—Pottery associated with the Colchester mirror (Lexden site), *c.* 10 A.D. (¼)

likely being A.D. 10–25.[13] As for the mirror and the cup, these will surely have been precious possessions of the lady thus richly interred, and we should allow at least a decade earlier as the time of manufacture of either, which brings us to the bracket A.D. 1–15 for both the bronzes.

Now the cup has an interesting feature, a simple "sleeve" ornament on the handle. Such decoration is, as we shall see, well developed on the Birdlip mirror handle: we may give it a decade to mature, and date the Birdlip mirror not later than A.D. 25. Mayer will be

FIGURE 58.—Cup, and pin, associated with the Colchester mirror. (½)

definitely B.C., and Desborough perhaps as late as A.D. 30. An elaborate and interesting silver-gilt brooch, one of the grave-goods at Birdlip,[14] is here illustrated (Figure 59) with a parallel from Ham Hill (Som.); both are derived from the "Aylesford" brooch type with internal chord, and represent a western, Dobunic, development, possibly under Belgic influence, since there are parallels (*Augenfibeln*) on the Continent. This is consistent with the date suggested for the mirror.

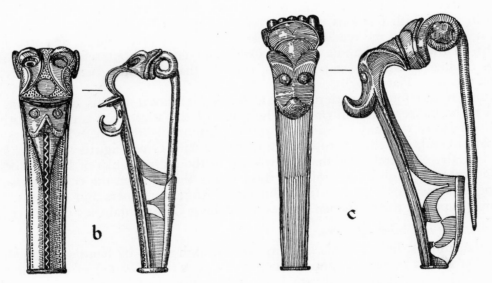

FIGURE 59.—b. Brooch: Birdlip (Glos.); c. Brooch: Ham Hill (Som.). (¼)

The zöomorphic decoration of the brooch consists of cast strips riveted to the bow. The "eyes" hold countersunk rivets, originally, no doubt, concealed by decorative inlay. At the waist of the bow is an elaborate projecting disc-moulding, below which is riveted a broad curved hook which tapers to a point. The catch-plate is pierced, and the head of the bow is expanded into a trumpet-terminal which secures the coils of the spring. The Ham Hill brooch is similar, but coarser, and typologically later.

Roman (?) influence on the mirror-art

A comment may here be in place. It is that we might go further in an endeavour to understand how these elaborate mirrors with fold-over designs, beginning with Colchester and culminating in Desborough, came to be wrought in the first twenty years or so of I A.D. than is implied in a vague reference to Roman influence. In their Celtic fashion, and highly specialized idiom, they reveal something of the delicacy of perception and execution, the serenity of mood, which characterizes Roman decorative art in the Augustan age (23 B.C.– A.D. 14), and the possibility of a link should be sought. The effect of this Imperial art movement on the Gallo-Belgic periphery of the Empire and beyond need not, of course, be assumed to end with the death of Augustus in A.D. 14. The proposition does not lack an analogy, that of the effect on ancillary crafts of the Gothic tradition in Britain of the first breath of the Italian Renaissance at the turn of the fifteenth and sixteenth centuries A.D.

I have particularly in mind the acanthus scrolls which decorate the outer wall of the *Ara Pacis Augustae* (*Plate 58b*). As Mrs. Strong remarks: "The scrolls became a typical Roman decoration; they adorned furniture and small objects". A network of such flowing curves, she remarks, "encircles a cup from the Treasure of Hildesheim", near Hanover. This cup is illustrated on *Plate 59b*.

That portable works of art of this quality and character trickled into south-western and south-eastern Britain in the half-century or so before the Claudian conquest is likely enough. Decorated silver cups, probably from Campania, were, as we have seen, with the Welwyn (Herts.) burial of this period.

To come down to detail, it is not easy to understand how the lace-like effect of the enrichment in the Desborough mirror scrolls could have developed *in vacuo*, but regarded as an attempt to create in the Celtic idiom the play of light and shade, the glitter, of silver plate decorated in relief with festoons of *Ara Pacis* quality—as on the dish and the bowl from Hildesheim—it seems to me readily explicable. Again, we are, I think, at a loss to explain the sheaths on the Birdlip handle and the Colchester cup without reference to the natural renderings of stem-sheaths on cup handles, such as that from the Bernay[15] (Eure, France) treasure on the same Plate (*59c*).

The mirror distribution pattern (Figure 67) is significant in this connection. Mirror finds tend to be concentrated in or near the ports of the south-east and the south-west of the island. It is not that any of our mirrors were imported—the type with decorated plates is unknown in Gaul, and the "Etruscan" mirror type with Greek figure-work had long been forgotten in Italy. It surely was that the women in the higher ranks of British society who were sophisticated enough to commission these costly things from the court craftsmen were those living in areas most open to the influence of Roman manners and customs. In their turn, we may suppose, the craftsmen studied everything Continental they could get hold of.

Studied formlessness in a mirror pattern

One other mirror, linked to the Birdlip–Desborough series by handle form—that found at Old Warden (Beds.) nearly a century ago—has a pattern (*Plate 60*) of different character, but wrought with similar skill and care. The dark ribbons of hatched work, produced by "rocking" the chasing tool, enclose shapes mostly bounded by the familiar two-simple-and-one-compound curves so familiar in "Mayer"; other combinations appear in scale with these, and there are faint reminders of the early bird-heads: eye-circles in beak-shaped frames. It is a late piece, as the moon-shaped figure in the centre (Figure 83, K84), "floating in a void", shows. The craftsman is surely building up a new "diffusive" style, *in which the voids are*

94

intended to please the eye as much as the pattern. The passion for novelty was, as we shall see in other advanced groups of creative bronze-work, as strong as it is today. The "grip" at the base of this mirror-plate has unique features, representing a pair of stylized bud-and-leaf (or bird?) forms bending outward from vertical stems and so emphasizing the kidney shape of the mirror. The enamel discs, now white, may originally have been red.

FIGURE 60.—Mirror I: Stamford Hill (Mount Batten), Plymouth. (⅔)

The enlarged detail, shown in one of the best photographs I have been able to secure, shows that the work is wholly freehand, and that the major pattern was traced with a fine point beforehand.[16]

95

If the Roman Conquest had not supervened, a new school of Celtic "B" design might have sprung from such a whole-hearted return to deeply-studied "formlessness", which has intellectual as well as emotional content. The mirror was associated with a characteristically rich late Belgic burial: parts of two large shale vases are preserved with it.

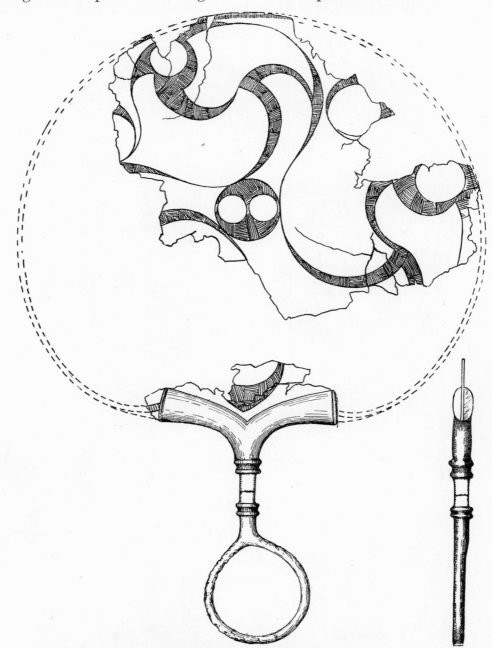

FIGURE 61.—Mirror: Billericay (Essex). (⅔)

Other mirror patterns

The unprovenanced "Gibbs" mirror (*Plate 57*) referred to on p. 90 may next be considered; though probably contemporary with Desborough, it has a simple handle of

"Mayer" derivation—its plate-pattern, indeed, shows descent in another (otherwise lost) sequence from "Mayer". The reader will notice how closely the *outline* of the double bands linking the upper with the lower roundels are reproduced, solidly patterned, in "Gibbs". In that lost sequence, moreover, the asymmetry of "Mayer" was increased; compare the twist given, in "Gibbs", to the central outlined shape of "onion" form in "Mayer". The structure of the pattern (Figure 50) is intentionally lopsided !

Stamford Hill,[17] an inhumation cemetery on a site overlooking the Mount Batten settlement on the promontory flanking the Plym estuary, yielded the mirror illustrated in Figure 60, and two handles of mirrors, one of which so nearly fits it—note the hollow, *Plate 56k*—that it (or another one like it) may be presumed correct. I had therefore redrawn the mirror to suggest what so obviously late an example looked like as a whole. We are dealing with a "silver age" of Celtic art, as the sophistication of a slightly oval frame shows; the freehand work is less accurate than in the great exemplars, but it has a delicate faded charm (the mirror was destroyed in the 1940 bombing of Plymouth). The difference between this mirror and the previous one (Gibbs) suggests that the Celtic craftsmen were emotionally thrust over and over again into the practice of symmetry by the beauty of imported works of, or influenced by, Mediterranean technique, slowly sinking back (or rising, according to one's point of view) into an asymmetry more acceptable to their *ethos*.

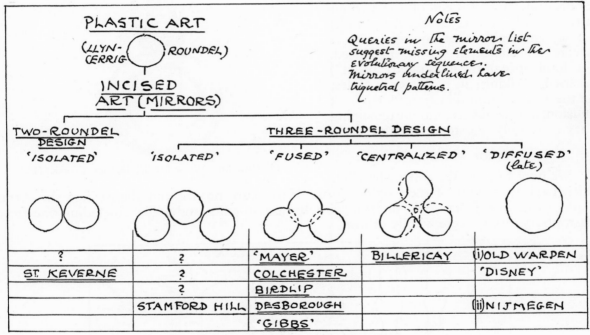

FIGURE 62.—Analysis of mirror designs.

The Billericay (Essex) mirror (*Plate 56F*), the only surviving example of the centralization of originally distinct triskeles, has been shattered and partly lost, but enough remains to justify the restoration of the whole structure with its anti-clockwise, wave-like movement. The large drawing (Figure 61) was made for me by my friend Mr. M. R. Hull in 1947 to show the sureness of the lay-out, the beauty of the flowing line, and the precise character of the infilling. The Llyn Cerrig shield-boss scroll (p. 43 above) is an important source-element of the design. The "kidney" shape is certain: see the fragment of marginal pattern on the left of the handle. This handle is quite unworthy of the piece: but it is contemporary.[18]

The Trelan Bahow—or St. Keverne —(Cornwall) mirror with debased ornament (*Plate 7*) reminds us that side by side with outstanding developments in pattern and technique, workshops finding a steady market in remote communities may, in mirrors as in other things, go on producing apparently outmoded patterns almost indefinitely. The surface of the bronze is badly pitted, but it shows just enough unusual detail—the marginal pattern, and the incised free circle in the main design (to the left of the centre)— to indicate that it is later—perhaps as much as half a century—than "Mayer", to which the rest of the pattern, like the handle, is closely related.

This completes the survey of the mirror-plate designs; a diagram (Figure 62) illustrates the descent of the various patterns from the Llyn Cerrig roundel —it is remarkable that enough mirrors survive to enable it to be produced. The dominance of the integrated ("fused") pattern is striking; it is the only series, for the last column illustrates *aspects* of diffusion, not a sequence, and the remaining types have only one representative each.

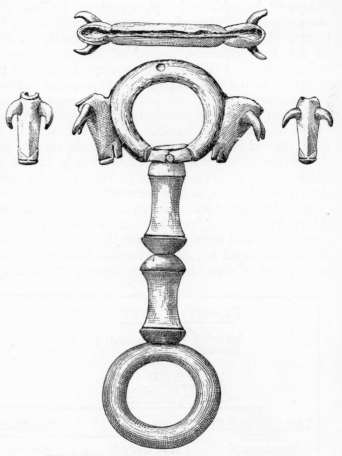

FIGURE 63.—Mirror handle: Ingleton (Yorks.) (⅔).

MIRROR-HANDLES

We now turn to the mirror-handles, which have an interest of their own. Most of them are bronze, but the earliest, the Arras (Yorks.) example (*Plate 7*) is of iron with bronze mounts, and a few, including one from Glastonbury (Som.) were wholly of iron.

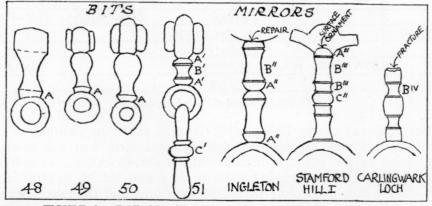

FIGURE 64.—Bridle bits: Llyn Cerrig (detail); and three mirror-handles.

There are four types: (i) "Bar", (ii) Shaped, (iii) (*a*) Looped, (*b*) Double-looped. The gradual evolution from simplicity to complexity, associated with a growing appreciation of

98

the artistic possibilities of the handle, is of interest.   The basic form is of Gaulish origin, as *Plate 7c* suggests.

Bar handles

The bar-type (already seen in *Plate 7a*, now in *Plate 56b*, J to M) develops a ring at the lower end, and expands to form a mirror-grip at the upper end.   *Plate 30a*, Stamford Hill (Mount Batten), and Figure 63, Ingleton (Yorks.), best illustrate these features, and show that the bar itself may become ornamental, having transverse reel and bun-shaped mouldings, quirked (Figure 83, J75).   In Figure 64, the three known moulded handles are shown together; these are probably *c.* A.D. 40 or later.   This dating is, incidentally, of importance, since it enables us to place a very handsome bridle-bit from Llyn Cerrig on the same Figure, as a late north-eastern product.   Its quality is well rendered in *Plate 5b*.

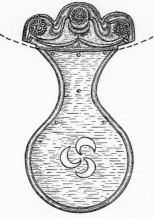

BALMACLELLAN

FIGURE 65.—Mirror handle:
Balmaclellan
(Kirkcudbrights.) (⅓).

Shaped handle

This type is represented only in one mirror, from Balmaclellan (Kirkcudbrights.) (Figure 65), probably made by a northern (East Riding, Yorks.) bronzesmith in the last years of independence: it is closely related to an Elmswell (Yorks.) panel (p. 105 below). Attention is drawn to the swag, looped in the centre and held by a pin, below the petalled rosettes and scroll-forms.

Loop handles (*simple*)

The type is a collared loop with out-bent expanding ends of circular section ("splays") transversely moulded, best illustrated by the "Mayer" handle (*Plate 57a*).   Development is seen in the "Gibbs" handle which had a ring below the loop (*Plate 57d*).   A series now follows in which the loop is not collared.   The curvilinear character of the unmoulded splays of the type specimen Rivenhall (Essex) (*Plate 56* N) is distinctive; and duplication is represented by the damaged Disney handle (*Plate 56* G).

Loop handles (*complex*)

The characters of this group are opposed loops *and* a terminal ring, often with decorative detail (Figure 66).[19]   Colchester is regarded as the type specimen; "Mayer" terminal mouldings are used as decorative elements on either side of the down-bent, delicately-curved splay, and the "Mayer" collar also is present.   The upturned scrolls, each encircling a hollow bronze boss, provide a satisfying finish to the handle, and adequate grip for the mirror plate. Old Warden (Beds.), a less distinguished handle design, suggests above the collar the diverging curves of Rivenhall and Billericay II; but structure is here masked by ornament.   Discs for enamel occur on the panel and within the terminal ring.

Two other handles of the group are, broadly speaking, similar to the above.   The lovely Birdlip handle has widely extended arms to the upper loop, a clue to the history of which is provided by the transverse mouldings, representing the terminals of a loop of "Mayer" character.   The upper and lower loops of Birdlip are linked vertically; within the terminal ring is a disc with red enamel, matching the design on the grip, of trumpets in relief with similar colour-units. Lastly, the "sheath" ornament on both loops—like a lily stem—is a notable enrichment (p. 93 above).

In Birdlip the varied elements are harmonized; but in Desborough (Northants.) these same elements—mirror panel in relief, double loops, ring with inner ring—are completely

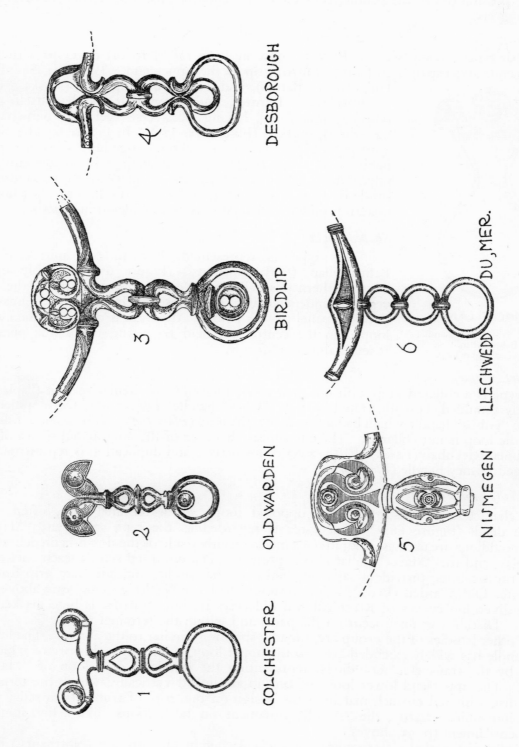

COLCHESTER

OLDWARDEN

BIRDLIP

DESBOROUGH

NIJMEGEN

LLECHWEDD DU, MER.

1

2

3

4

5

6

FIGURE 66.—Mirror handles: enriched series. ($\frac{1}{3}$)

100

integrated. This handle is one of the greatest plastic achievements of the Celtic bronze-smith in Britain. The tubular binding of the mirror-plate is conceived as gripping the upper, uncollared loop by the neck, its bent and curled-over ends suggesting the vigour and intensity of the compression.[20] Similarly, the neck of the figure-eight below is compressed by the ends of the terminal ring. The trumpet-like forms of the mirror-panel (assimilated to a Celtic "closed" palmette) are typologically the splayed arms of Rivenhall—hypertrophied, and joined at their upper margins.

The concepts so brilliantly developed in this closely-related group of four mirror handles gave rise, we may suppose, to many forms of like character. Two only survive, the Nijmegen[21] and Llechwedd Du[22] handles, and these are inferior; but they have structural interest (Figure 66).

Handle design of kidney-shaped mirrors

The earliest mirrors are circular, and this form survived until the close of our period; but the kidney-shape is a feature of I A.D. development.[23] The form of the handle was, in most cases, influenced, a downward bend to the splay being the usual modification. The change is fully demonstrated in the Colchester and Desborough mirrors. When the novelty had worn off and mirror designers reverted to the circle, there survived in this group certain vestiges of the kidney form; the Llechwedd Du grip rising to a point in the centre, and the upturned ends of the "binding" of Nijmegen.

Illusionism in mirror design and its bearing on workshop practice

Though the earliest of our Celtic mirrors, Arras and Mayer, probably had no binding, the majority have, or had, this "U" or "C" sectioned strip of sheet bronze covering the sharp edge of the mirror-plate. The treatment of the junction between the solid cast handle slotted for the mirror-plate and the hollow comparatively flimsy binding offered difficulty to the designer; at first the emphasis was laid on the functional differentiation between them, as in the Colchester handle. Thereafter, a solution of the problem was to treat the handle—the bronze casting—and the binding as a single unit, and then to decide where, in the interest of an effective slotting-in of the mirror plate, the solid casting should stop and the hollow binding begin.

The essence of the plan was to create illusion; to make the actual riveted joint (of binding and casting) invisible. A glance at *Plate 57* will show, despite later damage, distortion and differential patination, how neatly this was done in the case of Birdlip: another illustration on this Plate provides the same proof for Desborough. So completely masked were the two riveted joints of Desborough that in this formal pattern, distinguished for its fold-over symmetry, the bronze-smiths were able to make the cast bronze arms of strikingly unequal length for convenience of riveting, confident that this would never be noticed.[24] The intense effort to promote unity of design is shown by the fact that in both mirrors the delicate mouldings (beads) which are present on the binding extend on to the casting.

A minor change is associated with this integration of mirror handle and mirror binding. The binding is normally a slight and undistinguished feature, as *Plate 60* (Old Warden) shows; but if it is to be *merged* in the handle structure it must be stouter in appearance. So it is, and the job is accomplished with art; not by thickening the binding all round, but by gradually increasing the diameter as the handle is approached. This is seen on the Birdlip and Desborough mirrors.

Subsequent developments are of little interest. In the cases of Nijmegen (Figure 66, 5) and the late Type I mirror, Stamford Hill I, the ends of the binding are conceived as extending on to the face of the casting on each side; curved to a point in the one, straight and blunt-ended in the other. But some craftsmen grew tired of these practices; the grip of the late Llechwedd

Du mirror, for example, though it looks like imitation binding, has cross-mouldings at each end to show that it was not.

Summary of stylistic sequence

The evidence yielded by the detailed study of incised design on the mirror-plates is that the principal stylistic sequence is: "Mayer", Colchester, Birdlip, Desborough. The evidence yielded by study of the mirror handles is that the Colchester handle descends from a group best typified in this country by "Mayer", and that the Birdlip and Desborough handles are closely related to, but typologically later than, Colchester, in that order. Both lines of enquiry produce, to this extent, the same results.

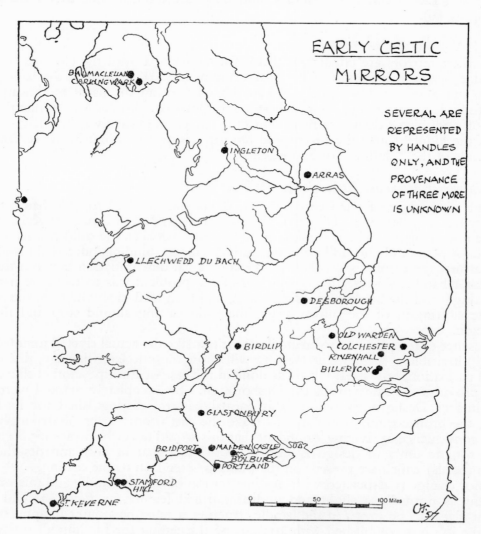

FIGURE 67.—Distribution map: Early Celtic mirrors.

The geographical distribution of mirrors

On Figure 67 the distribution of the mirrors and mirror handles is shown without complications: on Figure 67a with an indication above each of the type to which the handle belongs.

102

Type I, the bar handle, is on the limited evidence fundamentally northern; Arras and Ingleton are in Brigantian territory, Carlingwark in that of the Novantae. The spread of the type was, however, wide: it went southward to Devon, probably (as far as Mendip) by the Jurassic route: the drift is extensive, but explicable. The work of the late G. C. Brooke, followed by that of Derek Allen, on the distribution of Dobunic coins (Figure 68)[25] suggests

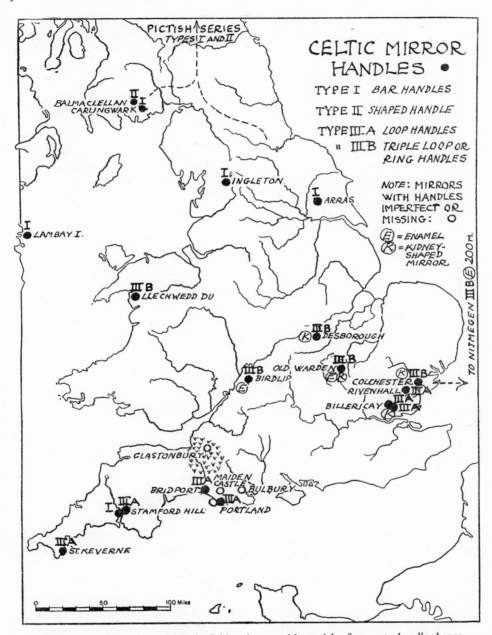

FIGURE 67a—Distribution of Early Celtic mirrors, with special reference to handle-shapes.

that in the period which here most concerns us, A.D. 1–50, this tribe with its busy metal-workers had access to a harbour settlement of the Durotriges at the mouth of the Stour (Hengistbury); that by this means it had trading contacts by sea with settlements on the

Tamar estuary (gold coins), and as far west as Camborne (gold coin). The raw material needed and obtained by the shippers was probably silver and tin.[26] I suggest, then, that the Stamford Hill and St. Keverne mirrors *and* the "Mayer" mirror, with other loop-handled (Type III A) mirrors from Bridport[27] and Portland, were made somewhere in Dobunic territory, and traded to the south-west.

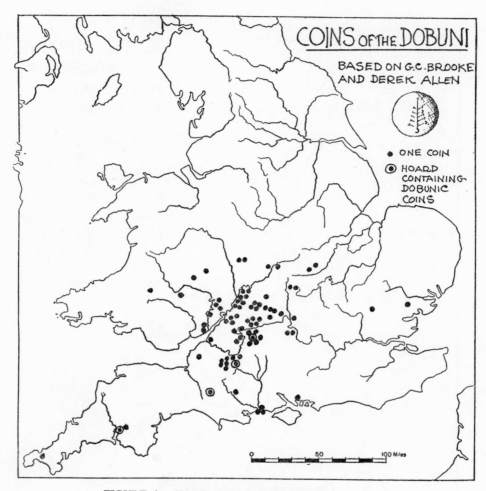

FIGURE 68.—Distribution of coins of the Dobuni.

Turning to south-east Britain, the III A group in Trinovantian territory is also definitely coastal; but different artistic influences were clearly at work to shape their handle forms, and manufacture in eastern Britain is probable.

The distribution of the multiple-looped handles, Type III B, differs from those of both concentrations of Type III A. The Type III B pattern includes, it is true, the same tract of the Essex countryside as the south-eastern concentration of Type III A; but Old Warden, Desborough, and Birdlip are from 50 to 120 miles inland, on or near the Jurassic belt, while Llechwedd Du, known to be post-conquest, illustrates trade from the lowland zone to the highland zone in Celtic works of art. The Dobunic coin map (Figure 68) is of interest in this connection as indicating the area in which ideas illustrated in the Colchester group of mirrors are likely to have been developed.

The application of enamel in the Belgic manner to the handle occurs only in Type III B forms ("E" on map). It was the artists of this Dobuno–Belgic style who created the kidney-mirror, "K" on map. More Belgic than Dobunic perhaps in this latter respect, for the fashionable mirror form in the *south-west* continued to be the circle, in the period covered by known examples such as St. Keverne and Stamford Hill I; moreover, the Birdlip mirror (the only one of the Type III B group that has no trace of the kidney shape) comes from the heart of Dobunic territory, on the evidence of the Bagendon site, and of the later capital, CORINIVM DOBVNORVM.

Belgic as the development may partly be, it has its artistic roots in the west; the characters of the linear and the plastic arts involved, taken together, suggest that "Iron B western" craftsmen were mainly responsible. This is not surprising; Dr. Jacobsthal has shown us how mobile the Early Celtic craftsmen were,[28] and our later British metal-workers, like their predecessors, no doubt attached themselves to the entourage of princes and nobles anywhere within reach who were able and willing to pay for fine metal-work.[29] We know, indeed, that the necessary purchasing power and appreciation of the accessories of courtly life, was concentrated precisely in the eastern region (from Desborough and Old Warden to the Essex coast) in the period with which we are concerned, as a distribution map of imports of wine and fine pottery from the Mediterranean, published some years ago, shows.[30]

(ii) "CASKET" ORNAMENT

Strips. Repetitive ornament in relief, curvilinear, on narrow strips or squares of thin bronze, was widespread in Belgic and Celtic Britain in the last century of independence. Some of the simpler patterns may have decorated chariot-bodies (p. 120 below), but richer examples are shown on (disintegrated) wooden caskets or boxes, as in the Stanfordbury (Beds.) room-burial. Strips likely to have been thus used occur in hoards of scrap-metal, as at Santon Downham (Suffolk) (*Plate 67c*); other well-known examples with scroll-patterns, in the British Museum, come from Rodborough Common (Glos.), and in Taunton Museum from Ham Hill (Som.). Several were found at Llyn Cerrig (Anglesey). Fragments, showing bands of debased duck-pattern in Severn "B" style alternating with paired comma-forms and knobs, from a flat-sided casket found at Otterbourne and now in Winchester Museum, are illustrated on *Plate 77a*. Two small "squares", on the same Plate, found at Silchester (Hants.), and possibly derived from the pre-Roman fortress, show familiar Celtic designs: a triquetral pattern is seen on a strip from Hod Hill (Dorset). Generally speaking, there is little merit in these small mechanically-produced ornaments; the "trumpet", rosettes, and broken-backed scrolls of the Santon strip perhaps show the best style available to the craftsman. The technique of manufacture is known from the discovery of an iron die at Wroxeter[31] (Salop).

The Elmswell panel, east Yorkshire. Whereas, in south Britain, the brilliance and originality of Celtic and Belgic art tended to fade out after A.D. 43, in the north—within the Brigantian confederacy and possibly beyond it—the craft-workshops were, as we have seen, active up to the 70's. That refugee bronze-workers, after the Claudian conquest of south Britain, reinforced the northern craftsmanship is rendered likely by the discovery, in east Yorkshire, of an important piece, in a southern style, more advanced than we have hitherto recorded. This is a panel of repoussé bronze on an iron base, surmounted by a strip of cast bronze with a pattern of champlevé enamel mainly of classical character (Figure 69), from Elmswell (east Yorks.), and is almost certainly the front of a casket suited to a lady of quality.[32] The panel is a shaped structure, with bold smoothly-rounded relief consisting of a central inverted palmette-form with scrolled tips, developing on either side an elongated trumpet scroll with lobes and coils associated. Berried rosettes point the pattern, and are the chief keys to the appreciation of the artist's intention in this complex design (Figure 83,

FIGURE 69.—Panel, enamel and bronze: Elmswell (East Riding, Yorks.) (¾).

L93). The enamel work is provincial-Roman, apart from the terminal trumpet scrolls. In short, it is a baroque ornament marking, with the Tre'r Ceiri brooch and the "Roman" helmet (pp. 107, 119 below), the end of a style as well as a culture[33]; the suggested date, *c.* A.D. 70, is certainly acceptable.

(iii) PERSONAL ORNAMENT

(a) Collars—insignia of dignity

Bronze collars seem in I A.D. to have replaced the gold torcs with expanded ends; an interesting series has been found, widespread in Britain.

Llyn Cerrig trumpet designs are seen on collars from the west and south, worn, it may be, only on ceremonial occasions: feast or ritual. An attractive example, possibly the earliest we have (the beginning of I A.D.) comes from Llandysul (Cards.), and is in Bristol Museum (*Plate 12d*). On the surviving half of the flat band of metal, trumpet units of Llyn Cerrig ancestry, bossed and folded up (Figure 83, L92), are linked by beautiful flying S-curves, terminating at the front in paired lentoids (Figure 83, H64), and at the neck in a lobe with beaded terminal and appendage. This is certainly a Dobunic piece.

A heavier and obviously later example (mid-I A.D.), somewhat relieved by gaiety and movement in the cast ornament, is the collar from Wraxall (Som.) (*Plate 61a*) whereon S-curves interlock, and scroll-and-trumpet forms, all in bold relief, curl round insets of enamel or glass—now lost[34]: the scroll-work becomes more elaborate and concentrated at three points. Beaded mouldings—double on the inner side—frame the pattern.

The Portland Collar. The photograph (*Plate 62a*) of this remarkable British Museum piece, 6¼ in. in diameter, shows that its ornament is influenced, in part, by the earlier "horned-helmet style". The decorative interest starts, of course, on the wearer's breast where bossy terminals, decorated with formal leaf-forms (with holes for glass studs) are flanked by barred ridges and rounded hollows. The emphasis on cross-alignment then gradually fades, giving place to wandering scrolls with trumpet terminals defined by relief varying in height, and stipple; these features also were studded with points of glitter and colour. The pattern is well suited to the slightly-rounded surface; it dies away on the neck of the wearer. Structurally the piece provides, by a change in the axis from the horizontal to the vertical plane—

reached at the hinged back—for a concentration of its weight where it is most easily borne, and for a close fit at the back of the neck: it opens easily and fits tightly when in position. This collar has classical parallels, and is said to have been found with a Samian bowl in a stone coffin; as R. A. Smith remarked,[35] it is not likely to be earlier than I A.D. A similar collar, weaker in design and possibly dating in I A.D., comes from Lelant at the tip of Cornwall. The north-east has yielded a neck ornament in two planes, hinged at the back like the Portland example; this is the Stichill collar from the banks of the Eden in Roxburghshire, figured on the same Plate, but on a smaller scale. It has a pair of tight scrolls with Llyn Cerrig trumpets in high relief, and bands of open scrolls of the same character in low relief, separated by heavy intervening mouldings at right-angles thereto. The two pieces, then, have resemblances other than structural.

The broken-backed curve. The development of this curve as a decorative feature[36] is shown in the equally late Galloway collar in a true northern style—from Lochar Moss (Dumfries.) (*Plate 29b*). The upper portion is a string of bronze Roman "melon" beads with collars graded to suit the curve; the lower shows a scroll pattern of a familiar form in which each boss serves two scrolls "one arriving, the other departing". The sweep of each scroll here, however, is abruptly closed by a change of direction—Leeds's "broken back"— through nearly a right-angle (Figure 83, K89): and each boss serves, as it were, two half-scrolls. Technically the piece is unusual; the band of open-work is riveted on to the main structure. The reader will note that like the Wraxall torc this band has a delicate beaded border. Also, there is a close resemblance, in the mode by which the pattern is terminated, to the sub-triangular beaded design on the neck of the Llandysul collar.

Clearly this art has a wide and chronologically extended highland-zone interest; contacts throughout I A.D. between south and north by the western sea route, when the land routes were unsafe, may account for its vigour.

(b) Brooches

In the late group with which we are here concerned three outstanding examples additional to the Birdlip brooch (p. 93) will be discussed and illustrated. One which, *in the round*, shows parallel developments to the relief work on two of the collars is the remarkable "Icenian" brooch found at Sandy Plantation, Lakenheath (Suffolk) (*Plate 41b*).[37] The quality of the scroll-work, the movement of the strange design, on so tiny a work is remarkable; two aspects may be detailed. The central "roundel" begins as a moulding on each arm of the central structure of the brooch, extending in opposite directions; the mouldings then become free and each ends in a "trumpet", and they interlock. The resultant pattern is formalized in Figure 83, G53. The two terminals of the brooch are modified trumpet-forms ending in a coil. The piece forms one of the starting-points (*c.* 40–60) for the great series of Romano–British "dragonesque" brooches of II A.D. in which the open central portion of the design is filled by enamel patterns, and the terminals are transformed into the snout and tail of a classical sea-horse.[38]

Excavation in 1904 of hut-groups in the hill-fort of Tre'r Ceiri (Caern.), 1,500 ft. above sea-level, produced an exceptional piece, the bronze-gilt brooch illustrated in *Plate 41d* and Figure 70.[39] The latter is 3/2 in scale, the overall length of the surviving part of the brooch— "humped" bow and (transverse) cover for the spring —being $1\frac{1}{4}$ in., and the extreme breadth $1\frac{3}{8}$ in. It is of the fan-tail group,[40] so called from its expanded foot. The trumpet forms in low relief with the berried rosettes and

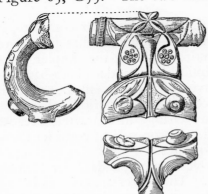

FIGURE 70.—Brooch, Tre'r Ceiri (Caern.). Spring-cover and humped bow: from three points of view. ($\frac{3}{2}$)

expanded "tails" (Figure 83, L94) are "contemporary" features, but the "snaily coils" on the crown of the bow represent an art-form two centuries earlier—a remarkable "Marnian" survival, suggesting (as does its site) that the piece is the work of an artificer outside the southern area of Roman control, its date being probably *c.* A.D. 60.

 Lastly, the Aesica brooch,[41] another "fan-tail" of gilt bronze found at Great Chesters (Northumb.) (*Plate 41c*), is a renowned masterpiece of the baroque phase of British Celtic art. It was probably made in the east Yorkshire area of the Brigantian confederacy—the country of the Parisii—in the late seventies, the uneasy last phase before the northern tribes were engulfed by Rome. That independence should end, and Celtic art in one of its most striking manifestations achieve a fantastic finality, within the compass of a few years, is (if correctly estimated) a curious conjunction, and accident of history.

Artistically, and to some extent constructionally, the brooch is in two parts: the first consists of the loop, headpiece, spring-case, and high bow; the second, the circular moulded plate under the bow and the flat fan. The front of the bow is attached to the plate only at one point, its centre, and so seems to be a functionless survival: but the plate is so narrow at its junction with the spring-case that the bow is structurally necessary.

The ornament is based on the Llyn Cerrig trumpet-pattern (*Plate 23a* and Figure 18): the writer, in 1946,[42] held that this piece was north-eastern, and the present study supports the view that a school of craftsmen worked in this area over a considerable period.

The relief of the main elements of the design, trumpet and scroll, is richly modelled, with smoothly-rounded surfaces flanked, interspersed, or linked with narrow bands sharply angled. Broad-based coils of inverted "V" section provide a simpler, less contorted element on the fan and circular plate, and two lyre-shaped scrolls unite at their heads to form the ornament on the bow. One, short, is headed by trumpets with bossy tips; the other, elongated and less involved, leads the eye downward and backward to spring-case and plate, where two elaborate trumpet-forms with curving tips that extend beyond the frame in uncontrolled *abandon* typify the artistic freedom enjoyed by the craftsman, and his delight in the unconventional.[43]

(c) Bangle

Lastly, a bangle of golden bronze for a young girl, $2\frac{1}{2}$ in. in diameter, is included to show a simple Belgic ornament of the period that poorer folk could acquire (*Plate 26d*). There is a triple band of punched ornament, and the overlapping terminals are notched. It comes from Borough Green, near Maidstone, in Kent.

(iv) HEARTH AND HOME

(a) The feast: tankards

The number of tankards known either by preservation of their hold-fasts, or complete, is considerable.[44] The distribution—in both west and east Britain—suggests that people of quality in a Celtic (or Belgic) community possessed one or more; and that the simpler types at all events were in daily use.[45] Tankards are usually stave-built like a modern beer-barrel—but straight or hollow-sided. The decorated examples all have Celtic ornament, but there is evidence that the type continued to be produced during the early Roman period—that from Shapwick Heath (Som.) (*Plate 63a*) for example—without any change in character, because no better containers than wooden ones for beer can be found. I proposed to consider them technically and as works of art, without further reference to dates.

Tankards have narrow bands of bronze (Pentuan), broad overlapping bands (river Thames at Kew) or are completely encased in bronze (Trawsfynydd). The staves are thicker below than above to allow for the deep inner horizontal slot needed to fit the wooden base securely and tightly. The rims, for obvious reasons, are always cased in bronze; the handles vary in character, and provide the chief decorative feature of the series.

In the Kew example *(Plate 63b)* the bands are seen to overlap vertically and (on the right) horizontally. The thinness of the bronze rim is notable—the stave ends being almost sharp. The above-mentioned hold-fast is here shaped like a pair of loops of angular section conjoined at the centre and expanding sideways at their bases: the opening is small, and a full tankard could not be lifted by grasping it in the ordinary way. Trial shows (as Corcoran pointed out in 1952) that it is intended for the insertion of one or two fingers of the flat (right) hand, the left palm being pressed on the opposite curve of the vessel. Lift and tilt: it will be found easy to drink in this way, and the risk of spilling the liquor—an important point when men drank deep—is reduced by the hold-fast of those locked right fingers: hence my term for the fitting in question.

The tankard from Shapwick already mentioned shows its handsome "turned" base and thick stave-ends; it is as well-wrought as it looks. The vertical joint of the complete casing of this piece is covered and secured by a bronze strip—seen in the Plate—to which the hold-fast is riveted; the strip, then, serves two purposes. The knobs at the centre of the hold-fast lean outwards; the inner side is very smooth and rounded, so the fingers slide effortlessly in. Nothing in the design or structure suggests that the piece is as late as its Romano–British associations might suggest.

There are two tankards (belonging to an eastern group) that double the security of the hold-fast—from Elveden (Suffolk) and Aylesford (Kent), both reconstructed in Sir Arthur Evans's paper on the latter cemetery.[46] The former is fragmentary: the reconstruction— reproduced in part on my *Plate 54b*—shows three medallions with triskeles in relief; late "trumpet" forms placed centrally, with horizontal mouldings above and below.[47] No other known tankard has decoration of this character, which in East Anglia suggests a date in mid-I A.D.[48] The Aylesford tankard is bronze-covered; its hold-fasts were formerly ornamented with five bosses (of enamel?).

The Trawsfynydd tankard. This famous tankard is the finest known: it is perfectly preserved, and its incurved shape is unique. By the kindness of the Director of the Liverpool Museums I am able to show it from unusual angles, and to illustrate constructional detail. *Plate 64* and Figure 83, H67 shows the famous "S"-loop of the openwork pattern in the "pointed ellipse" of the hold-fast; the adjacent knobbed coils with moulded terminals and with comma-shaped voids (each unit of each pair "moving" in an opposite direction and so presenting an equilibrium) are very remarkable (Figure 83, G59). Behind the hold-fast is the vertical decorated band covering the joint of the bronze casing of the tankard. This casing rises in a curve over the rim, and is seen inside, terminating, on *Plate 65a*. The two rivet-heads secure the upper coiled structure, the larger bolt-head the upper end of the hold-fast. The perfect preservation (in a peat bog) of the wooden staves is remarkable; neither this part nor the base on the same Plate *(65b)* looks 1900 years old. This base has a central circular plate of bronze with serrated edge and boss; its most striking feature is the double circle of bronze-strip closely folded and hammered into the ends of the staves. This is said to prevent expansion and leakage; but the effect will be *most* decorative (since the bronze would be shiny with wear) when the bottom of the vessel is seen, by diners opposite, in the space previously occupied by the owner's face.

This tankard is one of the few works of Celtic art, found in an unlikely region for manufacture, to which such a region can with confidence be assigned: it was, I hold, made in Dobunic territory. The evidence is in the structural ornament of the four moulded circles of the hand-grip. Each of the three curved "spokes" take over part of its rim, fading out when they reach the *outer* surface, like a wave on the sand (see photograph, top left): the "whirling" structure ends in a moulded knob. The technique closely resembles features near the junction of rim and handle of the Birdlip mirror.

The similar technique of the lower and upper roundels of the Battersea shield (the long-drawn-out replacement of one descending rib by a rising one) has already been commented on.

The criticism of hold-fast shapes in these British tankards is usually concentrated on the Trawsfynydd example, the argument being that usefulness has been sacrificed to beauty of design, for being angular in shape it is most uncomfortable to hold. We know that this criticism is irrelevant (p. 109 above); but why was this shape adopted? It was designed not for two fingers like the others, but for the whole flat hand; when inserted, the little finger on one side and the forefinger on the other fit perfectly against the upright sides of the grip which, as the photograph is designed to show, are smoothly rounded for their comfort. The hollow curve of the body of the vessel adds to the feeling of security in respect of the left palm as well as the right. Centuries of small improvements must surely have gone to build up this perfection. It is a late piece, of course: work of Iron "B" character hardly touched by Roman classicism.[49]

Hold-fasts: the technique of design. Many more tankard hold-fasts than complete tankards survive; an important, but damaged, series is that in the National Museum from "the Seven Sisters" hoard, Neath (Glam.), illustrated on my Figure 78, 6–10.[50]

The most interesting of these is shown nearly full size on *Plate 66*, with a restored copy beside it. Its ancestry, which includes Battersea shield detail, has already been mentioned (p. 28): here the features which show its late date (consonant with the hoard in general) should be stressed. They are the heavy moulded loop with terminal coil, and the massive trumpet with coiled tip, of Llyn Cerrig plaque derivation, on the circular flats (with holes for attachment) at the base of the "arch" on each side.

Of the other hold-fasts on Figure 78, the most interesting structurally is No. 8, having "three central open circles on the arch" framed by two interlocking segments of large circles, the arch being thus asymmetrical in outline. These shapes are "true"; but in a better preserved example of this strange Celtic asymmetry from Hod Hill (Dorset) they are not compass-drawn.[51] A hold-fast from Welwyn (Herts.) has scrolls on either side of a pointed ellipse, all in high relief: the arch ends in a "lipped" moulding, close to a terminal disc with eccentrically placed boss. It is an interesting Iron "B" piece in unexpected association (p. 65).[52]

(b) Modes of living

(1) *Belgic.* If the reader doubts the suggestion made in the preceding section that a native chieftain might have not only finely wrought tankards but "everything handsome about him" (despite the squalor), let me reinforce the funeral evidence for feasts (p. 108) by *Plate 67a*, wherein is seen an iron chain, $7\frac{1}{2}$ ft. long, to hang above an open fire. This remarkable hearth-fitting comes, it is true, not from a known Belgic house, but from a large collection of ironwork in a pit on the site of the Romano–British township at Great Chesterford (Essex). Its decorative character being barbaric, I have no hesitation in using it to illustrate well-to-do pre-Roman Belgic life in I A.D. Moreover, as Richard Neville pointed out in 1856,[53] chains of like character had in his day been found in small villas (Belgic farmhouses of Roman date, the writer would call them) at Ickleton and Bartlow nearby. There is another from *Corinium Dobunorum* (Cirencester), which we can assume to be of early Roman date. The next Plate (*68*) shows important elements (top, middle, and lower) of the Chesterford structure. It turns freely on a swivel to which cords of iron, festooned and hooked, are attached; thence a chain of double links descends, giving place at the centre of the piece to cords of iron pointed above and coiled below; interlocked at the centre in a "reef-knot with expanded or coiled ends". (We have, there can be no doubt, a pair of serpents intertwined: protectors of the hearth.) Two further chains of double links lead to the hooks for a cauldron. As much care, clearly, was bestowed on significant ornament as on function in this piece.

At this stage we are reminded, inevitably, of the evidence for feasts and drinking bouts in the burials of Belgic chieftains discussed in Chapter VI. At Snailwell (Cambs.), though the chieftain's body was burnt, his couch was present; so were "the wine jars, the mixing bowl, the oil jugs, the pork, the beef and the chicken."[54] The early I A.D. burials at Welwyn (Herts.) and Stanfordbury (Beds.), as we have seen, had wine jars and drinking vessels with many other rich furnishings, native and imported; these feasts of the dead were moreover set out in a rectangular excavated floor.

We can surely accept such lay-outs as expressing the reality of well-to-do Belgic life in the first half of the century, and affirm also that the landed man of the period lived then in a four-square house, not a round hut.[55] The fine pottery of the Belgae, illustrated in the Aylesford and Swarling (Kent) cemeteries supports this thesis. With its handsomely decorated utilities on hearth and table,[56] possibly also in its smoky squalor, the Belgic hall in south-east Britain will, no doubt, have resembled in plan a *small* early medieval hall in the same part of England, with central hearth and pendant cauldron.

What, then, can be inferred as to the siting of Belgic houses of chieftains and other land-owners in the countryside? Mr. Lethbridge, uncovering the Snailwell burial close to the springs that give a name to the modern village and parish, remarks that Belgic nobles in pre- and post-conquest times in the Cambridge region were probably buried near their dwellings. We do not find their heaped-up memorials even on knolls; the great Romano–British burial mounds called the "Bartlow Hills" are by a stream. There are burial "vaults"—four-square excavated floors, no doubt, like the others—by the Whittlesford (Cambs.) springs, and important finds are recorded by a stream at Lords Bridge in the same county. We are reminded of the Harpenden fish-head, the elaborate water-holding structure associated with which will surely have been part of the immediate environment of a dwelling. In short, the houses of the lesser Belgic landowners, as well as the greater, will have been in much the same places as the manor houses referred to in the previous paragraph.[57]

(2) *Celtic*. In the purely Celtic Iron "B" regions there is little except tankards and fire-dogs to suggest that any dwellings of the character envisaged in the previous paragraphs existed in pre-Roman times; the only habitations known are round huts such as have been recorded in detail at Glastonbury—a fine photograph of a 22-footer at Salmonsbury camp (Dobunic) was reproduced in *Antiquity* (1931, p. 490). Such fire-dogs as the Capel Garmon example and tankards as that at Trawsfynydd, however, seem to demand a more spacious setting than any excavated round hut of the period has yet provided; and in this unsatisfactory state the problem of the Celtic house must, regrettably, be left.[58] As for burial custom, the interment of important people on hill-tops was still practised by some Iron "B" folk; we may recall the rich Birdlip mirror burial, in a cemetery on the dominating Cotswold limestone scarp (760 ft.) overlooking the Severn plain, the Malverns, and the hills of Wales.

(c) *Magic or ritual*

"*Spoons*": Whether the enigmatic spoon-shaped objects (one pair of which, from Weston (Som.) has claims to an earlier date than this chapter covers (p. 36 above)), were used for ritual purposes generally, or associated solely with burial ceremonies is unknown. An incised cross or a small hole is seen on the spoon part of every example: and they were probably always made in pairs.

The character of the ornament on the grip is very varied. Some have concentric moulded circle patterns—possibly derived from Roman *patera* handles. One of a pair found in a grave (at Burnmouth in Berwickshire) has incised and hatched coils and moon-shaped figures—debased mirror ornament.[59] Another well-known pair from Penbryn (Cards.) is here illustrated (*Plate 70*): one "spoon", like Burnmouth, has the incised cross; both have holes. The relief ornament on the grip is a sadly debased example of the Llyn Cerrig trumpet style, with "stamped" roundels, probably of mid-I A.D. date.[60]   A spoon from "Cardigan" in Liverpool Museum is also illustrated; the uncertainties in the lay-out of the mirror-style ornament on the grip should be noted.   Carelessness in the decoration of grave-furniture is not uncommon in any period.

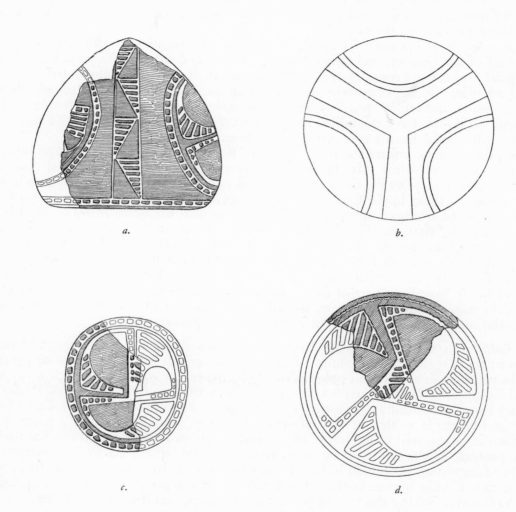

FIGURE 71.—*a.* Cone, liassic limestone: Barnwood (Glos.); *b.* Diagram of design, from above; *c.* Design on side, restored; *d.* Design on base. (All half-scale.)

"*Cone*", of limestone, ornamented: from Barnwood (Glos.).   This remarkable object, oval in plan, with a slight inward curvature at the base, of Liassic limestone, is only 3.6 in. high; it is covered with incised triskeles (Figures 71 and 83, F47).   The extreme formalism of these patterns points to a date in mid-I A.D., and the material indicates local (i.e. Dobunic) manufacture[61]; an object so shaped and so small, moreover, can have no purpose other than in magic or ritual, and the triskelar character of its patterning is therefore significant.

[1] There is no evidence as yet that the craftsmen had seen examples of the figure-work on Greek (Etruscan) mirror-backs of IV B.C. A few late examples, in Gaul, of mirrors in bronze or white metal are recorded by Déchelette, but none is ornamented in our fashion.

[2] This survey is based mainly on the author's papers in *Arch. Camb.*, 1945 and 1948, and *Ant. Journ.*, 1948.

[3] This admirable photograph was produced in the Liverpool City Museum, where the piece is preserved.

[4] A later mirror (*Plate 7b*) in which the same design was used, showing two unassociated roundels only, comes from Trelan Bahow in St. Keverne, a coastal parish near the Lizard: the Helford River, near by, is probably the port-of-entry. See p. 98 below.

[5] Jacobsthal, *Early Celtic Art*, p. 89. Other examples in this country are seen on the Cerrig-y-Drudion bowl, the Clevedon torc, the Battersea shield, and the Bapchild, Kent, and eight Westhall, Suffolk, terrets.

[6] Jacobsthal, op. cit., p. 84.

[7] See p. 27 above. The range of date suggested in 1945 was 50 to 25 B.C. The latter now seems most likely: a gap in the series, anyway, must be admitted.

[8] The handle of the mirror is discussed, with others, on p. 99 below.

[9] In Praetorius' drawing, reproduced in *Plate 57*, the left-hand circle is accidentally omitted.

[10] *Ant. Journ.*, 1948, p. 133.

[11] The note and illustration was sent to me by Mr. J. N. Taylor, Curator, Gloucester Museum, kindly inviting publication.

[12] Fox, *Arch. Camb.*, 1945, Figure 11 and pp. 216–18.

[13] In *Ant. Journ.*, 1948, p. 136.

[14] Charles Green, *Proc. Prehist. Soc.*, 1949, pp. 188–9 and Figure 1. I have used the author's description and discussion. It is relevant that the Birdlip lady was inhumed, not burnt: she will have been a member of a noble Dobunic family.

[15] Babelon, *Le Trésor d'Argenterie de Berthonville près Bernay (Eure)*, Paris 1916.

[16] I may claim to have rediscovered this mirror, as a result of my visit to Bedford in 1954, when the kindly Librarian, after a search, found the parcel in which it has rested unsought since Reginald Smith saw it in 1908. (It did not then belong to the city.) The quality of the ornament astonished me. The mirror was sent to the British Museum on my recommendation to be repaired, and was thereafter transferred to the new Cecil Higgins Museum, Bedford. My photographs were taken at Bedford before the repair. Two vases of Kimmeridge Shale come from Quints Hill: one is in the British Museum, dated 1855, the other in the Museum of Archaeology and Ethnology, Cambridge. See *Archaeologia* 61, pp. 333–4.

[17] *Archaeologia* 40, *Plate XXX*.

[18] The reconstruction is after E. T. Leeds, *Celtic Ornament*, Figure 15a.

[19] It should be noted that this doubling is a common motif in Celtic art; see Jacobsthal, op. cit., p. 86, B (*a*), "Two lyres, foot to foot".

[20] See "Illusionism", below.

[21] *Arch. Journ.* 85, 1928, p. 71 ff.

[22] *Ant. Journ.*, 1925, p. 255, Figure 1.

[23] *Ant. Journ.*, 1948, p. 128.

[24] The casting provides tenons in the case of Birdlip and Stamford Hill I, mortises in that of Desborough. The tightest possible joints were obviously required.

[25] G. C. Brooke, "The Distribution of Gaulish and British Coins in Britain", *Antiquity*, 1933, pp. 268–89; Derek Allen, "The Belgic Dynasties of Britain and their Coins", *Archaeologia* 90, pp. 1–46. The map in *Arch. Camb.*, 1948, p. 38, compiled by Aileen Fox, embodies corrections of the latter paper, arising out of correspondence with Mr. Allen.

[26] The distribution map of currency bars (my Figure 37), which are regarded as essentially Dobunic, shows a concentration near the south coast between Weymouth and Poole Harbour.

[27] The associations of this mirror, burial furnishings, are now known, and my dating, c. A.D. 25, confirmed. R. Farrar in *Proc. Dorset Arch. Soc.*, 1954, p. 90.

[28] *Burlington Magazine*, Vol. 75, p. 31.

[29] This survey of the mirror-style may be thought to have occupied a disproportionate space in text and illustration. Mirrors are, however, the only group of early Celtic works of art of the first rank in which a complete sequence—early, middle, and late—can be studied.

[30] *Proc. Prehist. Soc. East Anglia*, Vol. vii, p. 156, Figure 6c, by L. F. Chitty and C. Fox.

[31] For this, and for repetitive work of the same sort, see Donald Atkinson, "Report on Excavations at Wroxeter, 1923–7", *Birmingham Arch. Soc.*, 1942, *Plate 52* and pp. 216–17. Most of the known examples are listed in the Museum publication *Llyn Cerrig*, p. 89.

[32] P. Corder and C. F. C. Hawkes, *Ant. Journ.*, 1940, p. 338 ff.

[33] Note its position in the series of "trumpet lobes", *Llyn Cerrig*, Figure 24, 9.

[34] These bosses were attached to metal stems riveted at the back of the piece; the holes are seen in the photograph.

[35] *B.M. Guide*, 2nd ed., 1925, pp. 150–1.

[36] Discussed by E. T. Leeds in *Celtic Ornament*, pp. 52, 53.

[37] See W. Bulmer, *Ant. Journ.*, 1938, pp. 147–8 and 151, and Figure 2.

[38] R. W. Feachem, *Ant. Journ.*, 1951, p. 32 ff.

[39] *Arch. Camb.*, 1904, p. 9 and Figure 6: Corder and Hawkes, *Ant. Journ.* XX, 1940, pp. 350–1.

[40] R. G. Collingwood, *Archaeology of Roman Britain*, Type X, Figure 63.

[41] The structural character is dealt with by Sir Arthur Evans in *Archaeologia 55*, p. 179 ff. : and its ornament by R. G. Collingwood in *Archaeologia 80*, p. 37, with a fine illustration, *Plate XI*. See also Corder and Hawkes in *Ant. Journ.* XX, 1940, pp. 350–3.

[42] *Llyn Cerrig*, p. 50.

[43] The nearest parallel, in detail, is perhaps the Wraxall torc (*Plate 61*), whereon the scrolls and lobes are framed in narrow bands of relief work at a lower level; but it is much more advanced.

[44] The full account of these vessels is by J. X. W. P. Corcoran in *Proc. Prehist. Soc.*, 1952, p. 85 ff.: he lists twenty-five examples and provides a distribution map. Many hold-fasts are in the National Museum of Wales—Seven Sisters hoard. See my p. 110 below.

[45] Corcoran, loc. cit., *Plate IX*. Handled mugs of pottery were made in *Glevum* (Gloucester) and at Cirencester in the Roman period, I A.D. and part of II (*inf.* Aileen Fox): this suggests that the straight-sided type of drinking vessel was particularly popular among the Dobuni. See *Journal of Roman Studies*, 1943, p. 16, Figure 1, No. 3, and cf. Wheeler, *Maiden Castle, Dorset*, 1943, Figure 74 (227).

[46] *Archaeologia 52*, p. 359. Mr. Corcoran's reconstruction of the latter is to be preferred: loc. cit., *Plate XI*.

[47] The fragments of the piece are in Bury St. Edmunds Museum.

[48] A tankard is, of course, a sort of mug: and it is significant that at Glevum (*Journal of Roman Studies*, 1943, p. 16) mugs were being made in I and II A.D. in the local ware with countersunk cordons on the lines of the handle: they are described as a common I A.D. type persisting into II A.D. A similar mug comes from a Romano-Belgic level at Maiden Castle (1943 Report, Figure 72, No. 185) and others from the Durotriges' country at Weymouth (Jordan's Hill, in B.M.).

[49] The fold-over identity of each pair of triquetral forms in the hold-fast shows late date—a faint revival of classical influence in a school of design normally asymmetric.

[50] Adapted from the *Museum Guide to the Collections*, Figure 40.

[51] Illustrated by Corcoran, loc. cit., *Plate X, No. 5*, and *B.M. Guide*, 2nd ed., 1925, Figure 146.

[52] Corcoran, *Plate X, 2*.

[53] R. C. Neville in *Arch. Journ.* XIII, 1856, pp. 4–6. The piece is in the Museum of Archaeology and Ethnology, Cambridge. Professor Stuart Piggott reminds me that three metal-work hoards from south Scotland include chains of this type, which confirms their Celtic origin.

[54] There were sixteen pottery vessels at Snailwell, fourteen of them imported from Gaul. The slave trade (*Llyn Cerrig*, p. 37) provided, no doubt, much of the "foreign currency" required. Lethbridge, *Proc. C.A.S.*, XLVII, 1954, *Plates II–IV*.

[55] The earliest Belgic rectangular house structures known at present are post-Claudian, *c.* A.D. 49–70.

[56] And carved woodwork, probably, on wall-seats and door-frames. See my p. 111.

[57] At Bagendon, Glos., Mrs. E. M. Clifford, F.S.A., is excavating an important occupation site by a stream, within extensive linear earthworks. Belgic pottery points to an intrusive (cultural and dynastic?) settlement, possibly associated with the late inscribed coinage of the region (1955). House-plans have not yet come to light.

[58] At Exeter, it may be added, Aileen Fox found a wooden house with central hearth, early Roman in date but not in some of its features: *Roman Exeter*, 1952, pp. 8–12, Manchester University Press. See *Glastonbury Lake Village* I, *Plate XXVII* and Figure 9, for the remains of a rectangular wooden hut used as foundation material.

[59] *Archaeologia 77*, p. 106, Figure 11.

[60] Nineteen examples are known, widely distributed in Britain (nine England, two Scotland), in France (two), and in Ireland (five): a list is in Ellis Davies, *Prehistoric and Roman Remains in Denbighshire*, 1929, p. 222. See also *Ant. Journ.*, 1933, pp. 464–5.

[61] *Ant. Journ.* XIV, 1934, p. 60. Mrs. Clifford tells me the drawings which she kindly allows me to reproduce are not quite accurate, because the piece is not truly round-based.

CHAPTER IX. PERSONAL DISPLAY : OUTDOORS

(i) WEAPONS

(a) *Shield-ornament, St. Mawgan in Pyder (Cornwall)*[1]

Few pieces of quality of this late phase are known; a recent discovery at Mawgan in Pyder near Newquay in north Cornwall is therefore welcome. It is one terminal of the bronze spine formerly extending outwards from the boss, and so decorating an oblong shield (*Plate 67b*). The spine is nearly parallel-sided, and the central ribbon has a delicate wavy pattern; there are narrow grooves parallel to this pattern, and similar incised lines defining the margins of the bronze. The latter almost certainly continued round the whole ornamental structure.

The axial wavy pattern dies into a pelta-shaped end stippled for emphasis, sited where the expanded portion of the piece begins. The flanking bands each curve outward to form a tiny dual pelta-shaped pattern with tips modelled as "snailshells" in the Marnian tradition, and with holes (for decorative (?) rivet heads) at their tops. The bands continue on either side as narrow ribbons, expanding into scrolls which initiate the two successive coils forming the major pattern of the piece, making, in their course, a double curve across each of them. One of the ribbons leaves the second coil at the tip, ending in a "Llyn Cerrig trumpet" with ornamented boss, axially aligned.

The pattern within each coil is complex. Two opposed comma-forms, to left and right of the axis, fit into each of the double curves mentioned above; they are stippled, and help to define complete peltas, based on the coil, and expanding from it.[2] Here, again, the movement is alternate and interlocked. Put briefly, the continuous coil incorporates, successively, four peltas linked in pairs: the comma-shaped voids thus created are stippled.

The partially lost (marginal) elements of the pattern consisted of ribbon-work and stippled, triangular voids, balancing the series of comma-voids in the centre, and matching two such units at the base of the expanding terminal.

When the study of this work of art is completed, its mazy paths threaded, the counter-point[3] understood, the question remains—why such virtuosity? The piece is so small, the ornament so delicately contrived, its unity of plan discernible only by studying the planes of the pattern in various lights; as decoration of a shield such ornament should be at least twice the scale, for due effect.

It would seem that when complete control of the tool and the medium is attained, a stage in our early art may be reached (as it certainly is later) when the craftsman indulges the intellectual pleasure of intricate logical pattern-making (pattern interwoven with pattern) to please his fellow craftsmen, in a workshop with a long tradition. The shield may have been a parade-piece, anyhow; this bronze stiffening—with its ornament hammered up from the back—is paper-thin, but it should always be remembered that lightness in a shield was a merit: *deflection* of arrow or spear-thrust or sword-blow, by its interposition, was a classical defensive technique.

"Workshop with a tradition." Only so can the amazing long-life of a primary (late third century?) British Marnian motif, the "snaily coil", be accounted for. The recognition of this survival is supported by the fact that the decoration of the trumpet boss is also seen on early Marnian works; it is well shown on Figure 10.[4]

Where was the shield made? Certainly not in the Cornish peninsula. The folds show that it was scrap-bronze, in so far as the Mawgan Pyder settlement is concerned, and the parallels are far away. Indeed, I know of no close parallel to the refinements and ambiguities of design discussed here, but the double coil is the main feature of two of the harness ornaments in the above-mentioned "Seven Sisters" hoard (Glam.)[5] in our National Museum (p. 127 below). The design of one of these, a looped ring (*Plate 66b* and Figure 78, 2), amplifies an unusual feature of the Cornish piece, the deep groove running outward to the margins between two coils (*see arrow*), and it can with assurance be regarded as a later (*c.* A.D. 50) development of the school of Dobunic craftsmen which produced our shield-mount. This, then, will have come from a workshop at the south end of the Jurassic zone, *c.* A.D. 25.

(*b*) *Shield-boss*: *Polden Hill* (*Som.*) *hoard*

This shield-boss, from the famous hoard, is also of very thin sheet-bronze, and is badly crumpled. The boss is circular, with a slightly pointed dome and broad flat base on which there is a band of rhythmic ornament, which is reproduced in Figure 72. The interest of the pattern—four identical elongated scrolls in low relief—is centred on the four points where the "hook" of a scroll interlocks with its neighbour. At each of these there was a knob (of enamel (?) now lost), and the scroll-ends had trumpet forms (of Llyn Cerrig derivation) providing—as will be seen—a decorative and well-balanced complex. It again is a Dobunian piece, and the scrolls are related to the more extended pair on the Wraxall collar (*Plate 61a*).

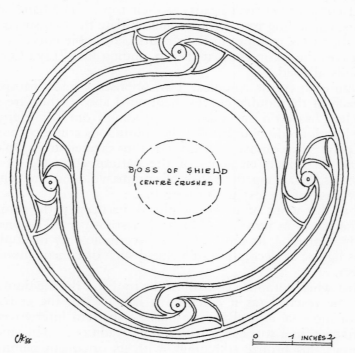

FIGURE 72.—Shield-boss, decoration of: Polden Hill (Som.).

Balmaclellan (*Kirkcudbrights.*)

(*c*) A possible shield-ornament is the flat semi-ring of decorated bronze with pointed tips from Balmaclellan (Kirkcudbrights.) (*Plate 61b*). This is incised with beautiful running scrolls in the mirror-style; the basketry ornament is formalized, as Figure 83, K83, shows. The moon-shaped figures floating in the voids of the angular central feature confirm late date, probably A.D. 30–40. Though a south-western piece in style (Dobunic) it was made in the north, as the archaic (Marnian) notch in the tips of the shaded coil of the third "roundel" on the right shows: the western sea-route is almost certainly involved in the transmission of the pattern,[6] and the central feature resembles, in outline, that of the Stichill collar (*Plate 62*).

The suggestion, of course, is that it was one of two terminals of a long shield, the boss, with short spinal extensions, being in the middle. As a lady's ornament stitched on to an upper garment—another suggestion—it could hardly have conformed to the contours of neck and breast.

(d) Bronze panel, Moel Hiraddug (Flints.)

The exciting diamond-shaped plate of thin bronze, with ornament in low relief, found with other objects in a hill-fort on Moel Hiraddug (Flints.) (*Plate 45b*) is probably another terminal for the central rib of a shield: it was associated with weapons. Its triskele pattern was used by E. T. Leeds in 1933 to demonstrate the principle of the broken-backed scroll[7]: the date should be early I A.D.

I think that the younger students of Celtic art will be baffled, as at first I was, by its unusual technique. The three bent-back arms of the triskele (Figure 82, D31) show sharply ridged, flat or slightly hollow planes throughout; the incurved bases of these arms and the spurs which frame the central smoothly-rounded "button" are similar in their crisp texture, as are the triple incurved points of the circular frame. The explanation of these features, surely, is that it is an exact copy of a piece of Celtic wood-carving in relief, like the Bulbury chariot fittings (p. 74 above). The central "button" was turned on a wheel; the rest reflects freehand chisel-work, by a master craftsman. Like the Bulbury find it indicates what we have lost; the range and quality of creative work in wood may well have equalled that in metal.

Direct copying of woodwork is possible, but unlikely; its manufacture as a frequently-used piece of decorative metal-work may well have been mechanical, wrought, that is, on an iron die (p. 75 above).[8] It is likely to have been made in the northern part of the Jurassic belt; the acutely-broken back and the rounded hollow at the "joint" are reflected on the later bronze armlet from Borgue (Kirkcudbrights.) (*c.* A.D. 100).[9]

(e) Sword-scabbards, Belgic and Brigantian

A group of scabbards found in Britain, approximately or actually parallel-sided, and with square mouth-profile, related to the Continental La Tène III type, has been regarded as definitely Belgic in origin[10] but as developing a specific character in north Britain. An attractive example of the Belgic group (*Plate 49b*) comes from the river Witham, near Lincoln : the curvilinear relief work on the cross-bindings of the scabbard head is handsome and carefully wrought; the formal incised ornament on the intervening panels—two segments of circles touching each other—is accordant, and the decorative scheme ends on the central portion of the sheath as a Celtic coil—rather stiff and formal: the design on the back is simpler, but equally effective. The chape is semi-circular in outline. In all, an example of good craftsmanship and adequate ornament of early I A.D. in south-eastern Britain. To the same Belgic series belongs a scabbard (with its sword) from Stanwick (North Riding, Yorks.), dramatically dated as pre-70 A.D.—it has reasonably been held—by its resting-place at the bottom of the inner ditch of the famous earthworks, beside the gateway. The mouthpiece ornament, compass-drawn, consists of two vesica-shaped elements, each containing a double ring-and-dot, the whole within a triple-lined semi-circular border. The chape is of narrowed U-form with quatrefoil ornaments on the upper ends; the bar is of a shallow "U" shape, and there is a terminal knob of Roman character.[11]

A third scabbard, from the Thames at Battersea, is illustrated on Figure 73. It has a similar barred mouth, and a bifid terminal to the functional rib at the back of the chape— the end of which is rounded.

On this figure also the northern type referred to above, termed "Brigantian" by Stuart Piggott, is illustrated. There are two swords with their scabbards, one from Sadberge (County Durham), the other from Embleton (Cumberland). The former shows that the

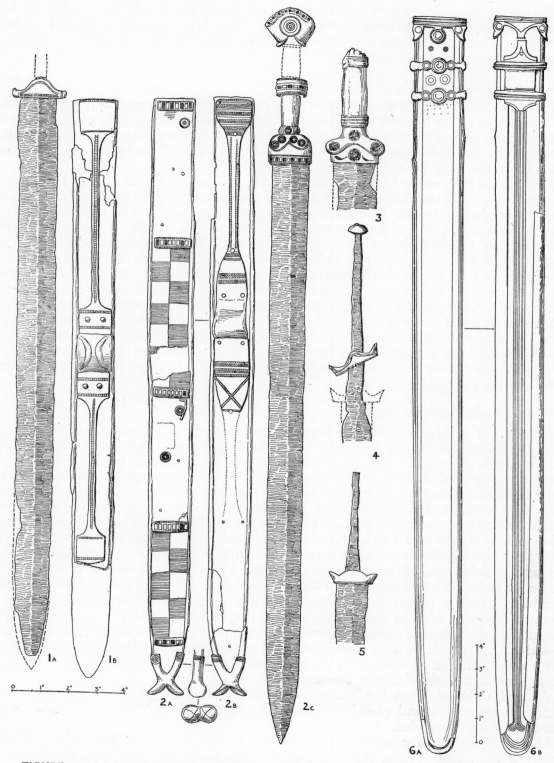

FIGURE 73.—Iron swords and bronze scabbards. 1—Sadberge (Co. Durham); 2—Embleton (Cumb.);
3—Thorpe (Yorks.); 4, 5—Newstead (Roxburgh.); 6—River Thames at Battersea.

flattened mouth of the scabbard involves the transference of the arched terminal with its ornament to the sword itself. This feature is more strikingly presented on the latter sword, the hilt of which is handsomely shaped: it has a cocked-hat pommel. Its bronze scabbard-plates are decorated in a rectilinear style which we shall see again in the Dobunic region, hatched chequer-fashion and with enamelled bindings on the front, and showing on the back narrow bands hatched diagonally. The chape is bifid.

This transference of ornament from scabbard to sword hilt is also seen on the Thorpe, Rudston, sword in York Museum, for the curved projecting bronze guard has retained its proper outline, emphasized by three enamelled studs; the fourth stud is on the intrusive, arched, sword-head, filling the hollow curve. One of these studs shows a hollow-sided "triangle", the others rectangular or lobed patterns.

Decorated scabbards from Stanwick (the second) and Cotterdale (Yorks.), and from Morton Hill, Edinburgh, illustrated in the article referred to, further enrich this interesting northern group. A photograph of the Cotterdale scabbard is reproduced on *Plate 74*.

(f) An anthropoid-hilted dagger

Late survival of the anthropoid-hilted dagger is demonstrated by a find associated with a burial by cremation, on Ham Hill (Som.). The piece, with a bronze buckle, rings and studs, in its bronze scabbard, is illustrated on *Plate 77*. An iron adzehead and an arrowhead were also found in the pit. All are preserved in Taunton Museum.[12]

(g) Helmet, unprovenanced: belt-plate, from York

A helmet of bronze in the British Museum (*Plate 62c*), unprovenanced, presents a difficult problem.[14] The shape is influenced by Roman types, but the bold curvilinear ornament in relief on the broad neck-guard is purely Celtic, in the north-eastern Llyn Cerrig plaque tradition, and the piece comes, there is little doubt, from a workshop at the northern end of the Jurassic Zone. A palmette in the centre is linked to bold elongated trumpet-forms on either side; the design is pointed by two bosses of enamel ("run-on", not pinned) round which the palmette tips curl, and from which a swelling lobe extends to the trumpet mouth. At each side are the remains of a plate similarly embossed, and cheek-pieces were also fitted. The date may be *c.* A.D. 70 and the owner a Celtic noble in Roman service: there has been a metal badge of some sort on the helmet, which needed rivets to keep it in place.

A well-known "soldier's belt-plate" in York Museum, with a trumpet-loop in high relief and an extended pattern of triangles in coloured enamels (*Plate 52c*) may be coupled with this, and assigned to the same decade.

Comment. In this series of bronzes, we have identified the shield-ornament from Cornwall, the Polden Hill (Som.) shield-boss, and the Dumfriesshire shield-ornament as works of western, Dobunic, schools; and the Moel Hiraddug piece as a Coritanian work from the Trent region. Sword-scabbards of Belgic type from Lincolnshire, Stanwick (Yorks.), and river Thames, Battersea, have been contrasted with a Brigantian type developed under southern influence, the examples being from Durham and Cumberland. The survival of the anthropoid-hilted dagger is noted, and an unprovenanced helmet is regarded as an Iron Age "B" piece made in north Britain under Roman influence.

It will be seen, then, that the study of Early Celtic art, as we move towards its close, becomes more assured in its conclusions—though *all* such attributions must at present be regarded as speculative. Since these pieces are very varied in style and so come from different workshops, they indicate the small percentage of creative work of I A.D. that is known to survive, in this field, rich as the material may sometimes seem to be.

(*a*) *Chariot-fittings*

It is possible that many parts of the chariot were ornamented; we have already studied a decorated hand-hold from the Llyn Cerrig collection (Figure 15). The type continued in use, throughout the life of the war-chariot, for a well-designed severely practical example comes from High Cross (Leics.) (*Plate 3d*).

The bent-ash sides and the jutting ends of the floor-frame of the chariot may have been masked with embossed strips or squares of sheet-bronze technically similar to those discussed on p. 105 above, and illustrated on *Plate 67c*. The horse-head from Stanwick (*Plate 52b* and p. 129) is the most likely piece to have been used for such a purpose; but no such ornament has yet been found with a chariot-burial in Britain.

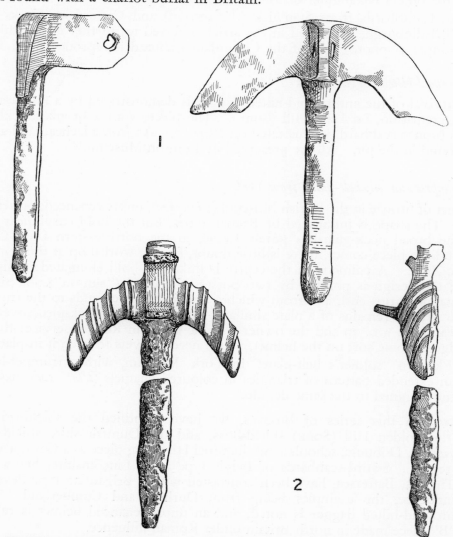

FIGURE 74.—Linch-pins: 1. Évreux, Normandy (iron); 2. Tiddington, War. (bronze and iron). (½)

Linch-pins. The heads of linch-pins (which prevented wheels from sliding off the axles) offered a field for ornament which was exploited in I A.D. The knobbed head of a Marnian type (holed for a wire attachment) became flattened and expanded, as in a handsome example from Kings Langley (Herts.) (*Plate 52*). The lobed pattern is defined partly by enamel, partly by incised lines on the bronze; it is in a familiar Iron "B" curvilinear tradition.[15]   An "arched" type, probably of Belgic origin (since Figure 74, 1 comes from Evreux), is also found in Britain; Figure 74, 2, illustrates another example from Tiddington (War.), the bold vertical ribbing of which well suits its function.[16]   A handsome and elaborate type, of iron (*Plate 39b*), comes from Great Chesterford (Essex), a Roman town-site which has yielded other Celtic pieces.   It is over 10-in. high, and may have been made for a "general service" vehicle. The Stanwick hoard provides a third pattern, with a large lipped ring atop of a domed head—a barbarous conjunction !

Mention has already been made of chariot and yoke ornament (pp. 73, 105); we turn now to first-century decorative work related to the ponies, their harness, and other furnishings.

(b) Pony-harness fittings
(1) *In central Britain*

The *Rainsborough* (*Northants.*) *harness-fitting*, illustrated on *Plate 66c* and Figure 53, is an interesting piece, showing the persistence of the lyre-form in our art, and being ornamented with fossil discs (encrinite stems) from the local limestone, was made in the neighbourhood. It is unique in character, and its function is not known.   The basal knob seen in the photograph is set on a stalk, and so is designed for a strap-loop: the piece was "threaded" on another ($\frac{1}{4}$-in.) strap at top and bottom: and there are three pyramidal spikes at the back—parts of the original casting.   The ornament is finely executed, though the piece is now in poor condition.

(2) *In south Britain*

In the last half-century of freedom, *c.* A.D. 1–50, fittings for the harness of chariot ponies are the principal bronzes, numerically speaking, that survive in this extensive region.   They show great variety in pattern—and probably in function—but well illustrate the thesis that regional differentiation in *south* Britain now hardly exists.   The designs may be curvilinear, asymmetric, or symmetric; or they may be geometric—a feature somewhat new to us—showing straight lines, equilateral triangles, and right-angles.   The first and second pieces discussed will be traditional, curvilinear, in character: the third and fourth partially geometric.

The "Ashmolean" triskele: a crest for a pony-cap.   A remarkable object of cast bronze in openwork, the relief being the same on both faces, is illustrated on *Plate 69a*.   This triskelar figure, asymmetric, is a development of the Llyn Cerrig plaque design, with the Llyn Cerrig bronze bosses replaced by applied settings, now lost.   It is badly damaged, parts of each side being broken off, including subtriangular voids illustrated in Figure 83, L97, and its provenance moreover is not known; it is south British in character, and probably came from the "Oxford Region".   The essential structure is a roundel, but the rim is expanded on either side, and it can only have been fixed by trunnions; it would then have been turned over and over by wind and movement.   It most probably decorated a chariot-pony's "mullen" or headstall: most striking, then, seen sideways, would have been the conjoined half-globes of bright colour in their bronze frames.   This is not an imaginative notion; the holes for the pins are plainly to be seen, and the brooch from the Thames at Datchet (*Plate 41a*) approaches the full technique required, in orange glass.

When the restored disc (Figure 75)[17] is studied together with the plaque the relationship is evident, but the abstract threesomeness of the latter has become naturalistic, a tree being represented, with one of the "coloured globes" (as I surmise) lying free beside the thickened trunk.   In the published account I have suggested that we may perhaps regard this dainty object as illustrating a widespread myth familiar to the Greeks, of the golden apples in the Garden of the Hesperides—the "Fortunate Isles".   The date of the disc if made, as I think, in the Dobunic area of the west where contact with Continental art and ideas was close, and where Iron "B" art still flourished, may be the beginning of I A.D.

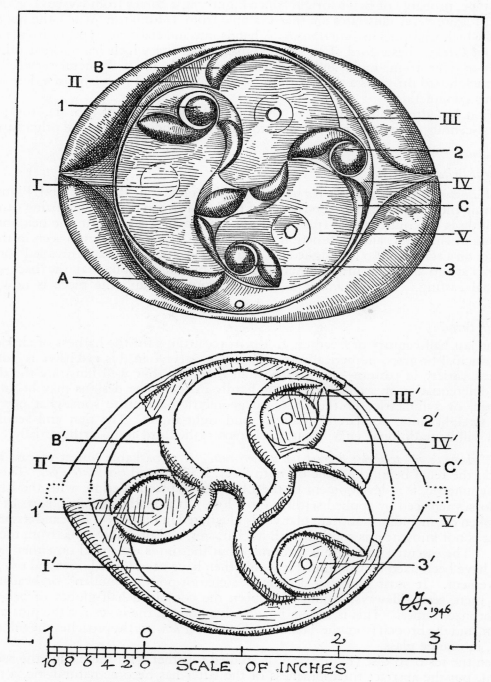

FIGURE 75.—Plaque: Llyn Cerrig. Triskele: Ashmolean Museum.
(Cf. Figure 18 and *Plate 69a*.)

When we see a non-representational design—the plaque roundel—evolving into a twisted "apple" tree without loss of any essential element of its asymmetric form—not even the spatial distribution of its three nodes—we must surely be observing the effects of a remarkable tradition and continuity of workshop practice among the Celts. The plaque roundel could hardly have been available for study when the disc was designed, but on a piece of metal hung above the bench its exact size must have been marked and its character outlined with a graver. Furthermore, we perceive that the device of the fallen "apple" on the disc is due to the pressure of an artistic convention; the third node of the pattern had to be at the bottom, and fruit does not grow on tree-trunks. As has often been said, we cannot analyse the creative spirit, but thus to glimpse in a pre-literate phase of British art the mechanics of its application is something worth retrieving from the darkness.

No parallels to this piece are known, but the detail of the lobes is found on two I A.D. bronzes made for chariotry—a pair of trace-hooks in the famous Polden Hill hoard[18]; *Plate 72b* shows one of them. On each hook are five settings with central rivets, three of which have smoothly wrought clasping lobes in relief similar to those on the disc, but of more advanced type, the tips being overlaid by a spur.[19] Two of the domed studs on the trace-hooks survive; their presence supports the view that our disc studs were half-spheres and not flat.

Horse-brooches in the Polden Hill hoard. The Polden Hill hoard also contains a small group of three pieces with a special function in the chariot-and-pony set-up. They are reproduced here from accurate engravings in an early volume of *Archaeologia*.[20] Two have curvilinear patterns, one linear; so both art forms are represented. The most remarkable is that on the left of *Plate 73*; the shaded portions were filled with red enamel, which has perished. The pattern has in the centre a "derived" palmette, islanded in bronze, and on either side elongated "trumpet" forms of Llyn Cerrig type, islanded in enamel (Figure 83, L96). It is in the high tradition of Iron "B" art; one of those intriguing pieces in which background and pattern are interchangeable; but the enamel element of the design is chosen to emphasize the unusual outline of the piece. It seems likely that the artist has used the lyre or opposed-scroll design at the stage reached by the Colchester mirror (Figure 54); but this bronze (illustrated *at the back* on the Plate) is also a brooch; the hinge for the pin is part of the casting, and so is the catch. The brilliant piece must then have been made to secure a horse-blanket—not one, of course, for routine use, but a brighter weave, a gay caparison for display.

It is of interest, therefore, to observe from a newly-discovered fragment of Diocletian's *Edict of Prices* (1955) that—300 years later—the value of the British rug (*tapete Britannicum*) was the highest in its class (an undecorated type is indicated, the quality of which will, no doubt, have resided in its raw material and technical excellence). Like the British woollen cloak (*birrus Britannicus*) rug-making was a speciality.[21]

Our elaborate caparison, then, will have been laid across the pony's back, one selvedge against the yoke, the other across the pony's quarters: it needed to be pinned at the centre of each, to prevent it sliding off on either side. Now the strap-holes on the back of the brooch, set askew, are for a crupper (that is the strap with a loop to go under the pony's tail, extended along the back and fixed to the yoke at the other end).

This is shown on Figure 76, at the bottom, where the brooch is drawn upside down. It was slid on to the loop—permanently when the strap was made, unless there was a buckle at this point—and could be lifted up sufficiently to push the caparison under the brooch-part, where it would then be made fast.

When fixed, the brooch lay as shown in the sketch of the pony's back as seen from the chariot, in the same Figure: the straight alignments of the brooch's outline faced the tail. They are slightly inclined outwards, presumably because the artist noticed that the selvedge of the material, being under the strain of its own weight on the curve of the rump, lay that way; the "loophole" of the brooch, a common Celtic motif, was surely here used because it would match the loop of the crupper. The whole shape, then, grew out of the craftsman's intimate knowledge of the precise function of the piece, and his sensitiveness to that relation.

Proof that this is a correct interpretation is in our hands. Two brooches were needed for each pony, and they had to be different in shape. Of the two other horse-brooches in the hoard, one, with a single strap-hole, is without any doubt made for the yoke-end.[22] It is shown on *Plate 73, 2A* and *B*, derived from the same source: a finely wrought pattern in red enamel, it is strongly linear in design—the first piece of this character we have studied. It

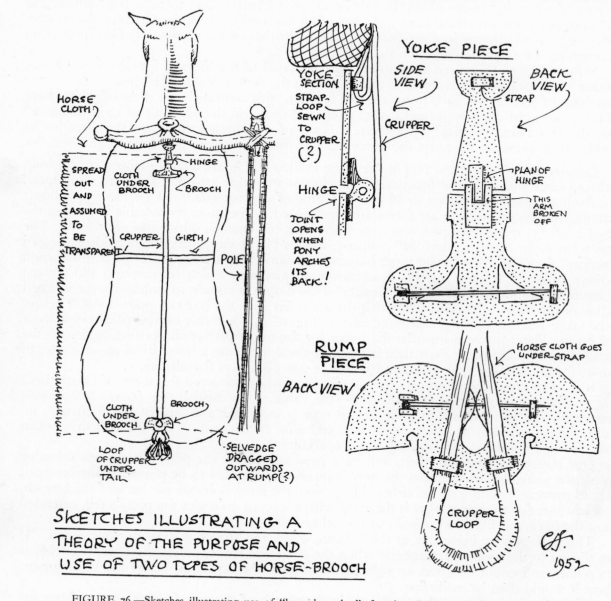

SKETCHES ILLUSTRATING A
THEORY OF THE PURPOSE AND
USE OF TWO TYPES OF HORSE-BROOCH

FIGURE 76.—Sketches illustrating use of "horse-brooches", found at Polden Hill (Som.). (*Plate 73a*.)

seems to reflect, in its classical idiom, one structural element in its immediate neighbourhood as seen from the chariot: the bar of the yoke. The broad brooch-part is the "yoke"; it was, as the engraving shows, separate from the narrow piece threaded on the strap, but would have been attached to it in antiquity by a bronze pin passed through pierced projections (two on this—one survives—and one on the other) forming a hinge.[23] This hinge is illustrated on plan and sectionally in Figure 76. It enabled the brooch, which is 7 in. long, to rise in the centre, forming an obtuse angle, when the pony arched its back to stretch or to feed. The sketch-section also shows a possible method of attaching the brooch to the crupper; its cast-bronze strap-hole seems too narrow to house the crupper itself.

No horse-brooches are known in Britain other than these, which will no doubt have been made for use in some Dobunic ritual or cult, a formal parade in which a vehicle was a necessary feature.[24] Tacitus's account (in *Germania* 40) of the rites associated with Nerthus, a goddess worshipped in the north (Sjaelland?) is relevant: she, on prescribed occasions, toured the countryside in a car drawn by heifers. Thereafter goddess and garments were washed in a sacred lake, by slaves who were killed when the ablution was completed.

In conclusion it will, I think be agreed that the second horse brooch shows distinguished artistry in its fusion of rectilinear and curvilinear elements of design, and in the proportions of the piece as a whole. It is surely the work of a Celtic craftsman trained in the Iron "B" tradition, but influenced by the new ideas.

Other decorative harness fittings in south Britain. We now return to more ordinary horse and pony fittings. The Belgae possessed equines suitable for cavalry, but their neighbours to the east, the Iceni of Norfolk and west Suffolk, certainly continued to use the chariot and therefore the native pony down to the revolt of A.D. 61,[25] and it may be that the Belgae (and, incidentally, the Dobuni) made use of both arms.

In a highly decorative type of harness ornament for chariotry, found in Belgic, Icenian, and Dobunic territories, a bronze plate was cast with shaped openings in the centre and with angular loops for broad straps at the back. The surface of the bronze was then cut away to form the required design (*champlevé*), and enamel poured into these hollows; fine incised linear ornament helped to define and enrich the enamelled shapes, the whole surface being thereafter ground smooth. Palmette forms, from "London" and Westhall (Suffolk) pieces are reproduced on Figure 82, B13 and 14. A characteristic design was reproduced in colour on the cover of my *Archaeology of the Cambridge Region* in 1923; another, more elaborate, from the same Santon Downham (Suffolk) hoard is here illustrated (*Plate 72e*). It is rubbed very smooth by long use, and was, in a sense, an *applied* ornament; for an extensive area of rotted leather was attached to the back. Only a colour-process block could bring out the pattern clearly, but the *quality* of the piece is, I hope, unmistakable. The enamel pattern is enmeshed in a network of finely incised lines as mentioned above; these are drawn with remarkable accuracy.

The elements of the curvilinear design are wholly of Iron "B" character; one unit is on the line of the strap between the two shaped openings, the other, duplicated, on either side: there is complete fold-over symmetry. "Onion" shapes in enamel, axially extended, dominate the central zone; four coils in pairs elaborately dissected, the flanks. Elements of the design are sketched on the Plate; the Llyn Cerrig trumpet-pattern, enveloping a stud of enamel, is notable, as is the *yin-yang* scroll arising from a coil of similar character.

The second example, "C" on the same Plate, from the Polden Hill hoard, shows the influence of Belgic formalism on this class of ornament. All the enamel having disappeared, the design is clear: two palmettes and two "S" coils (traditional forms) are associated with bands of zig-zag pattern, prominently displayed on the curved ends of the piece.

Bridle-bits. The cheek-piece of a bridle-bit of the rare "bar" type,[26] also from Polden (*Plate 72a*), is contemporary, as the triangle motif in its ornament shows; it has more character, and will have been an attractive ornament when the enamel was present. The effect is heightened by incised work on the bronze background.

A massive two-piece bit from the Thames, presumably near "London" (overall 12½ in.) in the British Museum (*Plate 71d*) obviously for a horse not a pony (cavalryman not charioteer) illustrates another aspect of Belgic metalwork of early I A.D. and the decay hereabouts of the curvilinear tradition. Paired lozenges (Figure 83, F51), and opposed trumpet forms in openwork, are the incongruous features of cruciform panels to which the knobs (showing sunk triangular panels) are attached; turned through a right-angle (as in use) these secure the inner loop of each half of the bit. The bars are square in section: there is no trace of enamel on the piece.

(*The spread of geometric ornament.* Expensive bronzes encircled with triangular geometric ornament were in this century exported to the tin-producing areas of Cornwall. The Trelan Bahow mirror is one example (*Plate 7* and p. 98); another is the bronze collar found in a tin-stream at Trenoweth, Lelant, and published in *Archaeologia* in 1812.[27] The curvilinear element of the ornament concentrated at four points on the circumference is similar to that on the Wraxall collar—but very debased; *c.* A.D. 70 is a likely date).

To return to our immediate subject: the two-piece bit on *Plate 72d*, from Polden, with its expanded ring-head subtly curved, with enamel spots—the bars also being grooved for enamel—affords a marked contrast; it is wholly Iron "B" in character.

Terrets. We now turn to the three bronze loops on *Plate 71*, of which (*a*) from Suffolk, in the Ashmolean Museum, was intended to be hung at the free end of a strap, but as the extra wear on the left side of the opening shows was actually fitted as a terret to carry one of the reins. The enamel having perished, its simple, symmetrical Iron "B" design stands out clearly.

A terret of the western "lipped" type (*Plate 71b*) comes from Oxfordshire, and is also in the Ashmolean. Its date should be early I A.D.; the enamel settings and elaborate relief ornament related to the "horned helmet style" (but adopting fold-over symmetry) shows that it belonged to an expensive outfit. This terret has an interesting find-spot: the Ditchley Roman villa.[28] Nowadays we are alive to the probability that farming operations were centred on these country houses, and that lost possessions of earlier (Celtic or Belgic) owners and cultivators of the land are likely to turn up in present-day excavations.

In another set of harness-bronzes found at Polden, from which I now take a heavy terret for illustration (*Plate 71c*), the linear ornament attains an angular character of which it might hastily be said that Celtic art was absent. This would be untrue: the flat-surfaced bosses have leaves, half open, rayed from their centres (a development of the Ditchley "lips") with triangular and pointed-oval enamels in two colours. These, and the string of similar units shaped in Belgic fashion along the curve of the ring and emphasized by double outlines, produce an astonishing effect, especially as there are subtle Celtic curves in the structure of the "leaves", well seen in the upper illustration. The expanded terminals, which will have rested firmly on a leather base (secured below by the loop) confirm the fine proportions of the piece, which is a credit to both Belgic and Celtic sources of its inspiration and to the artist who invented it. Belgic influence is, of course, archaeologically manifest in many other bronzes from the region after the beginning of I A.D., when a Belgic dynasty may have obtained control of the Dobuni (p. 140, Note 14, below).

Lastly, the types—six in all—of this useful and widespread fitting were illustrated by E. T. Leeds in 1933, and the reader is referred to Figure 33 of *Celtic Ornament*, which shows their character and distribution.

Hame-mounting, from East Anglia. An unusual piece of horse furniture (*Plate 69b*) can conveniently be mentioned here. It is (as I conjecture) an hitherto unrecognized fragment of a "hame-mounting"—one of a pair of stiffeners of bronze (such as were commonly seen, fifty years ago, in brass) rising to a knobbed point in double curve, on the heavy collars of English draught-horses carrying trace-hooks. It comes from the "Layard (local) Collection" in Ipswich Museum, without provenance; and is of continental, Marnian, pedigree[29]; the draught-horse, however, must be a Belgic introduction. The openwork design is obviously British and of early I A.D. date; my sketch (Figure 77) shows a bold "Llyn Cerrig" scroll, facing left, which will have been repeated above (facing right), and followed by a third "twist" at the top. The surviving portion is identical with the pattern on the linch-pin from Kings Langley (*Plate 52a*): turn it sideways! If the void-pattern is studied, "trumpets" with knobbed tails, facing in opposite directions, are certainly intended. Coloured cloth under the open-work will have emphasized the structural form (it was red in modern times, to my recollection).

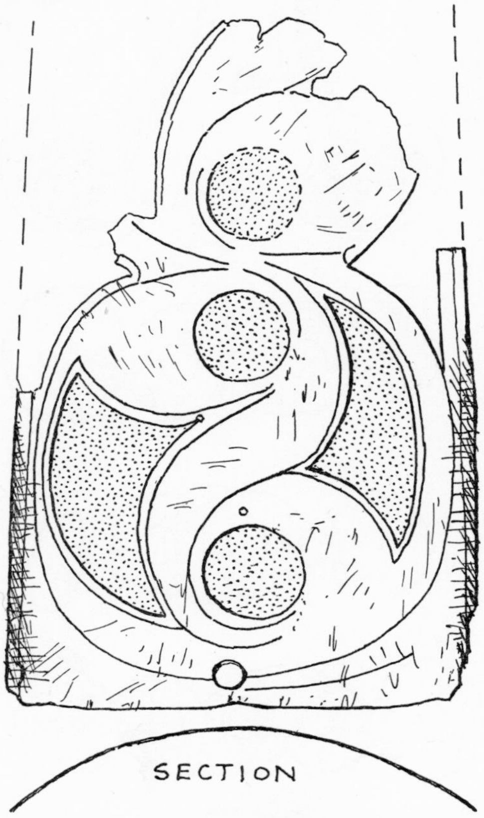

The traditional ornament illustrated in this Suffolk piece is also well seen on the small bronze boss in *Plate 12b* from Ixworth (Suffolk). This high-domed cap has a formalized Llyn Cerrig triquetral design in red enamel, each "trumpet" being identical (Figure 83, G60); the background, viewed from above, is a three-armed pattern with bent-back ends, in shining bronze.

Strap-link, Cheltenham. The last piece we shall look at from our southern region is a strap-link from near Cheltenham (Glos.) (*Plate 52d*). It shows the dynamic structure which may be associated with formal ornament in this closing phase of our art, wherever the ancient "B" tradition is still alive. Nothing could be less exciting than the two three-way figures on the circular panels, identical, typically Belgic,[30] and "moving" in the same direction; but how unexpected is the lateral compression of each of their frames, and of the unit carrying the leathers which the mind cannot but envisage as being under intense pressure! There are other (non-Belgic) decorative elements—the patterning here and there on the smooth bronze surfaces, and the boldly ornamented rims of the triquetras—to lessen the dominance of the main concept. The creative originality and distinction of mind and spirit which the Celt possessed is here fully brought out.

FIGURE 77.—Hame, open-work, lower portion of: Ipswich Museum. Site unknown. (⅔)
(Drawn by Cyril Fox).

Seven Sisters Hoard, Neath, South Wales

The Silures, as the close of the Age of freedom, seem to have acquired from the Dobunic folk a distinctive variant of southern art, strongly influenced by the classical formalism of the Belgic tradition. This new style is represented by the principal items in the local group of bronzes already mentioned (p. 110), the "Seven Sisters" hoard, found in Dulais Higher parish near Neath (Glam.), after a freshet had carried away part of a stream-bank; it was probably reduced in bulk when the collection served as playthings for a family of children, but the surviving pieces give a good idea of the range of shapes and variety of fittings formerly to be seen in a Silurian chieftain's harness-room, and of the unity of decorative design which characterized a "set". Romilly Allen published the whole collection in 1905, and there is an able summary by W. F. Grimes in the Museum's *Guide to the Prehistoric Collections*.[31] Tankard hold-fasts from the hoard (*Plate 66*) have already been discussed, but we cannot

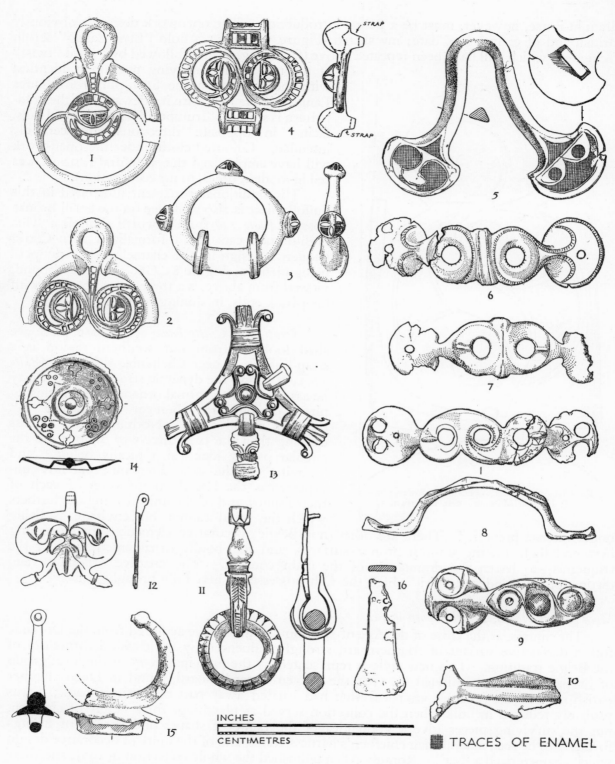

INCHES

CENTIMETRES

■ TRACES OF ENAMEL

FIGURE 78.—"Seven Sisters" hoard, Upper Dulais (Glam.) (N.M.W.). (Cf. *Plate 66a, b*)

128

neglect the ornamental features of an important set of harness fittings, and Mr. Grimes's drawings are here reproduced on a larger scale than in the *Guide*.

A pair of terrets of the usual shape show three bosses on their outer curves with quadrate patterns in enamel of two colours, the shapes being sub-triangular and pointed-oval (Figure 78, 3). The design of the next piece—one flat-backed ring of a bridle-bit (Figure 78, 1) has character which the first misses: the knobbed ends of the ring compress the neck of the loop which extends to form a centre-piece (a half-dome enclosed by a ring), reinforced laterally by curved strips of bronze. Here the enamel decoration, in small panels mostly rectangular, is concentrated: two groups are used in the Grammar (Figure 83, 50 and 66).

The other ring of the same bit (Figure 78, 2) is more elaborate, being made for the visible, off-side of the pony: it is broken and partly lost, but the essential elements of the design are preserved (this important piece is also illustrated on *Plate 66*). The loop-stem dies into an S-coil which has half-domes at each centre; spots of enamel ornament the domes (pointed ovals) and the scrolls (rectangular). It is a fair comment on this set, however, that the decorative treatment is wholly unrelated to the structural stresses set up when the ponies are halted at speed! There is a harness mount of the same set, with attachments on either side having angular loops for straps (No. 4); all the elements in this piece had panels of enamel.

The source in Belgic (?) Gloucestershire of this cellular style of ornament in the Seven Sisters hoard is clear: the Barnwood (Glos.) limestone Cone already mentioned provides a precise parallel, and could have been made only in the oolite region where it was found (Figure 71a).

The variety of the "southern" art of the period as illustrated in South Wales is shown by two other pieces in the Seven Sisters hoard; a trace-hook (No. 5) with somewhat debased enamel patterns at each expanded terminal (Figure 83, H65), and an elaborate three-sided fitting, flatbacked, for as many straps (No. 13). The terminal coils of each incurved side of the latter are reflected in the central openwork pattern, and cross-ridged bronze-work ties the structure together at each end of the triangle. It is, in short, a highly integrated, mannered design appropriate to the "silver age" of our insular Celtic art.[32]

More closely related to the current southern idiom (with which we are now familiar) than any of these works is a well-known harness-mount from Chepstow (Mon.) (*Plate 70c*), with linear ornament—triangular enamel patterns (Figure 83, F49)—at the ends, like the Polden Hill bronze (*Plate 72c*) and traditional scrolls (Figure 83, H68); this also is in the National Museum. The reader, then, will recognize that, like the greater collection of works of Celtic art in Anglesey, and the scattered finds in western coastal districts, the whole of the Seven Sisters hoard and the Chepstow mount were made in lowland Britain: these, of course, in the adjacent Dobunic territory.

Viewing this southern art, in east and west and centre, *as a whole*, one may say that neither the popularity of the new rigid geometric forms, nor the capacity of the older free curvilinear forms to survive and flourish, can be in doubt. The art of the Celtic and Belgic communities in south Britain was active right up to the Conquest, and, in the history of art, that transfer of power must still be regarded as a disaster.

(*c*) *A north-eastern school, Stanwick (Yorks.).* The main source of information about Brigantian art of I A.D. associated with chariotry is concentrated in the famous group of bronzes found at Stanwick (North Riding, Yorks.).

This collection (material from chariots in burials?) was found close to the great fortress which, Sir Mortimer Wheeler suggests,[33] was the scene of the final defeat of the Brigantian Confederacy prior to A.D. 74.

From the mass of material at Stanwick thus made available,[34] one example of a particular type of harness-mount (purely decorative, and attached to leather by a split-pin or some such device) from each of *three sets*, has been selected (*Plate 74*).   The back, as well as the front, is illustrated, in order to show how fascinating is the study of the interplay of tradition and invention which went on at the Celtic craftsman's bench.   Such a sequence shows how ruthless, how insistent, in any Age is the customer's demand for novelty.   The series might indeed be twentieth-century.   The first piece, Edwardian baroque.   Next, a simplified pattern—1920-ish—produced between the wars; it avoids the lush curves of the older style. The last specimen is an unemotional presentation—note the "new look", the flatness: post-war work, obviously.   But let us study the piece a little more carefully; the craftsman is using a pre-war mould, for it has the same half-circle section (3, right) as the others (1, left, and 2, left); he has but turned the casting over, and tooled up the flat back (3, left).   The customer's whimsy must be recognized and met, but good material should not be wasted.

GENERAL COMMENT.   A monograph on the large and varied group of bronze horse-trappings—central, southern, and northern—discussed in this section, mostly of the first half of I A.D., but which, on the borders of the Highland Zone (north-eastern Yorkshire and possibly Northumbria), were certainly made for a generation after the Roman conquest of the lowlands, is overdue.   Very little attention, moreover, has been given to the technical problem of function, on which the varied modes of attachment to leather of the bronzes could throw much light.

Tailpiece: *The "Dolphin" series of bronzes.*   It has been suggested that a number of "harness mounts" we have considered, those with small circular loops at the back, were functionless decorations on leather pony-harness for chariots.   This is almost certainly the case with a remarkable group of objects, light in weight, hollow-backed, shaped like a dolphin's body, illustrated on *Plate 75, a, b,* and *c,* from the British Museum collection.   These are sometimes in pairs, and I think "pairs" are standard.   The first comes from a "Roman villa" and is an actual fish; the Celtic examples *b, c,* and *d,* probably dating in I A.D., are, I suggest, copied or derived from earlier Roman imports.   The standard British type is represented by *c* and *c*[1] from the Polden Hill hoard; there are holes for fastening the missing "heads", and decorative bosses, now lost, were attached to the fish-tails.   These objects look like hooks but are unworn at the loop, and the metal is too thin for such service.   The Tooley Street, London, example (*b*) gave the clue to their use: there is an iron pin at the back of the *single* knob with a big washer, and space enough for stout leather between.   These objects were attached, then, to parade harness *in pairs*[35] and were functionless, like many other harness mounts.

There is a tailpiece to the story.   When the source-type, a dolphin's body and tail with the *head* as a separate casting, had been forgotten, an enterprising British craftsman modelled a piece with a duck's head at the tail end (*d*).   Whether he cast a duck's tail for the necessarily separate head end may never be known.

NOTES TO CHAPTER IX

[1] The author was invited to write this up for the publication by Mrs. L. Murray-Threipland; his account is here much abbreviated.   See *Archaeological Journal*, CXIII, p. 80.

[2] The coil is perhaps 0.25 mm. above the plane of the rest of the pelta-shape; perceptible, therefore, in certain lighting only.   The intentional ambiguity in design met with in many Celtic works of art is here well illustrated.

[3] "The art of adding one or more melodies as accompaniment to a plainsong, according to certain rules"; a word which admirably suits manifestations in another medium of expression, such as I am trying to describe.

[4] It also is seen on other late pieces, e.g. the eye of the snakehead of the Snailwell, Cambs., armlet: cf. T. C. Lethbridge in *Proc. Camb. Antiq. Soc.*, 1954, p. 36.

[5] Romilly Allen, in *Arch. Camb.*, 1905, p. 132: W. F. Grimes, *Prehistory of Wales*, 1951, Figure 40 (2, 4).

[6] Confirmation of the use of this route in early I A.D. is provided by a gold coin of Boduoc found near Dumfries in Galloway: Evans, *Ancient British Coins*, p. 135, and my *Plate 80, 21*. It is also relevant that Ptolemy records "Damnonii" on the western Scottish coast, in the region of the Clyde.

[7] W. J. Hemp in *Arch. Camb.*, 1928, p. 283: E. T. Leeds, *Celtic Ornament*, 1933, p. 56.

[8] The moulded angular border of the piece was "run off" by a subsequent process.

[9] J. Anderson, *Scotland in Pagan Times*, Figure 13.

[10] Stuart Piggott, *Proc. Prehist. Soc.*, 1950, pp. 17–22, Figures 9 and 10, and *Plate II*: Greenwell, *Archaeologia* 60, p. 257, Figure 8.

[11] Illustrated (by Piggott) in *Stanwick Fortifications*: Sir Mortimer Wheeler, p. 48 ff. and *Plate XXVI*.

[12] R. H. Walter, F.S.A., in *Ant. Journ.* III, 1923, p. 149.

[13] J. W. Brailsford: Address at Prehistoric Conference, Madrid, 1954 (not yet published).

[14] See *Llyn Cerrig*, p. 51, lines 17–19, and my Figure 69—the Elmswell, East Riding, Yorkshire, panel.

[15] J. B. Ward Perkins has studied the class in *Ant. Journ.* XX, p. 358 ff. and *Plate LVI*. Few examples have artistic quality.

[16] This pattern flourished in Roman times: developments with animal heads, very effective, are known from Camulodunum, Verulamium, and Hassocks, Sussex.

[17] This illustration is reproduced from *Ant. Journ.* XXVII, 1947, p. 1 ff. The letters and figures attached to each feature of each design (B–B: 1–1) represent comparable, or identical, elements.

[18] *Archaeologia* xiv, *Plate XX, 2 (1814)*. The Polden Hill hoard, Somerset, from which these hooks are derived, is the richest representation of early Celtic art, techniques, and ornamental patterns in the region. It is very varied in its make-up (as the examples already mentioned show), and has been a quarry for modern students; but it has never been given the monograph it deserves. It was found in 1814 in Knowle Bawdrip parish, at the western end of the ridge, Mr. W. A. Seaby, F.M.A., tells me. It is definitely late: *c.* A.D. 1–60 would perhaps cover its range.

[19] The larger settings of encrinite stems, three in number within the frame of the "lyre" of the Rainsborough harness fitting, *Plate 66c*, are bordered by similar moulded lobes in relief; the tips of the upper one turn outward with an air of *abandon*. The date of this piece should be in the second quarter of I A.D. (see p. 121 above).

[20] See Note 18 above; also Fox, *Proc. Prehist. Soc.*, 1952, pp. 47–54.

[21] Professor Ian Richmond in *Journal of Roman Studies* XLV, 1955, p. 114. Note that the reference is *not* to a *horse*-rug, but it shows the craft of rug-making was extensively practised.

[22] The third brooch is for the crupper, and of a different design.

[23] One is broken off, as is shown on the original engraving, my *Plate 73*. The type is known in iron; there is an example from Ashdown, Berks., in the British Museum (80/6/18). It is a very thin casting, and is possibly funerary.

[24] For the possible character of this ritual, see the *Proc. Prehist. Soc.* 1952 reference. The territory of the Dobuni in Roman times was a great centre for Celtic cults—the Mothers, the three "hooded-men", the horned man (Cernunnos?), and the Jupiter Column cult at Cirencester, *Sul Minerva* at Bath, *Nodens* at Lydney. Epona, a goddess (of fertility) associated with horses, must not be left out of account, though there is at present no evidence of her cult in western Britain. In relief sculpture on the Continent (Gaul and Germany) she is shown bestriding a horse or seated sideways on a horse; on one of the latter representations she has a "horse-blanket" under her (*Germania Romana*, Bilder Atlas IV, Taf. XXI, 3, from Leonberg). In the same publication (XXI, 1) a relief from Stuttgart shows two registers: in the upper she is seated with horses standing on either side; in the lower a four-wheeled waggon with driver and three horses awaits her; there is a throne on the waggon.

[25] *Roman Britain*, Collingwood and Myres, p. 99 ff.

[26] Another such from Great Easton, Leics., is in Leicester Museum.

[27] *Archaeologia* XVI, p. 137 ff. and *Plate X*. A good drawing is in Hencken, *Arch. of Cornwall and Scilly*, Fig. 29.

[28] C. A. R. Radford in *Oxoniensia* I, 1936, p. 55, and Figure 10.

[29] Jacobsthal, *Early Celtic Art, Plate 108, No. 171*, and Vol. I, p. 85. There is a pair in the Museum of Archaeology and Ethnology, Cambridge, of iron; Romano-British work.

[30] *Ancient British Art*, Piggott and Daniel, Figure 44. The pattern is closely related to that on the head of the linch-pin discussed on p. 121 above, from King's Langley.

[31] Romilly Allen, *Arch. Camb.*, 1905, pp. 128 ff.: W. F. Grimes, *Prehistory of Wales*, p. 118, and Figures.

[32] It will be observed that three of the pieces in the collection, Nos. 11, 12, and 14 on Figure 78, are Romano-British. The hoard was hidden, then, not earlier than the end of I A.D.

[33] "The Stanwick Fortifications", *Soc. Ant.*, 1954, pp. 2–3 and 20–21.

[34] The Stanwick bronzes were unearthed in 1844; twenty of the objects were published in 1846, and again in 1906, and nine more in the second issue of the *British Museum Guide to the Early Iron Age*. No assessment of the whole of this remarkable collection is in print; but the late E. T. Leeds illustrated one of the sets in *Celtic Ornament* (Figure 31) and the writer discussed the harness-type mentioned in the text in 1951 (British Association, Presidential Address, Section H).

[35] Or possibly, seeing how flimsy they are, to the horse-blankets already mentioned. An example from Camerton, Som., in Bristol Museum, suggests that they were widely distributed in south Britain.

CHAPTER X. SIDE-LINES

(A) PEASANT ART

In our high civilization the significance of the term "Peasant" or "Folk" Art, as applied to certain work of the seventeenth to nineteenth centuries, is well understood. It implies objects of metal, wood, or pottery—and needlework, serving the simple requirements of village households, made by village craftsmen and craftswomen in their own homes or yards.

In Early Celtic communities possessing, it would appear, an unusually widespread artistic sensibility and a less complex social organization, the difference between art-for-a-living in specialized workshops and art in the backyard incidental to the production of homely necessities—such as pottery, the simpler iron tools, and wooden vessels, turned or framed—will have been less marked, in quality and also (perhaps) in character. The only decorative shapes and patterns familiar to the Celtic peasants may have been not those of a *past* generation, as formerly with our people, but the current style of the chieftain's outfit for bed and board and transport.

(i) Woodwork

In an earlier chapter (p. 117) it has been suggested that there may have been a sophisticated art of wood-carving rivalling that of the metalsmiths. Here are two minor examples (*Plate 76*) from hut-sites in the Glastonbury Lake Village, showing two-dimensional patterns, which are with good reason held to have been made within the community for its own needs: the fine drawings are by the late Dr. Bulleid, republished by kind permission. The second design, a running triquetra on a fragmentary tub of ashwood, lathe-turned, 12 in. in diameter, is competently wrought in swinging curves and coils, truly drawn. The "solid" elements of the pattern are carefully cross-hatched with dots in the interspaces; Dr. Bulleid remarks[1] that the main outlines were incised and then deepened by burning with a sharp heated tool, the lines being finer on the original than in the drawing.

This design may appear to be no more than a delicate example of a common motif: alternate scrolls springing from a wavy stem. It has, however, a long history; the blunt ends of the scrolls are palmette derivatives, and the triangular projections are, in Britain, of Marnian origin. Both elements are present in the Sutton scabbard design (*Plate 21*); here they survive only as outlines undifferentiated in their shading from the rest of the pattern.[2]

The first piece is a thin strip of wood with a carefully wrought step-pattern. The elements are L-shaped with chequer-work shading, open and close alternately: it is difficult to find a parallel in the literature, and the only comparable patterns in our series of bronzes are on the early shield-boss from Grimthorpe (*Plate 23*) and the swastikas on the Battersea shield (*Plate 17*).

These minor examples of decorative woodwork then suggest, since they will surely have been made in or near the lake village, that craftsmen in this medium, even in a rural community, were knowledgeable as well as skilled. Acquaintance with both north-eastern and south-western art motifs is evident.

(ii) Ironwork

The only piece of ironwork known to me that might come into the category of "peasant" art is the straggling ox-shape built of iron strip, ½-in. in breadth, found during the excavations at Bigbury (Kent) in 1864, and referred to on p. 75 above; viewed at all angles the creature has an endearing air of absurdity (*Plate 26c*). It was regarded by the excavator as a fire-dog of which one half had been broken off; this seems to me likely, but the piece is very small for the purpose.

(iii) BONEWORK: WEAVING COMBS

Much attention has been given, in the Glastonbury and Meare volumes particularly, to the decoration of bone weaving-combs. These represent a peasant craft, but there is little of interest in the simple linear patterns incised on the handles, and they are not illustrated here.

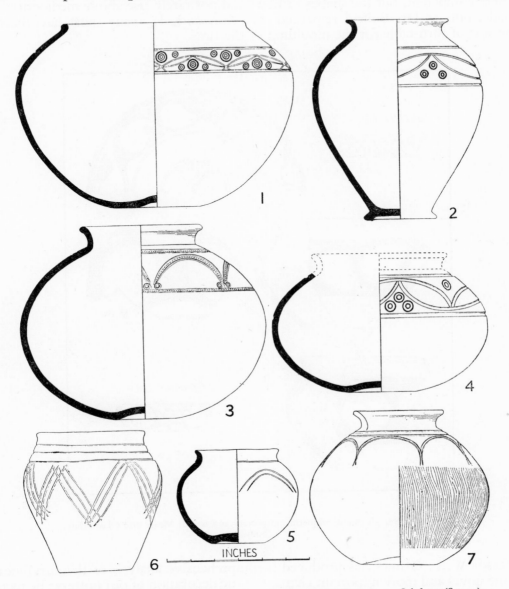

FIGURE 79.—"South-Eastern B" pottery. 1, 2. Canewdon (Essex); 3. Saltdean (Sussex); 4. Langenhoe (Essex); 5. Maidstone (Kent); 6, 7. London.

(iv) POTTERY

The beauty of form achieved by the Iron "C" (Belgic) potters in contact with Roman culture has led me to illustrate examples of their vases and bowls as elements of the notable art of this people (Figure 41). The Iron "B" potters of the west have not produced work of such refinement, but the decoration which some of them lavished on their wares seems to represent a peasant art which was widespread; the derivation of much of it from western Gaul is referred to, and a list of early sites given, on p. 55.[3]

Pot-making is often a women's craft; a search for finger-tip impressions—accidental, in the wet clay—might indicate if this were so in Celtic "B" communities. The technique is everywhere competent, but the shapes of bowl and pot rarely rise above mediocrity. All are hand-made, but, as Dr. Bulleid remarked (in *Glastonbury*, I), many must have been placed on some sort of turn-table for the moulding of the rims.

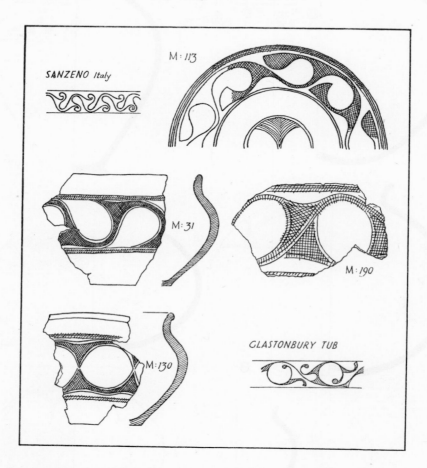

FIGURE 80.—Running triquetra, on pottery and wood: Meare and Glastonbury (Som.).

Professor W. F. Grimes has produced a comprehensive analysis of the curvilinear style which is the novel and more important element of the decoration of our pottery; he recognizes linear—sometimes rectilinear—ornament as a survival from earlier cultures. (The ability with which such survivals were at times incorporated with "Celtic" patterns is illustrated in my *Plate 76* (P97): this and P105 may well have been by the same potter.)

Grimes recognizes three groups—a South-Eastern, an East Midland, and the Western. The former, already defined by Ward-Perkins, is illustrated (in Figure 79) by pots and bowls from Essex, Kent, Sussex, and London (after that author). The style has a limited range—interlocking arcs and annulets are the principal elements—but the shapes are profoundly influenced by Belgic tradition.

The East Midland series is typified by a well-known group of bowls found within the fortress of Hunsbury, near Northampton, having two zones of a returning spiral pattern (*Plate 77c*), associated with rosettes. Both elements are found elsewhere in north-eastern art—the rosettes on the Ulceby bridle-bit (p. 35 above) and the scroll on a pot-sherd at Draughton (Northants.). The latter motif is related to the "double comma" or "*yin-yang*" scroll, a common Continental form seen on the Aylesford bucket.

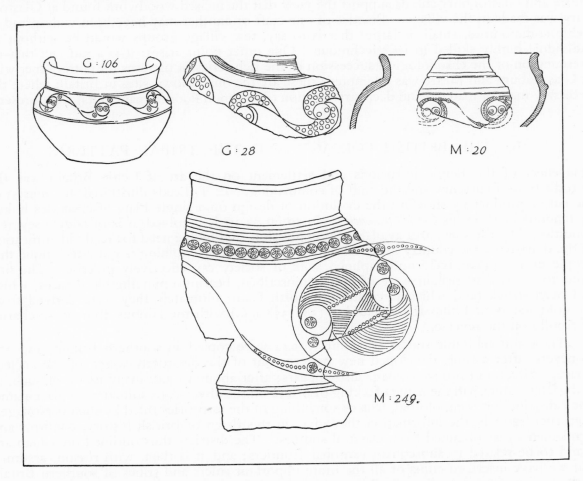

FIGURE 81.—Continuous S-scrolls: Glastonbury and Meare (Som.). (¼) Cf. *Plate 76.*
(After W. F. Grimes.)

The "Western style" necessarily, at present, centres on Glastonbury and Meare; it includes the coastal sites mentioned on p. 56, and decorated sherds found here and there in the upper Thames region, of which that from Yarnton (Oxon.) in the British Museum, is the best known. The more elaborate patterns are based on the metalwork of the period, those influenced by the mirror-style being particularly interesting: Figure 80, reproduced from Grimes's paper,[5] defines the connexion, and shows the development at Meare, more broadly visualized in Figure 81.[6] This illustrates the continuous S-scroll so commonly met with in the style (shown on a larger scale on *Plate 76*, P128), together with the unique elaboration of the motif (M249). The central feature is in saltire, like the limbs of a St. Andrew's cross; elsewhere the scroll-pattern is shaded so as to produce a rotating effect.

More common, of course, than these high-lights of a remarkable tradition are pots such as 15A in my *Plate 76*, whereon a wave-motif is rapidly drawn in the soft clay, dimpled and cross-hatched. The study of its descent from the adjacent P128 pattern (already referred to) is recommended to the interested student.[7]

GENERAL COMMENT. The skill and assurance shown by the potters of the above-mentioned Meare and Glastonbury sherds support the view that the incised woodwork found at Glastonbury was made in the village. Practice of one craft or another may have been widespread in Celtic communities, small or large: that is to say, few village groups would be without an individual highly skilled in *some* technique. One other point arises: it is a sad fact that no presentation of the chronological succession of the rich series of patterns on pottery met with at Glastonbury and Meare was attempted: these are the only known sites in Britain where the necessary mass of material and deep stratification (floor upon floor in many huts) were present.

(B) THE BRITISH COINAGE AND THE TRIBAL PATTERN

One effect of the Belgic intrusions and settlement on the art of Celtic Britain was the introduction of currency and the craft of coinmaking. E. T. Leeds illustrated the interest of the native product by showing the evolution of design on a single Plate of examples linked by tenuous lines, in his *Celtic Ornament*.[8] In so far as art is involved, it is of course severely conditioned by the small area available for expression, and by the need for ready identification of the dynasty or the country in letters and pictorial symbols: coining is not a technique that people in a comparatively undisciplined state of society can effectively practise. The first coins to be used in Britain were of gold, uninscribed, bearing unintelligible devices, which had been struck (and which circulated) in north Gaul; ultimately they were derived from the gold staters of Philip II of Macedon (382–358 B.C.) with the famous four-horse chariot of Apollo on the reverse.

These unintelligible staters of about 50 B.C. were copied in southern Britain, and the moneyers, after a time, developed new patterns out of the disorderly wreck of the ancient device. Silver and bronze coinage also appears; after about 10 B.C. many issues of such, as of the later staters, had the name of a king or prince on the obverse, or sometimes a place-name. Their distribution then, plotted, tells us something of the territories ruled by such personages, from such capitals; the information they give, in this dawn of British history, confirms and supplements that obtained from classical sources. The districts thus outlined on a map are found to be related to subsequent cantonal frontiers; and it is then, with reason, assumed that we have inscribed coins of all the more important rulers and tribes of southern Britain in the half-century preceding the Roman conquest.

These inscribed coins fall into two classes, the division being cultural and geographical. One covers the south-eastern (Belgic) region, revealing a group of tribes or confederacies and their rulers rapidly advancing in culture under Roman influence—the Atrebates, the Catuvellauni, the Trinovantes, and the Cantii. The tribes outside and beyond these consist of the Durotriges and the Dobuni in the west, the Iceni in the east, and the Brigantes in the north: their coinage shows little "variety or invention". Beyond them no pre-Roman coinage is known, though strays reach Wales and the south-west in the course of trade.

Thus, then, the tribal areas of Britain, shown on my Map C, have been worked out; it does not show later territorial extensions such as that of the Brigantes. This book is concerned with art, not dynasties; the studies mentioned in the footnote[9] will give the interested reader all the historical detail needed, together with a much wider range of illustration.

MAP C.—Distribution of inscribed coins, and tribal or communal areas, in Britain: *c.* 1—50 A.D.

The coin series

We begin, then, with the uninscribed series, in mid-I B.C. The laureate bust of Philip on the obverse of our earliest coins—probably of the Atrebates—is represented by an elaborate cruciform pattern,[10] but the reverse is closer to the original; it shows a presentable horse, at a gallop; associated with symbols or ornaments in the "field", the background. The specimen illustrated (*Plate 78, 5*) comes from the Whaddon Chase hoard (north Bucks.), dating about 40 B.C. An uninscribed gold coin from Llandudno (Caerns.) is in the National Museum.[11]

The earliest inscribed coin is that of Commius, Caesar's enemy or one of his family (*Plate 78, 1*). The same Plate shows coins of other members of this Atrebatian dynasty; Tincommius (TINC, *2*) and Verica (VERICA: VIRI, *3, 4*); there is an abbreviated patronymic on each reverse. In these the Roman influence is manifest; we shall indeed see in this series every gradation from coins which could have been made by Roman moneyers in the service of British dynasts—but which are, perhaps, more likely to be the work of Britons trained in their workshops, such as *No. 4* on this plate with a vineleaf, and the thoroughbred horse on the reverse—to those obviously of native origin. In the latter group intelligent adaptations of the classical technique (portrait busts, as in *Plate 78, 8*; *79, 15*; or devices, *79, 16*; *79, 14*, of an eagle and a Victory) are not uncommon.

Returning to our sequence: on *Plate 78* also are three early inscribed Catuvellaunian coins minted at Colchester, of Tasciovan. *No. 6* is a barbarous survival; *No. 7*, of silver, has a boldly conceived portrait-head with curled hair and beard; the mounted rider on the reverse is, in comparison with this, a poor effort. *No. 8* shows a laureate head of classical type—assiduous copying by a native moneyer.

On *Plate 79* the Catuvellaunian series is continued. There is one of the unexplained TASCIO-RIGON group and one of ANDO(COMIVS), followed by a series of five (*Nos. 11–15*) in gold, silver, or bronze, issued by the famous CVNOBELIN (*c.* A.D. 10–40) from the CAMVLODVN (Colchester) mint.[12]

The obverses of the first three of this series show wholly or in part the cruciform pattern previously discussed, which may in one favoured area have given rise to the famous corn (wheat or barley) symbol of the fourth (*No. 12*), a grandly simple concept with four letters of the mint equally spaced to give due breadth to the pattern. (It has been suggested that the vine-leaf design already mentioned is an Atrebatian imitation—Evans notes that it is not a Roman type.) The reverses on this dynastic series *9–12* are all of horses: single and prancing with a rider presumably the king, or a pair with the wheel-symbol of the chariot; the mounted arms of the Celtic host were decidedly aristocratic. These horses, whatever the defects of presentation, are spirited creatures.

The first coin in the series on the right of this Plate, *No. 13*, unique and remarkable though barbarous, shows a bearded head with "pipeclayed" locks and drooping moustache— no doubt the blond, full-blooded, broad-faced type met with in our countryside today. Evans remarks that it is "thoroughly British" and probably represents Hercules. The designer may have come from Western Gaul, for the boar-crest on the reverse has an Armorican formalism,[13] and full-face parallels have been found at Angers, in that region.

The obverse on the next coin of Cunobelin, *No. 14*, is of special interest, showing as it does the winged griffin of the Cambridge relief (p. 81 above) which enters so powerfully into Celtic religion; it was struck at Camulodun. The winged, partially draped, Victory of the reverse should be noted, as belonging to a very different category of the classical repertory (Evans, p. 342). The portrait bust, *No. 15*, "bare and beardless" (possibly based on the Young Augustus) with the inscription CVNOBELINVS REX in full shows above all other coins of his reign how far imitation of the Mediterranean tradition went in early I A.D. Evans notes that the butting bull, common on Gaulish coins, is also seen on the coins of Augustus.

The last Catuvellaunian coin illustrated (*No. 16*) has a head (of Caratacus as Hercules ?) and the inscription CARA on the obverse with an eagle strangling a serpent on the reverse. Whether or no the coin is correctly identified, this is a suitable symbol.

The coins on *Plate 80*, considered as a group, underline the fact that only in the Belgic or Belgicized[14] areas in Britain (see Map C) does the representation of man and animals attain reasonable adequacy. The Cantii were in this category,[15] and we have in *No. 17* a coin of DVBNOVELLAVNVS (obverse only) and in *No. 19* one of EPPILVS, both of this tribe; they show fairly adequate representations of spirited horses, the latter copied from a Roman republican original. The reverse of this coin shows a recognizable Victory winged and draped: Evans remarks that she is "far more of a virago than on the Roman coins, and equates her with ANDRASTE—whom, as Dio tells us, BOUDICCA addressed in A.D. 50, when she had assembled the Iceni for vengeance.

The coinage of the Brigantes of the north is illustrated (*No. 18*) by a I A.D. obverse of DVMNOCOVEROS; the horse is "liquidated", and the Roman script barbarized. The Dobuni of the west are often not much better, as the reverses of *Nos. 20* and *21* show. The obverse of *21*, however, vies with the Catuvellaunian "TINC" issue: "BODVOC" is set out in good classical script and "probably ends the issue" of this tribe. (Evans notes its artistic inferiority, as not being in a sunk panel.) The fern-like symbol of the obverse of *20*— a barbarous issue—is thought to imitate Cunobelin's ear of corn. This coin was found at Mount Batten, Plymouth: the type is peculiar to the west of England, and is probably post-Claudian.[16]

Some of the coins of the Iceni of East Anglia (*Plate 80, 22–25*) have cruciform obverses of the school already discussed, on both inscribed and uninscribed issues. A horse is the common obverse; it often has a bushy tail, and shows movement but little art. Compare the portrait in *24* with that of Tasciovanus in *8*: Evans, however, remarks that this head has character, "but it is hard to say whence it was originally derived". The forelegs of the boar in *23* are indefensible: "East Anglia" had, it would appear, little direct contact with the Continent—and was culturally backward despite its wealth in goldwork (p. 45 above).

Comment. In sum, the Early Celtic coinage of Britain shows considerable variety. It has rarely any merit outside the more civilized southern region. The treatment of man and animals is here under powerful classical influence; but there are barbaric interpretations of such motifs of great interest (those of Man in *78, 7, 8* and *79, 13, 16* have already been considered). Horses are vigorously portrayed; the small pony associated with early Celtic life in Britain had, in this phase, given place to a cavalry breed among the aristocracy of the more advanced states, which is perhaps distinguishable on the coins. The common cruciform pattern shows a considerable variation and a sense of style in many examples: among later works the ear of corn (*79, 12*) is outstanding as a symbol and in presentation. Lettering rarely reaches excellence (*78, 2* and *4*; *80, 21*), and is then Roman; it is often very inferior.

This is routine comment; the entry of numismatic art into the proto-historic phase of our insular culture deserves a deeper probe. When one considers the remarkable development in Armorica of the traditional obverse of western Gaul—the human head with contorted masses of hair—it is certain that our dynasts could have imported, had they wished, better moneyers for the uninscribed series.

As for later issues: we have a basis for comparison in the rapid development of the mirror-style in British bronzework—under the spur, surely, of intelligent and selective buying by high-born ladies—and these show nothing of the sort. There must have been a lack of interest among Catuvellaunian (and other) court-circles in securing recognizably British– Celtic presentations of dynastic succession and tribal symbols. In only three of the eight Catuvellaunian coins in my series (chosen, admittedly, for entirely different reasons) is there evidence of a school of moneyers: these are *No. 6* (TASC), *No. 10* (AND), and *No. 12*

(CVNO). If the equine reverses are carefully studied, a progressive technique, in the same tradition, is apparent. Sir John Evans was alive to this aspect, in his great survey, of course; he speaks (p. 291) of the diversity of style *and execution* (my italics) in the Cunobelin series, although it is probable that "by far the greater number of them were minted" in the same place, Camulodun.

NOTES TO CHAPTER X

[1] *Glastonbury* I, p. 312 and *Plate L.*

[2] For other parallels, see Stuart Piggott, *Proc. Prehist. Soc.*, 1950, p. 15.

[3] The developed style is manifest at Kents Cavern, Torquay, and Hengistbury: inland sites include Wookey Hole, Cheddar, and Ham Hill, Somerset.

[4] "The La Tène Art Style in British Early Iron Age Pottery", *Proc. Prehist. Soc.*, 1952, pp. 160–75.

[5] *Proc. Prehist. Soc.*, 1952, Figure 9, p. 170.

[6] *Proc. Prehist. Soc.*, 1952, Figure 5, p. 166.

[7] The photographs of pots in my *Plate 76* are reproduced from the Glastonbury volume by permission of the Glastonbury Archaeological Society, through the good offices of Mr. St. George Gray, F.S.A.

[8] Leeds, *Celtic Ornament*, p. 63 ff. and Figure 26.

[9] Based on Sir John Evans, *Ancient British Coins*, 1864; Derek Allen, "The Belgic Dynasties of Britain and their Coins", *Archaeologia* 90, 1944; and R. P. Mack, *The Coinage of Ancient Britain*, 1953. Also on C. A. Ralegh Radford, "The Tribes of Southern Britain", *Proc. Prehist. Soc.*, 1954, p. 1 ff. The casts were supplied by the British Museum, and I am particularly obliged to Mr. John Kent, Assistant Keeper in the Department of Coins and Medals, for helpful kindness. The number below each coin on the plates is the list number in R. P. Mack, wherein there is a reference to Sir John Evans's work, for every coin known to him.

[10] Mr. Sutherland points out that in primitive coinage the tendency is to cover the whole face with ornament.

[11] Illustrated and described by W. F. Grimes in *The Prehistory of Wales*, Plate XIX.

[12] The site of the mint is thought to have been discovered: "Camulodunum", Hawkes and Hull, *Soc. Ant.*, 1947, Index "mint".

[13] See J. Evans, *Ancient British Coins*, pp. 322–3. The exaggerated crest is Etruscan in origin: Jacobsthal, *Early Celtic Art*, Plate 222a.

[14] The latest Dobunic coinage probably represents an intrusive Belgic dynasty; there is archaeological evidence for Belgicization at Bagendon, Glos., now being excavated by Mrs. E. M. Clifford, F.S.A.

[15] The tribal status of the Cantii is now in question. See C. A. R. Radford, footnote 9 above, p. 7.

[16] Evans, p. 73.

CHAPTER XI. REFLECTIONS

The character of Early Celtic art

When the early art of the Celts in Britain is considered as a whole, all the 300 years of it, we may justly conclude that though deflected from time to time by the beauty of imported works in the realist, or symmetrical, classical traditions, the native artist-craftsman's approach to creative work was fundamentally different. His pattern-work, indeed, was essentially dynamic; on the move, as it were, or on leash. This dynamism did not mean disorder; far from it. Asymmetry was preferred to fold-over symmetry, a balanced lay-out being aimed at, often involving unexpected subtlety and variety in the placing of related elements. The two methods of approach are not peculiar to Britain; they can clearly be seen on many Plates of Dr. Jacobsthal's Continental *corpus*. But it is significant of the greater freedom of spirit and outlook the physical isolation of Britain encouraged or permitted, that we have a higher proportion of asymmetric, non-classical patterns of merit than Celtic Europe seems to have produced.

Of the seven most important works of the first creative phase in Britain, *c.* 230–150 B.C. with a late survival of the authentic style in *c.* 75 B.C. (five from the rivers Witham and Thames) dealt with in Chapter III, four are asymmetric; a variety of lesser works of early date, together with others of late II or early I B.C., underlines the strength of this attitude to formal art.

In the next half-century, *c.* 75–25 B.C., the tradition weakens; the two-dimensional triskele pattern, for example, is associated with a symmetrical linear framework of curved lines, best seen on the Hunsbury scabbard (Figure 24); this gives the whole structure the appearance of "opposed scrolls". The same feature, more closely integrated with the roundels, and therefore to be dated a little later, is seen on the Mayer mirror. The symmetrical framework of this and other contemporary pieces, however, is associated with a fundamental asymmetry in the roundels themselves.

This development may properly be regarded as foreshadowing the revival in Britain at the close of the century of the classical palmette and lyre patterns and of complete fold-over symmetry, best illustrated by the Colchester mirror: two powerful influences brought it about. One was the settlement in eastern and southern Britain of the Belgae; the other, commencing no doubt with Caesar's invasion, was the increasing interest of British princes in Rome and Roman ways.

The import of manufactured goods and works of art from Roman Gaul may well have been the chief stimulus. To the native craftsman—who would have known little or nothing of the history of his trade—such symmetry was, for a time, an unalloyed delight; hence we possess and cherish the dazzling craftsmanship and beauty of line and form of the Birdlip and Desborough mirrors: peaks of the later insular achievement. I have elsewhere related the enrichment of the ribbons on the Desborough mirror-back to the banded glitter of relief ornament on Augustan Roman silverware, and other correlations could be suggested.

Nevertheless, as far as the Iron "B" craftsmen were concerned—the inheritors of the old Celtic tradition in west-central and north-eastern Britain—the practice of fold-over symmetry, though it dominated the "routine" (and to some extent debased) work of I A.D. which we have examined, did not, until the Roman conquest was complete, become universal practice in the workshops. Consider the unprovenanced, but certainly British, "Gibbs" mirror (Figure 43) of about A.D. 10, where the internal asymmetry of the roundels of the earlier pieces has spread to the frame (and the roundels themselves are disintegrating): look again also at the remarkable Old Warden mirror, so recently rediscovered, and restored to its pristine brilliance.[1] The Celtic craftsmen seem to have been indeed, from II B.C. onwards, thrust over and over again into the practice of symmetry by the beauty of imported works of Mediterranean derivation, slowly sinking back (or rising, according to one's point of view) into an asymmetry more acceptable to their *ethos*.

This aspect of our art can be generalized. It was at one time an accepted principle among ethnologists that barbaric art withers and dies in contact with the products of a higher civilization; the "backward" country is "opened up", and cheap trade goods are imported *en masse*.

In antiquity, the more common phenomenon in Continental countries beyond the Mediterranean fringe, was probably that a trickle of imports, of high quality and therefore expensive, continuing over a considerable period of time, reached the chieftains and their families, a process which in the case of the Celts in western Europe had quite the opposite effect. It provided the craftsmen attached to great households with new ideas in design and technique, stimulating, not killing, the urge to creative effort. This effort was not confined to *pure* pattern-making. Living creatures were, from the outset, embodied in the bronze-smith's designs, as the duck-heads on the Torrs pony-cap and the boar outlined on the Witham shield show: ox-heads on fire-dogs, buckets, and chariot-yoke, and helmet-crests such as the Hounslow boar, carry on the tradition, as does the notable pair of rams' heads from Harpenden. Most of these bronzes are, however, in a sense examples of patterning—stylized exaggerations! Consider the ox-head from Ham Hill (*Plate 48*): the nostrils, with their Celtic "coils" and the enlarged "almond" eyes, suggest that a decorative design was the artist's aim. Even the harshly-angular Felmersham bronze is surely an artist's comment on the queer form that the life-force may take when its envelope is water-borne, combined with an appreciation of the essence of fishiness. The Stanwick mask, again, presents by a masterly use of simple motifs, full-fed horsiness, bland and smug. The only exceptions to this delightful series of interpretations of living creatures occur in representations of Man: the demonic Brigantian terret-design from Brough, and the tragic mask on the Aylesford bucket, will at once occur to the reader. There are also the comparatively agreeable Celtic face on the Grimston sword-handle and the moustachio'd masks from the Welwyn bucket (*Plates 18* and *33*). But two of these examples, it should be remembered, are probably Continental pieces.

This is, incidentally, a reminder that it was the Belgic intrusion which produced craftsmen specializing in naturalistic animal modelling. They also developed the technique of enamel-work, which spread widely over southern Britain in early I A.D., but was still absent in the north—judging by the Stanwick hoard—in the middle of that century.

A remarkable feature in the west, the introduction in II B.C. and the development (principally in Somerset in the second half of I B.C.) of curvilinear incised decoration on pottery, was probably inspired by the painted scroll-work of Brittany ceramics; and since wheel-made wares of refined and beautiful forms were introduced into the east by the Belgae in the same century, we owe the quality of British wares largely to the Continental achievements.

To sum up these aspects of our art- and craft-work: so far as we can determine the chronological succession, there is no period, from the close of the third century when British Celtic craftsmen were first at work down to the third quarter of I A.D. when the zest to invent new forms and patterns in metalwork failed in the craft workshops. Circumstances were perhaps fortunate: when the stimulus of the Scythic and Etruscan (Greek) primary traditions in Celtic art may be thought to have worked themselves out, invaders affected by Roman culture and then Roman art works of the Augustan era provided, directly or indirectly, novel realism with fresh devices in pattern-making. Though repetitive work of little value increased in volume in the last century of freedom, originality of design was never wholly lacking down to the end, in the north-east, about A.D. 80.

Early Celtic art in Britain, then, maintained a high level of technical competence associated with originality in concept and design in both three- and two-dimensional art for three centuries. This judgment is based on metalwork, but there is little doubt that the wood-workers produced, for the chieftains' halls, art of equal quality and, it may be, much greater quantity.

Distribution of Early Celtic art

Turning to distribution, Map B—which records the sites of the Celtic pieces dealt with—has enabled me to develop in more detail the geographical survey with which this book begins. It may be regarded as giving a fairly accurate picture of the distribution of the dwellings of the upper class—the purchasers and users of these necessarily expensive things. Such would be buried with a deceased chieftain, lost, or discarded, within a limited distance from the home; the only disturbing factors are the possible losses in fighting, particularly at river-fords, and the presumed custom of dedicating valuable spoil to the gods by casting it into rivers or pools. Such dedication is held to have preserved the Llyn Cerrig (Anglesey) material, and *may* account for the early bronzes from the river Witham and the lower reaches of the Thames.

Most of our Celtic finds lie to the east of forest-clad and largely impassable river valleys: the Swale and Yorkshire Ouse, the upper Trent, and the Severn above the tidal estuary. The Pennine Chain was a formidable barrier.

Within this alignment the principal finds are in the East Riding of Yorkshire, in or near the middle Trent and the Witham rivers, in the Great Ouse[2] and Thames basins, on the northern coast of Norfolk and the coast of Essex; in Kent and in a broad belt from Gloucestershire and Somerset to the Dorset coast. This great region is the Lowland Zone of Britain, but there are within it extensive areas practically without find-spots of Celtic art-works —the chalk belt in Hampshire and Wiltshire, still largely occupied by folk of Iron "A" descent, and east Norfolk and east Suffolk, nominally or actually Icenian territory.

The Highland Zone is, as was to be expected, for the most part barren of finds of Celtic art: the sites where such *are* found may be small settlements of Marnians—or later British Celts; or settlements of non-Celtic people willing to barter with them. These are, it will be observed, markedly coastal. Cornwall (particularly Land's End) and the south Devon coast are naturally one of the outer regions where finds occur, but neither the number nor the quality of those from Cornwall suggest that the Cornish chiefs—or their villagers—gained much from the wealth of their country in tin. Settlement of Celtic folk on the South Wales coast (Glamorgan and Monmouth) is proven; they may also have, then, dwelt on the lower Towy and in the Lleyn peninsula. We think we know why Anglesey, the Druidic centre, is so rich; but the concentration of finds in the Clwyd basin is not readily accounted for. It was a favourite and wealthy region in the dawn of the Early Iron Age, then, no doubt, and perhaps now also, an *entrepôt* for an Irish trade to Britain in gold and copper. As for the settlements in the Dumfriesshire region, near the Solway Firth: the finds bracket the whole period of British art from III B.C. to I A.D.—Torrs to Balmaclellan—and a vigorous British Celtic life thereabouts is certain. Yet there are few finds across the backbone of northern Britain linking the East Riding settlements with the Irish Sea coast: the Aire–Ribble and Tyne–Solway routes were not apparently used. The approach may have been by Cotterdale and the Eden Valley.

We still, it is clear, have much to learn in every aspect of the geographical problems of the Highland Zone. It should be remembered that the map deals only with products of the period covered which are regarded as works of art—also that the survey does not cover the important settlements in northern Ireland (there is, it should be said, no evidence that our Solway Firth settlement was a part of this movement). Neither does it cover, effectively, the lodgments of Early Celtic art in Scotland—other than that in Dumfriesshire; but Burnmouth and Stichill (Map B) are in Berwick and Roxburgh, respectively.

There is a little-appreciated aspect of our study which should have place in a summary. It is that we possess an advantage for the understanding of Early Celtic art in Britain over any Celt contemporary with it. Such a map as mine covers a long period of time and human effort, and never was such a range of metalwork as is illustrated in the book likely to have been seen in a semi-civilized community by any one bronzesmith, goldsmith, or patron. On the other hand, two particular problems beset the modern student which any mature individual of the Celtic metal-working or ruling class could have known a lot about: where the more important works in the Lowland Zone were made, and what the internal traffic routes were by which goods and craftsmen reached the various centres of occupation. The latter query is today the easier to answer.

A route familiar to students of the pre-Celtic Ages, the Icknield Way, was almost certainly in use from the Thames to the Little Ouse at Brandon, but there is no evidence from the distributional standpoint that traders from the south used the Norfolk sector (35 miles in length), unless it is held that the presence of the Snettisham, North Creake, and Ringstead finds at its northern end provide this. For my part, I think not: these finds are at the most convenient point in east Anglia for the *north-eastern* trading interests (p. 56 above and Map B). Of greater importance throughout the whole period was the Thames itself, from the tidal estuary to its upper reaches in the Oxford Region, dotted with finds, in places richly; as a highway it provided a link, as in the Bronze Age, we may be sure, between the metalliferous areas in the west (the Mendips) and perhaps also the Forest of Dean, and the eastern settlements on or near its banks. The rich occupation of the upper Ouse countryside was mostly late in our period.

On the theoretical importance of the Jurassic Way from the Mendips to the Humber, on or near the probable western margin of Early Celtic occupation and sovereignty it is not necessary to dilate here, since it has entered so fully into previous pages of the book. East Norfolk was *perhaps* accessible from it by a known Bronze Age trackway which ultimately crossed the (later) Fenlands, *via* the site of Peterborough,[3] but there is no distributional evidence other than the Wisbech bronze.

The siting of the craft workshops. A feature of Celtic art is its variety, and throughout this book the importance of recognizing—if it be possible—schools of craftsmen, and of indicating the areas or regions within which they worked has been in mind. Some success has been attained in the former aim, less in the latter. The earlier pieces have been closely studied from this point of view, but I confine my comment here to a single record of such detail, recurrent in a late phase. This is the discovery that a striking minor feature of the Battersea shield ornament—the gradual replacement of a dominant rib of the design by another which moves up on one side of it—the replaced rib fading out on the other side—recurs in the design of the Trawsfynydd tankard and on one tankard handle of the Seven Sisters (Glam.) hoard.

It has been recognized that this hoard is Dobunic: that the Trawsfynydd tankard also came from a workshop at the southern end of the Jurassic Way, probable in itself, is well-nigh proven by this parallel. Details in the design of these pieces, moreover, recur on the Birdlip mirror, recognized as an outstanding western work.

Is it unreasonable to suggest that one of the chief creative craft-shops in Britain, that wherein the Battersea shield was made early in I B.C. (p. 29 above), was not on the lower Thames but near the upper Thames, that rich area of occupation flanking the Jurassic Way, "the Oxford Region": densely inhabited in the Bronze Age and yielding (as we have seen) many important Early Iron Age bronzes—including foreign ones? The reader will recognize the implications of this conclusion; it involves the whole of the *early* group of river finds (the latest example of which *is* this shield), for, as has been shown (p. 29), the Witham and the lower Thames bronzes form interlocked groups. We are *not*, I hold, dealing with two centres far distant from each other in Lincolnshire and on the lower Thames, but with two workshops related and therefore probably adjacent. The position of the finds, then, since the Witham is unfordable at Tattershall Ferry and the Thames very difficult to ford as low as Battersea and Wandsworth (not to mention the find by London Bridge), may be held to result from the Celtic custom of dedicating fine things to river gods rather than to losses near busy production centres. The close connection artistically between the early Witham and the early Thames finds generally is thus possibly solved: it is due to the interchange of ideas between craftsmen working in a limited area under the patronage, surely, of the highest in the land.

The further conclusion to which we are led by our studies, implied in the present argument, is that one of these schools of early craftsmanship on the borders of Dobunic territory, close to or on the Jurassic Way, continued in being long after the manufacture of the last great work of art in the high Marnian tradition—the Battersea shield—achieving the Birdlip mirror, the Trawsfynydd and Seven Sisters tankards, as well as other works of art, perhaps, still to be found in the west.

This leaves the two Torrs' art-works as the only examples of a true early northern (Parisian) school on the grand scale: the Sutton (Lincs.) scabbard shows how persistent and creative one aspect of this northern art was, the Llyn Cerrig plaque and the Ulceby bit another, and nothing should disturb its agreed original provenance. The Torrs, early lower Thames and river Witham works of art are then allocated to three craft-centres, one in the north-east and two in south Britain. The creators, later on, of the Llyn Cerrig plaque–Ulceby bit style are (more tentatively) grouped in an eastern atelier (in the Ancaster (Wolds) region?) where we have supposed that the goldsmiths of the period were working (or, at least, *trained*). This is in the northern part of the Jurassic Zone, near the middle Trent valley—a point where our craftsmen's gold supply will have reached settled Celtic territory, if Wicklow were its source, the vale of Clwyd an *entrepôt* of the trade, and the Needwood Forest torc-find a hint of its course across the Midlands. The "ifs" in this problem, as in others, are sadly frequent. For example, the intertribal commerce of the time must have been extensive, but its fundamental bases are unknown. What, for example, the Iceni traded for the gold-work massed at Snettisham (or the raw metal out of which this was wrought) is difficult to say: a fine breed of chariot-pony perhaps (since the horse-motif dominates their coinage) nourished on Suffolk heaths—such as Newmarket Heath? The aloofness of the Icenian dynasty and people from the southern tribes in A.D. 43—resulting in their becoming, willingly, a client kingdom of Rome—could, at all events, be held to reflect important economic north-eastern interests.

There is another possibility. It is that the Druidic hierarchy may have organized the gold traffic along the route mentioned above, primarily for their own ritual purposes: if so, it would partly explain why remote Mona became the centre of this British cult, and suggest that the port for the gold trade to the Continent was in Norfolk. The fanatic antagonism to Rome, illustrated by the dreadful scenes in Anglesey in A.D. 59 when the legionaries under Suetonius destroyed groves and priests and worshippers, will then have been fed by economic as well as religious and political motives.

The end of Early Celtic art

Speculation has necessarily had its place in this commentary on the making, maintaining, and distributing of our Early Celtic art; none is needed in discussing its end, for this was obviously caused by the Roman conquest. There will have been a lessening of the freedom and wealth of the patrons of the craftsmen and absence in consequence of opportunity or desire for personal display: mass-production techniques also, it may be, were introduced from Gaul. The survey carried out in this book, then, has reached its term: by A.D. 80

Early Celtic art in Britain up to the Tyne–Solway line is finished. Were another chapter to be added, the subject would be Romano–British art, which (with rare exceptions) is a very different matter.

There is then no more to do except, as a last gesture, to honour the craft-communities which in the fully Celticized half of our island, during so many generations, transformed stubborn metal into memorable beauty of form, or incised it with ravishing pattern; communities whose latest representatives, after the victories of Claudius and of Vespasian, "were, with their virtue, dispersed and molten into the great stiffening alloy of Rome."[4]

NOTES TO CHAPTER XI

[1] The only person competent to assess its significance who saw it between 1870 and 1950 was, I think, the late E. T. Leeds.

[2] For the Ouse region, see W. Watson's sketch map of the principal finds of Belgic bronzes, *Ant. Journ.*, 1949, p. 38.

[3] See *Personality of Britain*, Map C, and the map of Icenian coins in R. P. Mack, *Coinage of Ancient Britain*, Figure 17, p. 114. Mr. T. C. Lethbridge points out that prior to the geologically very recent drowning of the fenland adjacent to the Wash, north-western Norfolk could have easily been reached by land from Lincolnshire. This is confirmed by my Map C.

[4] Robert Bridges, *Testament of Beauty*, I, pp. 769–70, with reference to the Greeks. The Celts were spiritually akin, and I make no apology for applying to them also these lapidary lines.

A 1 to 8 PALMETTE AND 'LYRE' PATTERNS

B 9 to 15 PALMETTE-DERIVATIVES

C SUB-TRIANGULAR, CURVILINEAR, FORMS

D 24 to 33 DOMED 'TRUMPETS' AND RELATED FORMS

E 34 to 41 INCISED PATTERNS (EARLY) —SPIRALS AND 'BATWINGS': VARIED ENRICHMENT

FIGURE 82.—Grammar of British Early Celtic Ornament: I. (See pp. 149-50).

F 42 TO 51 RECTILINEAR PATTERNS: SOME WITHIN CIRCLES

G 52 TO 60 OTHER PATTERNS DEFINED BY CIRCLES

H 61 TO 68 — CIRCLES OR SEGMENTS OF CIRCLES

J 69 TO 74, 'LOBE' PATTERNS 76 AND 77

BALUSTER

S-SCROLLS

SUB-TRIANGULAR FORMS

WAVY: BROKEN-BACKED: WORMY: LIPPED:

97 TO 101: THREE-SIDED 'VOIDS'

K 80 TO 86 'MATTED' SHAPES

L 92 TO 96 TRUMPETS AND ROSETTES

SNAIL

LOBE DOME TRUMPET

DOME A ROUNDEL A ROUNDEL A DOME A LOBE A DOME A TRUMPET B ROUNDEL B TRUMPET A TRUMPET B ROUNDEL B TRUMPET A 96

FIGURE 83.—Grammar of British Early Celtic Ornament: II.

148

KEY TO FIGURES 82 AND 83

GRAMMAR OF CELTIC ORNAMENT IN BRITAIN[1]

(See Introduction, p. xxviii)

PALMETTES AND DERIVATIVE PATTERNS
FIGURE 82.
Row A.

1. Palmette: Classical product, with lyre scrolls (Etruria).
2. Palmette: Shield, R. Witham, Lincs.
3. „ „ „ „ „
4. Palmette and scroll: Bowl, Cerrig-y-Drudion, Denb.
5. „ „ „ Scabbard, Wisbech, Cambs.
6. Lyre-scroll: Harness mount, Rainsborough Camp, Northants.
7. Palmette and scroll: Scabbard mount, Stand-lake, Oxon.: (*a*: linear ornament; *b*: relief ornament).
8. „ „ „ Gold ring, Queen's Barrow, Arras, E.R., Yorks.

Row B.

9. Palmette derivative: Mirror, Colchester, Essex.
10. „ „ „ Horn-cap, Brentford, Middlesex.
11. Palmette and scroll: derivative: Shield, R. Thames, Battersea.
12. Palmette, derivative: Shield, R. Thames, Battersea.
13. Palmette and scroll: Horse-trapping, "London".
14. „ „ „ „ Horse-trapping, West-hall, Suffolk.
15. „ „ „ „ Bit-ring, Yeovil, Somerset (central feature restored).

SUB-TRIANGULAR CURVILINEAR FORMS
Row C.

16. Arm-ring: Newnham Croft, Cambs.
17. „ „ „ „
18. „ „ „ „
19. „ „ „ „
20. Pony-cap: Torrs, Kirkcudbrightshire.
21. Spoon: Weston, Som.
22. Duck-head terminal: Horn-cap, Brentford, Middlesex.
23. Trumpet pattern, with hollow triangles: Dagger-sheath, R. Witham, Lincs.

DOMED TRUMPETS AND RELATED FORMS
Row D.

24. Trumpet scrolls: Plaque, Llyn Cerrig, Anglesey.
25. „ „ „ „ „
26. „ „ „ „ „
27. „ „ „ „ „
28. „ Spear-head, R. Thames.
29. „ „ „ „
30. Three-way coil: Boss, Wood-Eaton, Oxon.
31. Trumpet-scroll derivative: Plaque, Moel Hiraddug, Flints.
32. Curved triangles: Torc, Clevedon, Som.
33. Comma and circle: Mirror, Colchester, Essex.

INCISED PATTERNS, CURVILINEAR, EARLY
Row E.

34. Scabbard-locket: R. Witham, Lincs.
35. „ „ „ „
36. Long shield: R. Witham, Lincs.
37. Round shield-boss: R. Thames, Wandsworth.
38. „ „ „ „
39. „ „ „ „
40. Horns: Torrs, Kirkcudbrightshire.
41. Oval boss of shield: R. Thames, Wandsworth.

RECTILINEAR PATTERNS (SOME WITHIN CIRCLES)
FIGURE 83.
Row F.

42. Shield-boss: Grimthorpe, N.R., Yorks.
43. „ „ „ „
44. Shield: R. Thames, Battersea.
45. Horn-cap: Llyn Cerrig, Anglesey.
46. Mount of wooden tub: Welwyn, Herts.
47. Cone, of limestone: Barnwood, Glos.
48. Scabbard: Wisbech, Cambs.
49. Enamelled terret: Chepstow, Mon.
50. Enamelled harness-mount: Seven Sisters, Glam.
51. Bridle-bit: "London" (B.M.).

OTHER PATTERNS IN CIRCLES
Row G.

52. Diagram: source of "comma" forms, and "yin-yang" scrolls.
53. Brooch: Lakenheath, Suffolk.
54. „ Newnham Croft, Cambs.

---

[1] *Note.*—Black areas on patterns represent enamel or other settings.

Row G—cont.
55. Shield: R. Thames, Battersea.
56. Bridle-bit: Ulceby, Lincs. (plan and section).
57. Scabbard: Bugthorpe, Yorks.
58. Chariot fitting: Bulbury, Dorset.
59. Tankard: Trawsfynydd, Merioneth.
60. Boss: Ixworth, Suffolk.

PATTERNS DEFINED BY CIRCLES OR SEGMENTS THEREOF
Row H.
61. "Snail-pattern": on brooch: Danes' Graves, Yorks.
62. Shouldered pin: Danes' Graves, Yorks.
63. Brooch: Newnham Croft, Cambs.
64. Collar: Llandysul, Cards.
65. Strap-hook: Seven Sisters, Glam.
66. "Dangle": Seven Sisters, Glam.
67. Tankard, Trawsfynydd, Mer.
68. Harness-mount: Chepstow, Mon.

LOBE PATTERNS AND SUBTRIANGULAR FORMS: A BALUSTER
Row J.
69. "Marnian" coil in low relief: Shield, R. Witham, Lincs.
70. Lobe in high relief: Shield, R. Witham, Lincs.
71. Torc, tubular: Snettisham, Norfolk.
72. Horned helmet: R. Thames, London.
73. ,, ,, ,, ,,
74. Shield: R. Thames, Battersea.
75. "Baluster", moulded: Mirror, Ingleton, Yorks.
76. Plaque: Llyn Cerrig, Anglesey.
77. Scabbard: Sutton Reach, R. Witham.
78. ,, ,, ,, ,,
79. ,, ,, ,, ,,

MATTED SHAPES, 80–86
Row K.
80. Torc, gold: Clevedon, Som.
81. Scabbard mount: Standlake, Oxon.
82. Mirror: "Mayer".
83. Shield mount: Balmaclellan, Kirkcudbrightshire.
84. Mirror: Old Warden, Beds.
85. Trumpet, modified: Mirror, "Gibbs".
86. Mirror: Billericay, Essex.

VARIOUS: UNCLASSIFIED
87. Wave pattern: Torc, gold, Needwood, Staffs.
88. ,, Shield, R. Witham, Lincs.
89. Broken-backed "curve": Collar, Lochar Moss, Dumfries.
90. Early coil: Scabbard, Standlake, Oxon.
91. Lipped motif: Harness-ring, Arras, Yorks.

"CLOSED TRUMPETS": BERRIED ROSETTES
Row L.
92. Collar: Llandysul, Cards.
93. Casket front: Elmswell, Yorks.
94. Brooch: Tre'r Ceiri, Cards.
95. Harness mount: Westhall, Suffolk.
96. ,, ,, Polden Hill, Som.

VOIDS, SEMI-TRIANGULAR
97. Plaque: Ashmolean Museum, Oxford.
98. ,, Llyn Cerrig, Anglesey.
99. ,, ,, ,, ,,
100. ,, ,, ,, ,,
101. Shield boss: Llyn Cerrig, Anglesey.

EARLY CELTIC ART IN BRITAIN

THE AUTHOR'S BIBLIOGRAPHY : 1923 TO 1952

1923. *The Archaeology of the Cambridge Region*, chapter V, pp. 70–120. Stanfordbury finds: shale vase. Old Warden: fine pottery.

1924. "A Settlement of the Early Iron Age at Abington Pigotts, Cambs." (bronze ring with embossed ornament), *Prehistoric Society of East Anglia* IV, 1924, p. 211 ff.

1925. "A Late Celtic Bronze Mirror from Wales" (Note), *Ant. Journ.* V, 1925, p. 254 ff.

1926. "A Late Celtic Fire-dog (Lords Bridge, Barton, Cambs.)" (Note), *Ant. Journ.* VII, 1926, pp. 316–18.

1927. "A La Tène I Brooch from Wales: the typology and distribution of these brooches in Britain", *Arch. Camb.*, 1927, pp. 67–112.

1928. "The Early Iron Age in England and Wales (summary of paper read 19 February 1928: the importance of the Jurassic route and zone)", *Camb. Antiq. Soc. Communications* XXX, pp. 52–3.

1929. "A La Tène I Brooch from Merthyr Mawr, Glamorgan" (Note), *Arch. Camb.*, 1929, pp. 146–7.

1933. "The Distribution of Man in East Anglia", *Proc. Prehist. Soc. of East Anglia* VII, p. 149 ff (Early Iron Age imports, pp. 158–60).

1939. "The Llyn Fawr Hoard, Rhigos, Glamorganshire" (in collaboration with H. A. Hyde, M.A., F.L.S.), (a "transitional" group), *Ant. Journ.*, 1939, pp. 369–404.
"The Capel Garmon Fire-dog" (Note), *Ant. Journ.*, 1939, pp. 446–8.

1940. "The Distribution of Currency Bars" (Note), *Antiquity*, 1940, p. 427 ff.

1945. *A Find of the Early Iron Age from Llyn Cerrig Bach, Anglesey* (Interim Report, National Museum of Wales).
"A Shield-boss of the Early Iron Age from Anglesey", *Arch. Camb.*, 1945, pp. 199–220.

1946. *A Find of the Early Iron Age from Llyn Cerrig Bach, Anglesey* (Definitive Report, National Museum of Wales).

1947. "An Open-work Bronze Disc in the Ashmolean Museum", *Ant. Journ.*, 1947, pp. 1–6.

1948. "The Incised Ornament on the Celtic Mirror from Colchester, Essex", *Ant. Journ.*, 1948, pp. 123–37.
"Celtic Mirror Handles in Britain", *Arch. Camb.*, 1948, pp. 24–44.

1949. "A Bronze Pole-sheath from the Charioteers Barrow, Arras, Yorks." (Note), *Ant. Journ.*, 1949, pp. 81–3.
"An Embossed Bronze Disc in Corinium Museum" (Note), *Arch. Camb.*, 1949, pp. 277–8.

1950. "Two Celtic Bronzes from Lough Gur, Limerick, Ireland" (Note), *Ant. Journ.* XXX, 1950, pp. 190–2.
"Note on Celtic Bronzes, Milber Down", *Proc. Devon Archaeological Exploration Society*, Vol. IV, 1950 p. 44.

1951. "The Study of Early Celtic Metalwork in Britain" (British Association, Edinburgh Meeting; Presidential Address, Section H), *The Advancement of Science*, No. 30.
"A Group of Bronzes of the Early Iron Age in Yeovil Museum" (Note), *Proc. Somerset Archaeological Society* XCVI, pp. 108–11.

1952. "Triskeles, Palmettes, and Horse Brooches", *Proc. Prehist. Soc.*, 1952, pp. 47–54.

INDEX I : SUBJECTS

INDEX II : PLACES

13

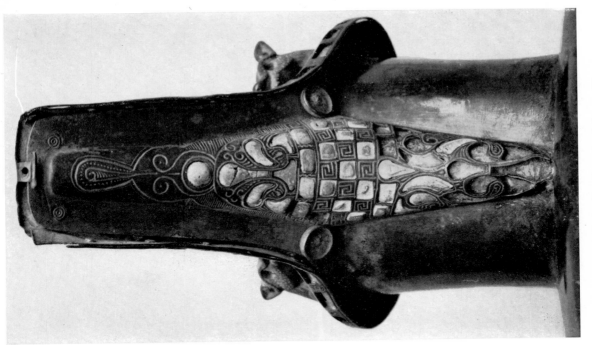

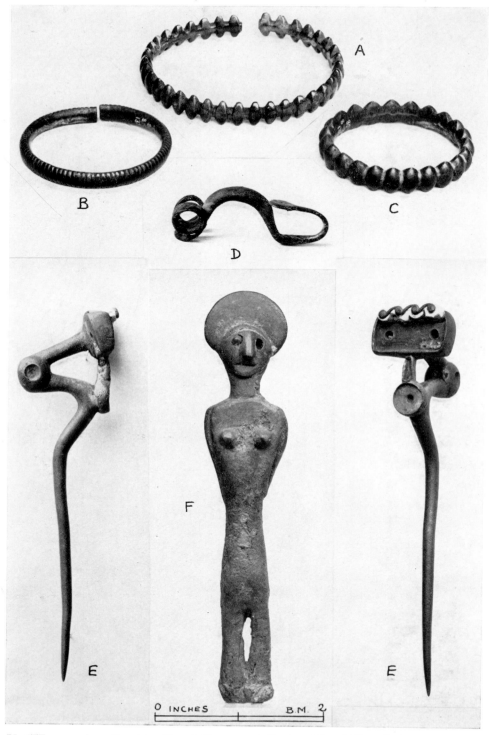

PLATE 2.—*a. b. c.* Bracelets: Danes' Graves, and Cowlam (East Riding, Yorks.). (Pp. 6, 19.)
d. Brooch, bronze: Cowlam. (P. 6.)   *e, e.* Pin, shouldered: River Thames (Hammersmith). (Pp. 9, 18.)
f. Statuette: Aust-by-Severn (Glos.). (P. xxiv.)   (All bronze.)

PLATE 3.—*a*. Horn-cap, bronze: River Thames (Brentford). *b*. Base of cap. *c*. Section ($\frac{5}{6}$). (*Drawn for the Museum.*) *d*. Horn-cap, bronze: High Cross, Leicester. (See pp. 3 and 120.)

PLATE 4.—Horn-cap: Brentford. Detail of central pattern. (P. 3.) (*Drawn for the Museum* $\frac{2}{1}$.)

CENTIMETRES
INCHES

PLATE 5a.—Bridle-bit, bronze: Kings Barrow, Arras (Yorks.). (P. 7.)

PLATE 5b.—Bridle-bit, bronze: Llyn Cerrig (Anglesey). (Pp. 55, 99.)

PLATE 6.—Model of British chariot, based on material from Llyn Cerrig (Anglesey). (See also Figure 40, p. 58, and pp. 7, 59.)

Photograph : National Museum of Wales

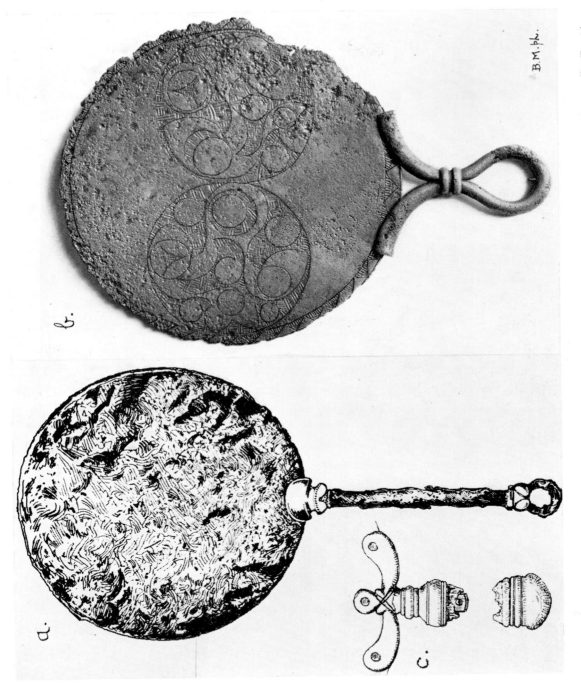

B.M. ph.

PLATE 7.—a. Mirror, iron with bronze mounts: Lady's Barrow, Arras (Yorks.). (P. 7.) b. Mirror: Trelan Bahow (Cornwall). (P. 98.)
c. Bronze mounts, La Motte St. Valentin mirror: France. (P. 7.)

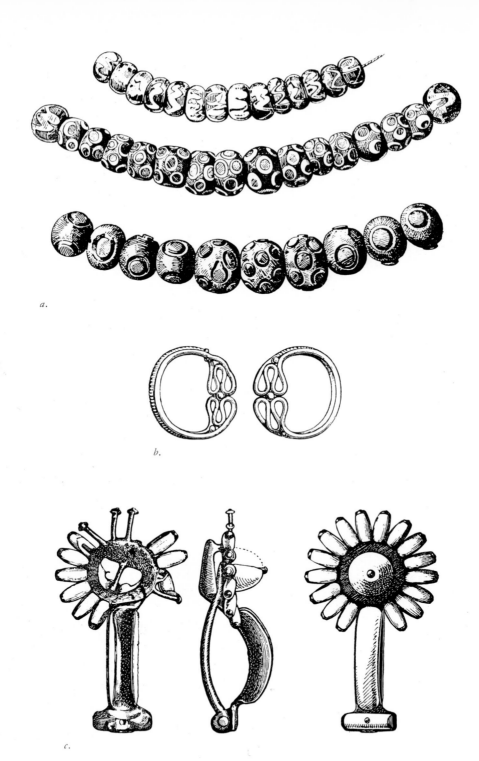

PLATE 8.—a. Glass beads: Queen's Barrow, Arras (Yorks.). (P. 7.)   b. Gold ring, Queen's
Barrow, Arras (Yorks.). (Pp. 7, 19.)   c. Brooch with coral settings: Harborough cave
(Derby.). (P. 9.)

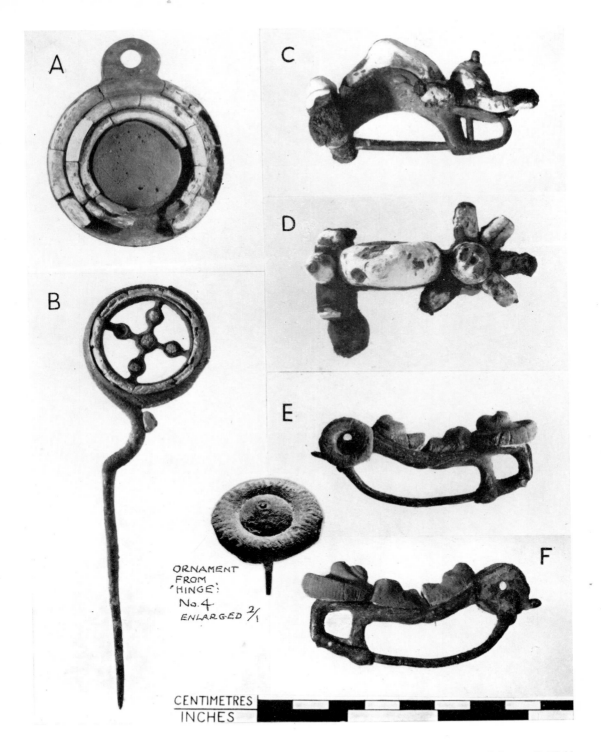

ORNAMENT
FROM
'HINGE'
No. 4
ENLARGED 2/1

CENTIMETRES
INCHES

PLATE 9.—*a*. Pendant, with coral inlay: Queen's Barrow, Arras (Yorks.). (P. 7.)   *b*. Pin: Danes' Graves, Driffield (Yorks.). (Pp. 7, 18.)   *c and d*. Brooch, with coral inlay: Queen's Barrow. (P. 7.)   *e, f*. Brooch, involuted: Danes' Graves. (Pp. 9, 19.)   *Inset*, detail of hinge, enlarged.

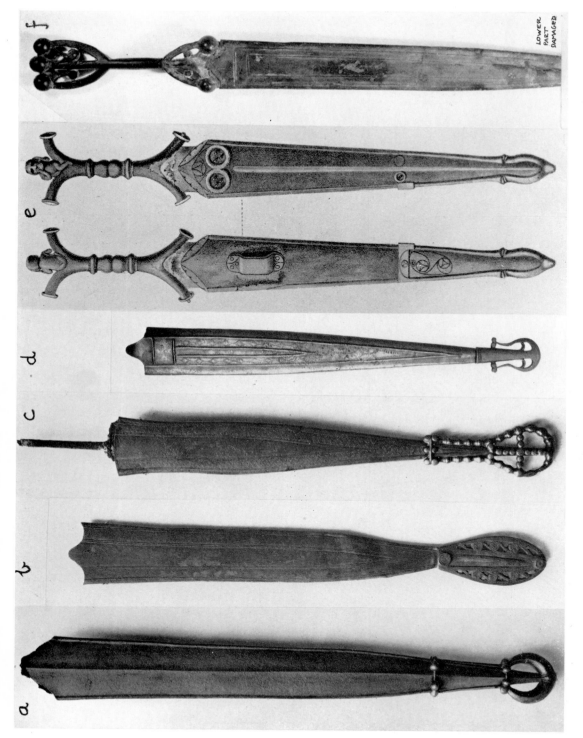

PLATE 10.—Sheaths and daggers. (P. 3.) *a, b,* River Thames (Wandsworth). *c.* River Thames (Richmond). *d.* Minster Ditch (Oxford). *e.* River Witham (Lincoln). (See also Figure 23, 8, p. 38.) *f.* Hertford Warren (Suffolk). (P. 30.)

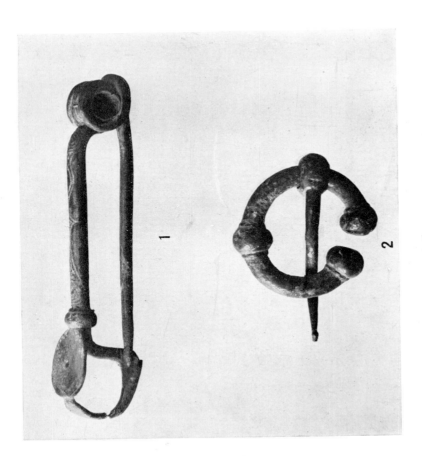

b.

c.

1

2

a.

PLATE 11.   Brooches: Sawdon (North Riding, Yorks.).   (See Figure 5, p. 8.)

a. Brooches: Sawdon (North Riding, Yorks.).   (See Figure 5, p. 8.)

b. Bracelet: Barrow 43, Arras (Yorks.).   (Pp. 9, 19.)

c. Disc, with red enamel: Bugthorpe (Yorks.).   (P. 43.)

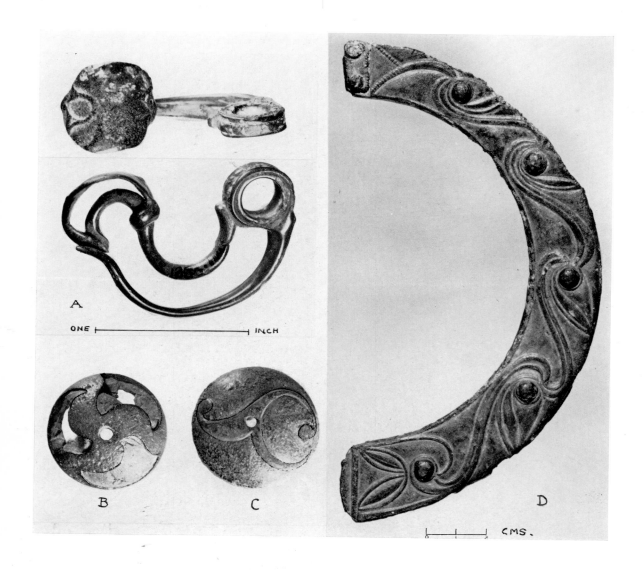

PLATE 12.—a. Brooch, involuted: Beckley (Oxon.). (See Figure 9b, p. 13.) b. Disc with enamel inlay: Ixworth (Suffolk).
(P. 127.) c. Disc with relief ornament: Wood Eaton (Oxon.). (P. 53.) (See Figure 9a, p. 13.) d. Collar: Llandysul (Cards.).
(P. 106.)

PLATE *13.*—Shield-boss: River Thames, Wandsworth. (P. 26.)

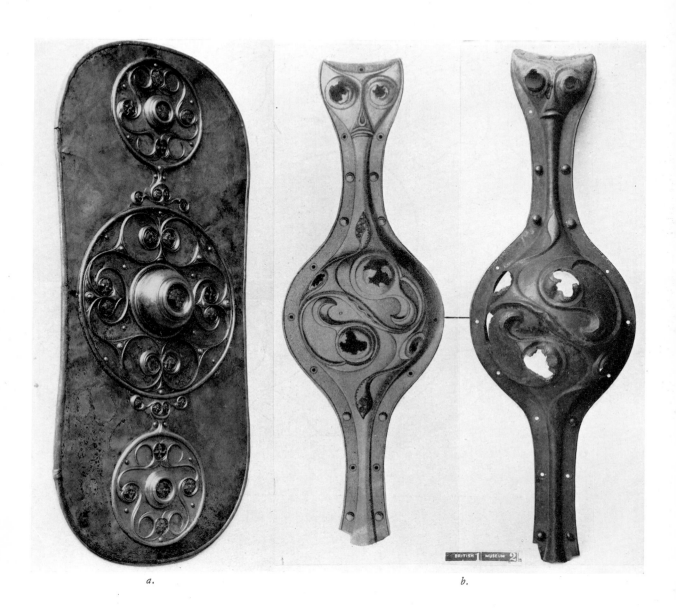

a.   *b.*

PLATE *14.*—*a.* Shield: River Thames (Battersea). (P. 27.) *b.* Shield-boss: River Thames (Wandsworth). (P. 26.)
(*Drawing and photograph.*)

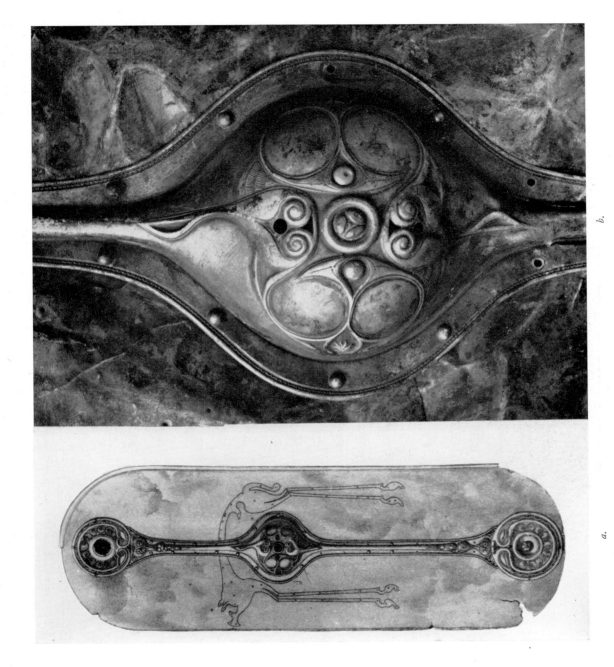

b.

PLATE 15.—a. Shield: River Witham (Lincs.). (Pp. 26, 27.) *b.* Detail of boss.

a.

PLATE *16*.—Shield: River Thames (Battersea). Detail of boss, with red enamel inlays. (P. 27.)
(See *Plate 14a*.)

PLATE *17.*—Shield: Battersea. Lower roundel. (See *Plate 14a.*)

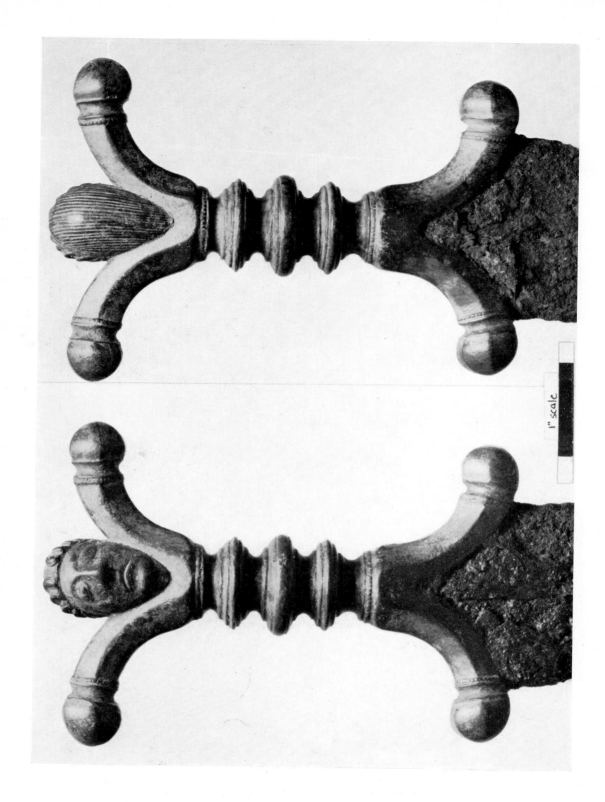

PLATE 18.—Hilt of short sword: North Grimston (East Riding, Yorks.). (P. 30.) (See Figure 23, 6, pp. 38, 72.)

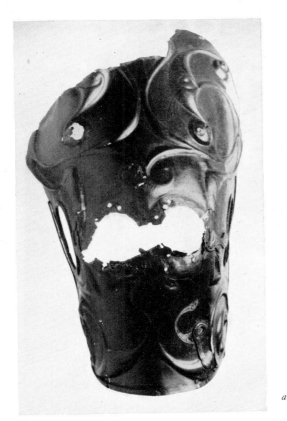

a.

b.

c.

PLATE 19.—a. Pony-cap: Torrs (Kirkcudbrights.). (P. 22.) b. In use. c. Detail of ornament.
(See also Figure 16, p. 23.)

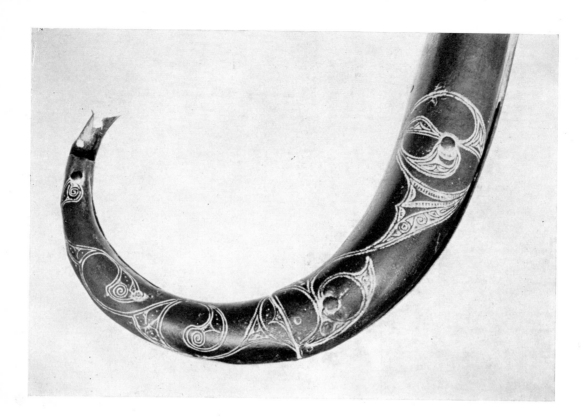

a.

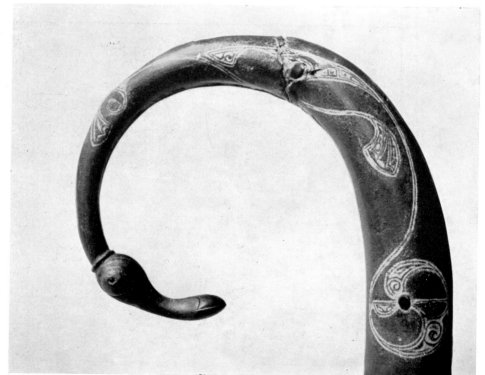

b.

PLATE *20.*

a–b. Tips of
drinking-horn
mounts: Torrs
(Kirkcudbrights.).
(P. 24.)
(See Figure 17,
p. 24.)

Note.—(*a*) As held for drinking; (*b*) Standing on table, empty.

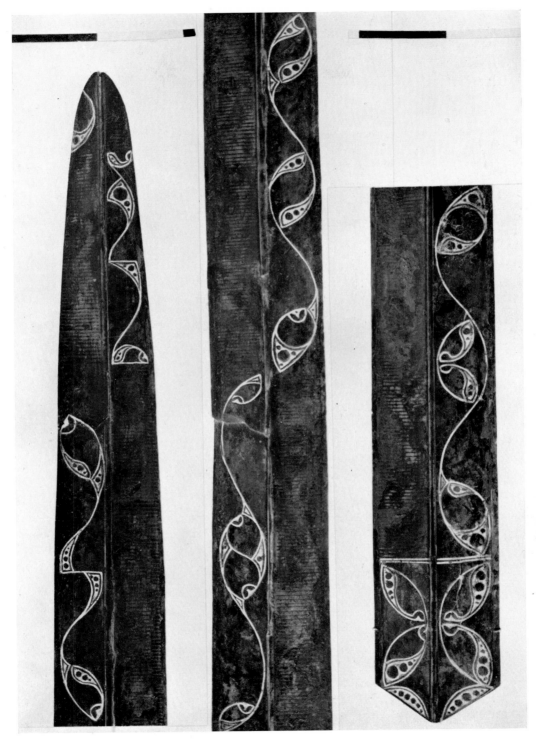

PLATE *21*.—Scabbard: Sutton Reach, River Trent (Lincs.) (P. *32*.). (*Photographed in three lengths.*)
(The black bars are 1 inch in length.)

b.

a.

PLATE 22.—a. Sword and scabbard mounts, details: Standlake (Oxon.). (Pp. 13–14.) *b.* Sword and scabbard-locket (l. 63 cm.): River Witham (Lincs.). (P. 25.)

a.

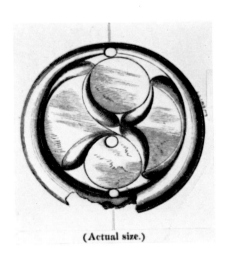

(Actual size.)

b.

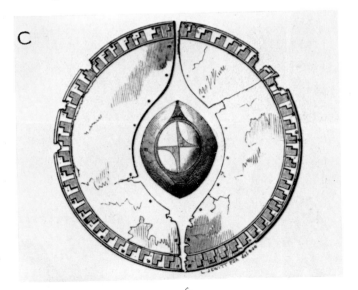

c.

PLATE 23.—*a.* Crescentic plaque (part of): Llyn Cerrig. (See Figure 18, pp. 33, 108.) *b.* Roundel: Grimthorpe (Yorks.).
(See Figure 19, p. 35.) *c.* Shield-boss: Grimthorpe. (P. 35.)

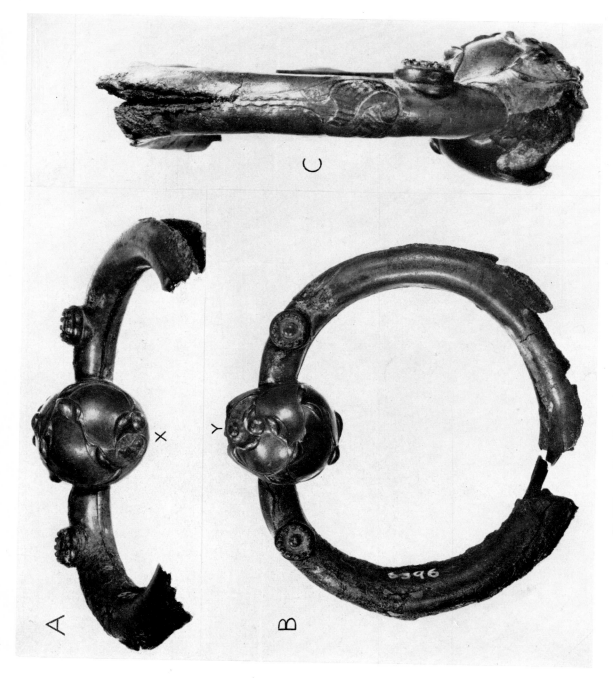

PLATE 24.—Horse-bits, portions of: Ulceby (Lincs.). (P. 35.) (See Figure 21a.)

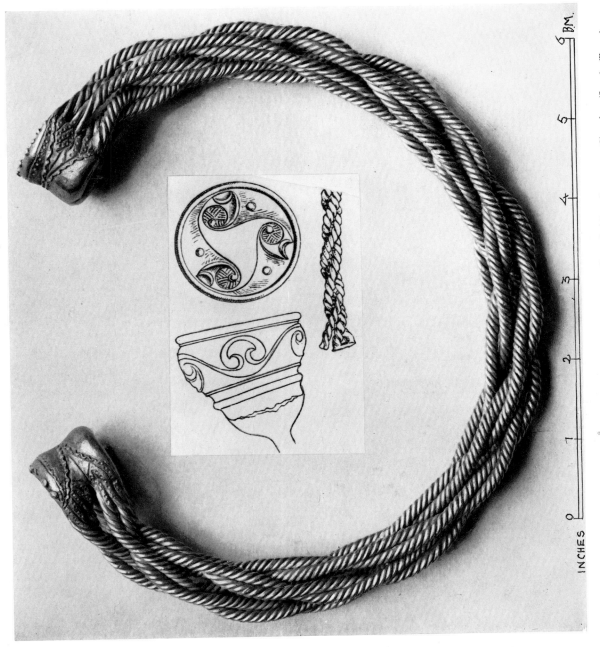

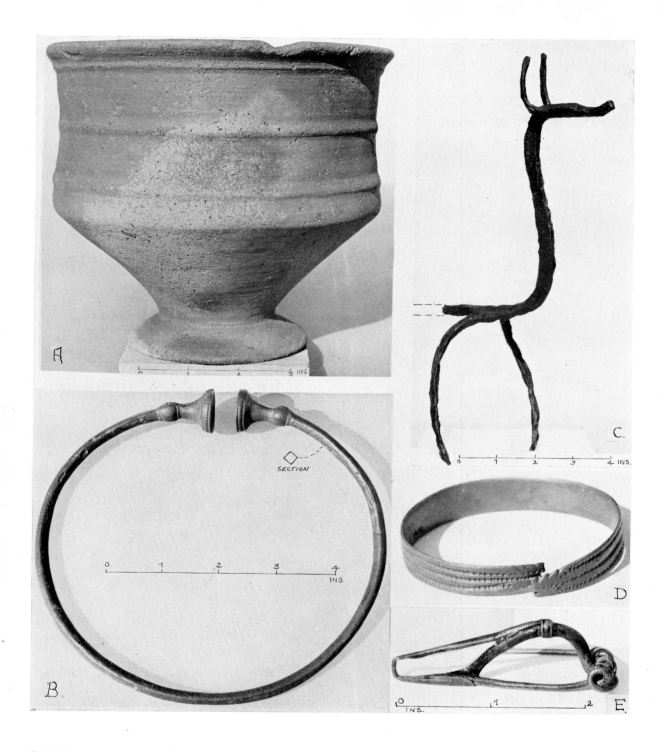

PLATE 26.—*a*. Pottery tazza: Aylesford (Kent). (P. 63.) *b*. Torc: River Medway, Aylesford. (P. 66.) *c*. Ox, strip-iron: Bigbury hill-fort (east Kent). (Pp. 75, 132.) *d*. Bracelet: Borough Green, Maidstone. (P. 108.) *e*. Brooch: Roman villa site, Maidstone Barracks. (P. 18.)

a.

b.

PLATE 27.—*a*. Handle of tub: Harpenden (Herts.) (P. 77.) *b*. Horned helmet: River Thames. Detail. (P. 49.) (See also Figure 36, p. 50.)

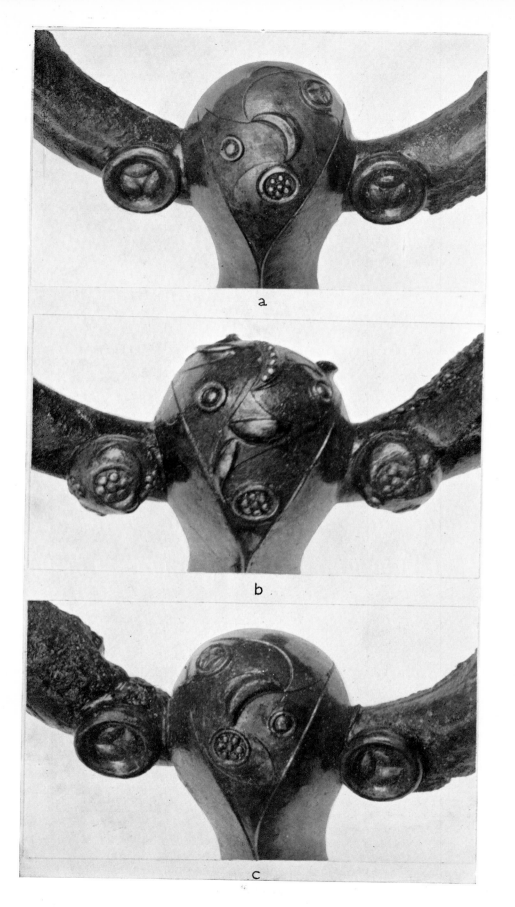

a

b

c

PLATE 29.—a. Gold torc terminal: Cairnmuir (Peebles). (P. 48.) *b.* Torc: Lochar Moss (south Dumfries.). (P. 107.)

a.

b.

c.

d.

PLATE *30.—a.* Mirror handle No. I: Stamford Hill (Mount Batten), Plymouth. (See Figure 64, p. 98.) *b, c, d.* Tazza, pedestal urn, bowl with cover: Essex. (P. 63.)

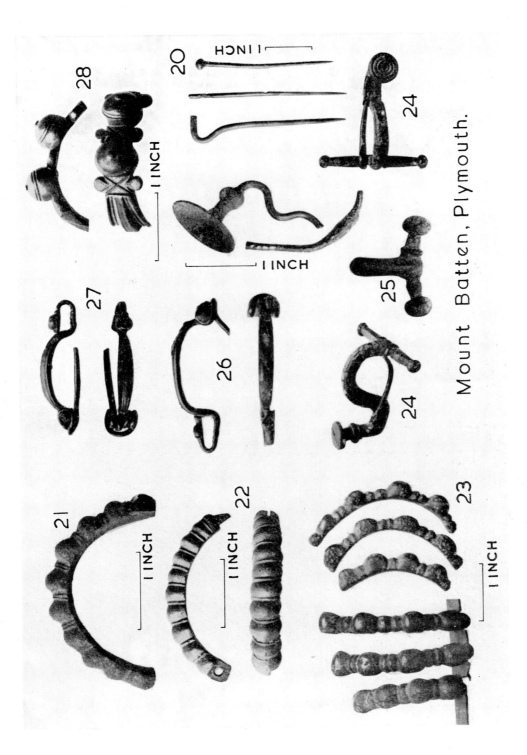

PLATE 31.—Brooches, bracelets, and pins: Mount Batten, Plymouth. (P. 14.)

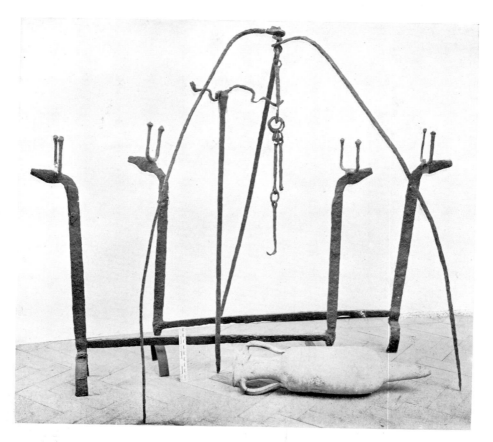

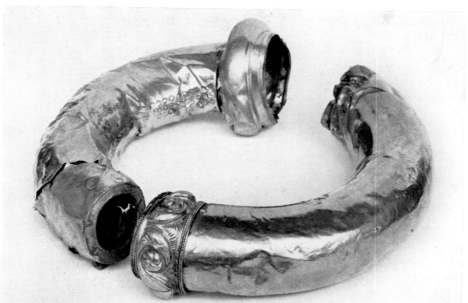

PLATE 32.—a. Iron fire-dogs, tripod, and imported amphora, from Stanfordbury (Beds.). (P. 65.)
b. Gold torc: Hoard A, Snettisham (Norfolk). (P. 48.)

PLATE 33.—a. Bucket: Aylesford (Kent). (P. 68.) *b.* Masks: Welwyn (Herts.). (P. 65.)

PLATE *34.*—The "Marlborough" vat (Wilts.). (Pp. 68, 70.) *a, b.* Original reconstruction. *c, d.* Facing heads on handles. *e.* Opposed animals, third register.

a.

b.

c.

PLATE *35.*—The "Marlborough" vat (Wilts.). (P. 68.) *a.* Head, first register. *b.* Sea-horses, first register. *c.* Animal, probably second register.

b.   *a.*

c.

PLATE *36.*—The "Marlborough" vat (Wilts.). (P. 69.)   *a, b.* Head of a god, horse to right, probably second
register.   *c.* Head of a god, horse to left.

PLATE 37.—*a and c*. Silver bowl: Gundestrup, Jutland. *a*. Detail of one panel. (Pp. 70, 72, 81.)
b. Disc-brooch: Santon Downham (Suffolk), with griffin in relief. (P. 70.)

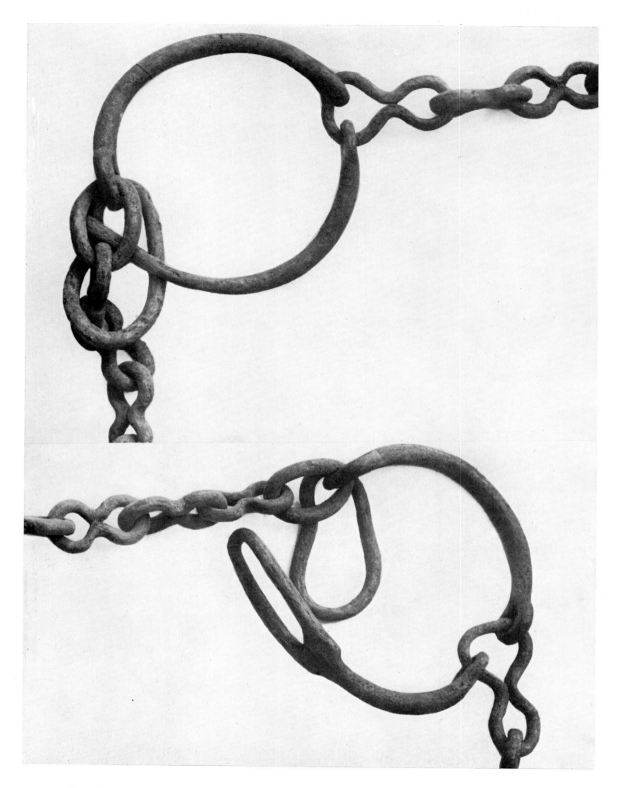

PLATE 38.—Iron gang-chain: Llyn Cerrig (Anglesey). (P. 66.)   (See also Figure 45, p. 68.)

b. Iron linch-pin: Great Chesterford (Essex). (P. 121.)

1 INCH

PLATE 39.—a. Iron spear-head with bronze mounts: River Thames. (P. 49.)

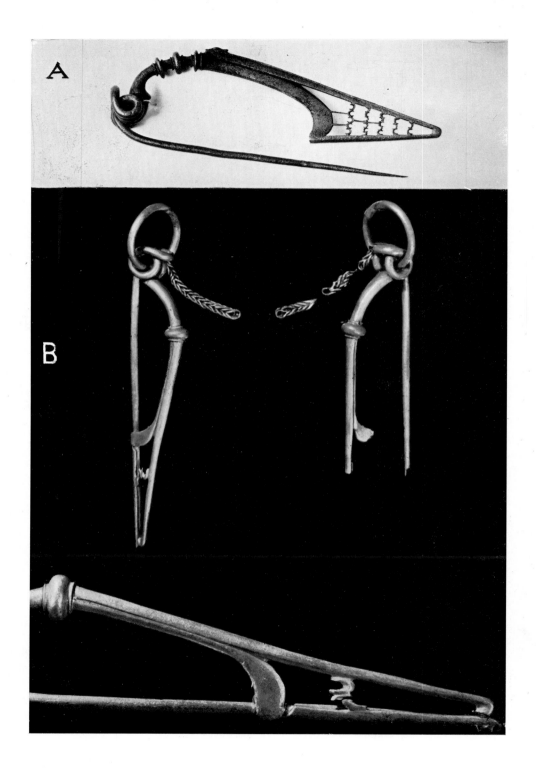

PLATE 40.—*a.* Brooch from River Thames. (P. 66.)   *b.* Brooches, silver: Great Chesterford (Essex). (P. 66.)

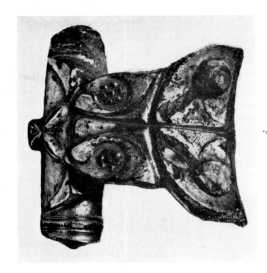

_d._

_e._

_c._

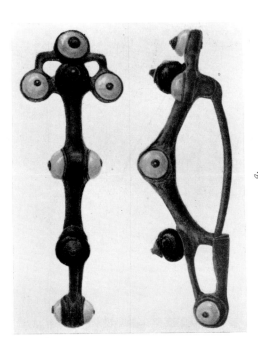

_a._

_b._

PLATE 41.—Brooches, later forms: _a._ River Thames, Datchet (Bucks.). (P. 55.)   _b._ Lakenheath (Suffolk). (P. 107.)   _c._ Great Chesters (_Aesica_) (Northumb.). (P. 108.)
_d._ Tre'r Ceiri (Caern.). (P. 107.)   _e._ Llanferres (Denbigh.).   (P. 80.)

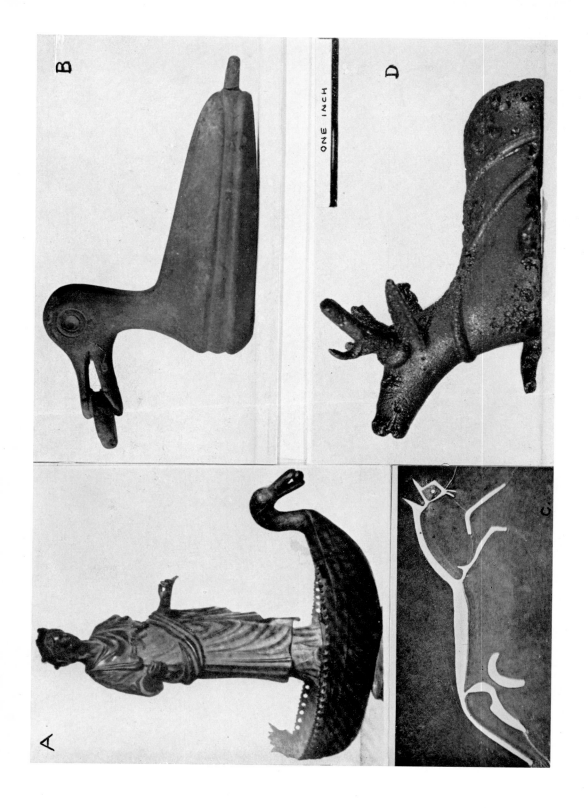

PLATE 42.—a. Bronze barge with goddess: River Seine. (P. 79.) *b and d.* Duck and Reindeer: Milber hill-fort (south Devon). (Pp. 79, 82–3, Note 31.) *c.* Hill figure, The White Horse: Uffington (Berks.). (P. 70.)

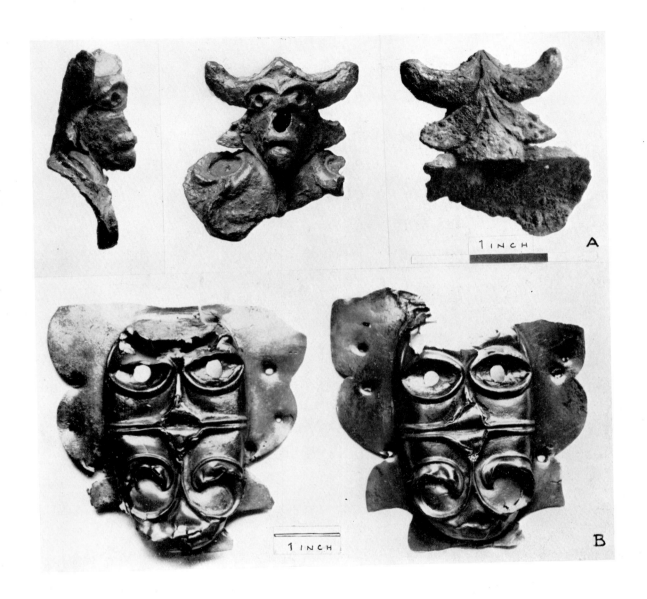

PLATE 43.—Human masks. *a.* Terret, Aldborough (Yorks.). (P. 73.) *b.* Stanwick (North Riding, Yorks.). (P. 73.)

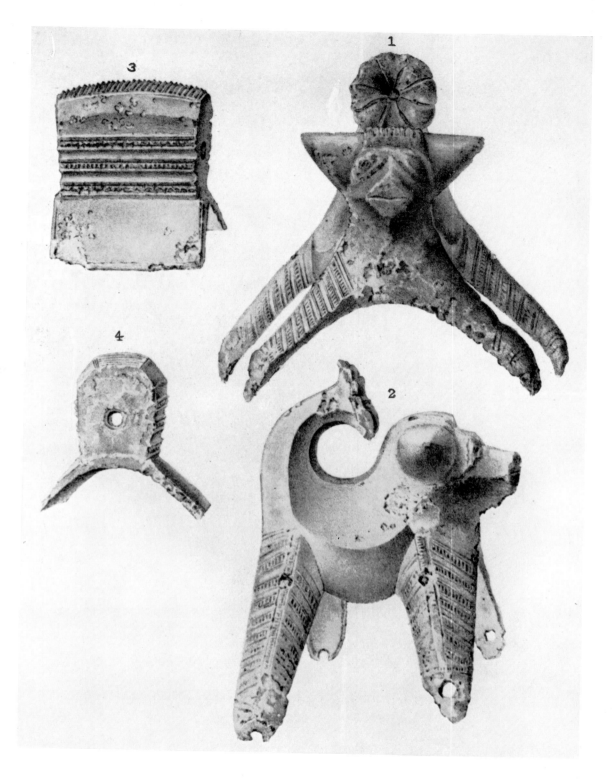

PLATE 44.—Chariot fittings: Bulbury (Dorset). (P. 73.)

PLATE 45.

a. Tazza, portion of, Kimmeridge shale: Barnwell (Cambridge). (P. 63.)

b. Bronze plate, embossed: Moel Hiraddug (Flints.). (Pp. 75, 117.)

a.

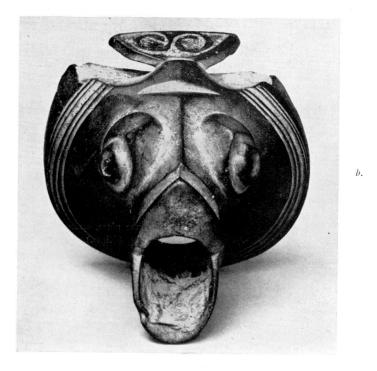

b.

c.

d.

PLATE *46.*—*a, b.* Spout (fish-head) : Felmersham-on-Ouse (Beds.). (See Figure 49, p. 80.) *c, d.* Bucket mounts, cow heads: Felmersham. (See also Figure 46, and p. 73.)

PLATE *47*.—Iron fire-dog: Lords Bridge, Barton (Cambs.). (P. 75.)

a.

INCHES

b.

c.

PLATE 48.—a. Iron fire-dog: Capel Garmon (Denbs.). (P. 75.) b. Ox-head: Ham Hill (Som.). (P. 73.) c. Ox-head: Dinorben (Denbs.). (P. 73.)

PLATE *49*.
a. Iron fire-dog, end view: Capel Garmon (Denb.). (P. 75.)

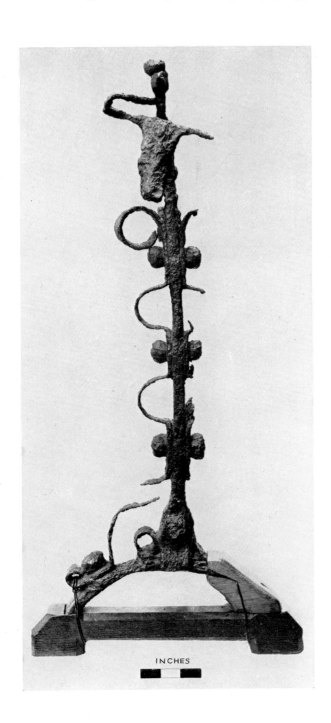

b. Sword scabbard, upper half, front and back views:
River Witham (Lincs.). (P. 117.)

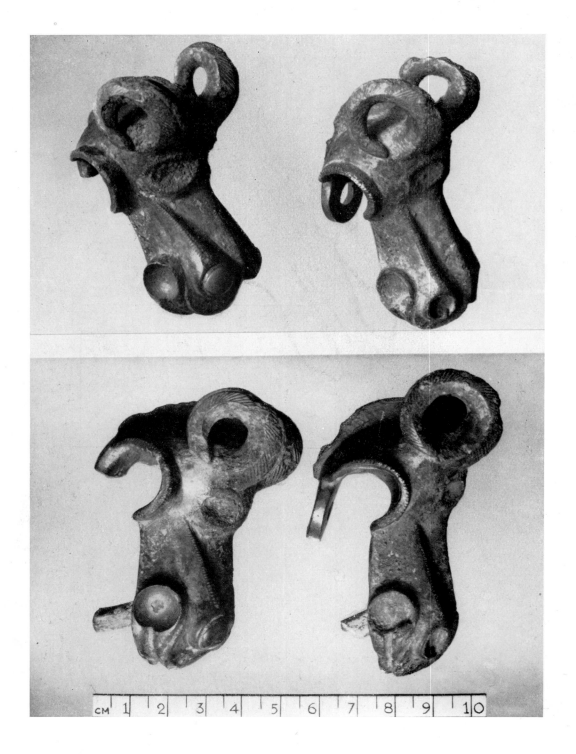

PLATE 50.—Rams' head mounts, pair of: Harpenden (Herts.). (Pp. 76–8.) (See also Figure 47, p. 77.)

PLATE 51.—Bowl, with inverted ram's head mount: Youlton (Cornwall). (P. 79.)

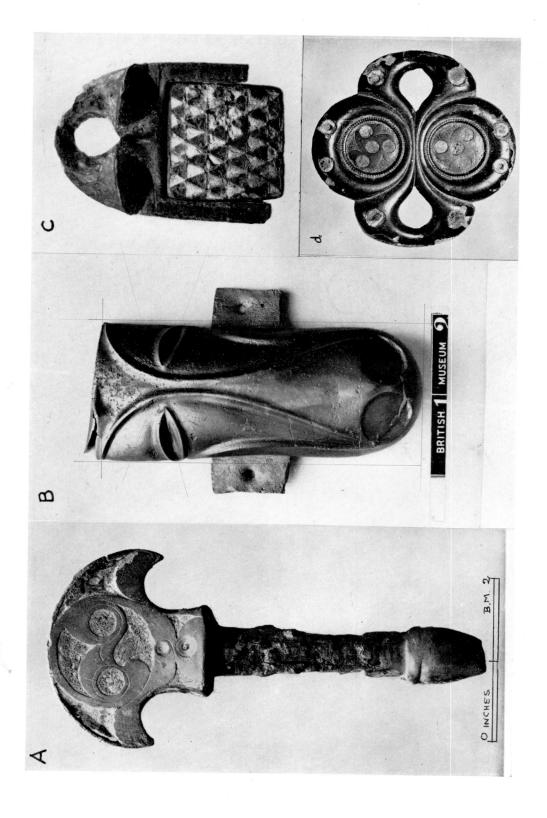

PLATE 52.—*a*. Linch-pin, enamelled: King's Langley (Herts.). (Pp. 121, 127.) *b*. Horse mask: Stanwick (Yorks.). (Pp. 76, 120.) *c*. Belt-plate, enamelled: York. (P. 119.) *d*. Harness-mount, enamelled: Cheltenham (Glos.). (P. 127.)

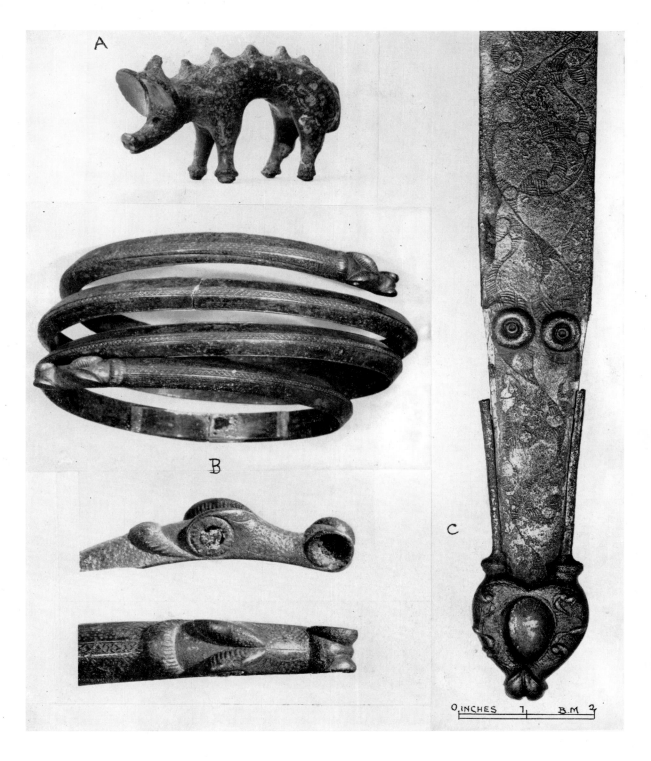

PLATE *53.—a.* Boar: Hounslow (Middx.). (P. 76.) *b.* Armlet, coiled, with ram-and-snake-headed terminals: Snailwell (Cambs.). (P. 81.) *c.* Scabbard, lower portion: Bugthorpe (Yorks.). (P. 41.)

PLATE *54.*—*a.* Silver cup: Welwyn (Herts.) (P. 63.) *b.* Tankard, upper part, restored: Elveden (Suffolk). (P. 109.)

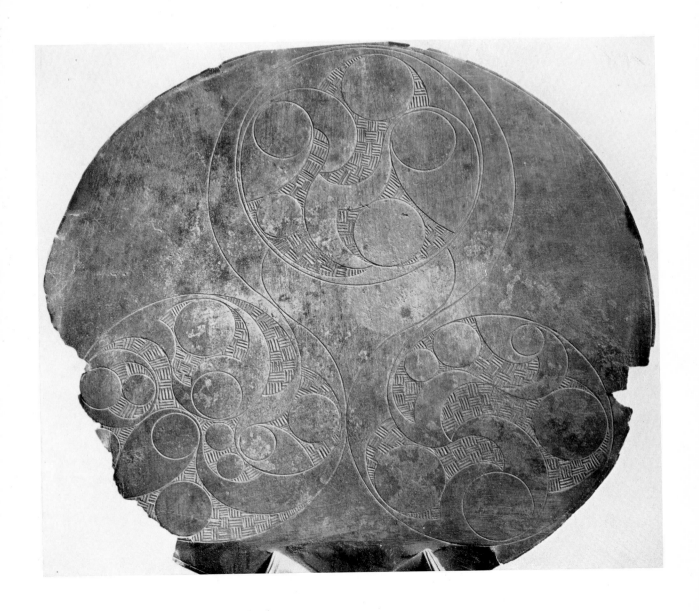

PLATE 55.—The Mayer mirror plate. (P. 85.) (See also *Plate 56a.*)

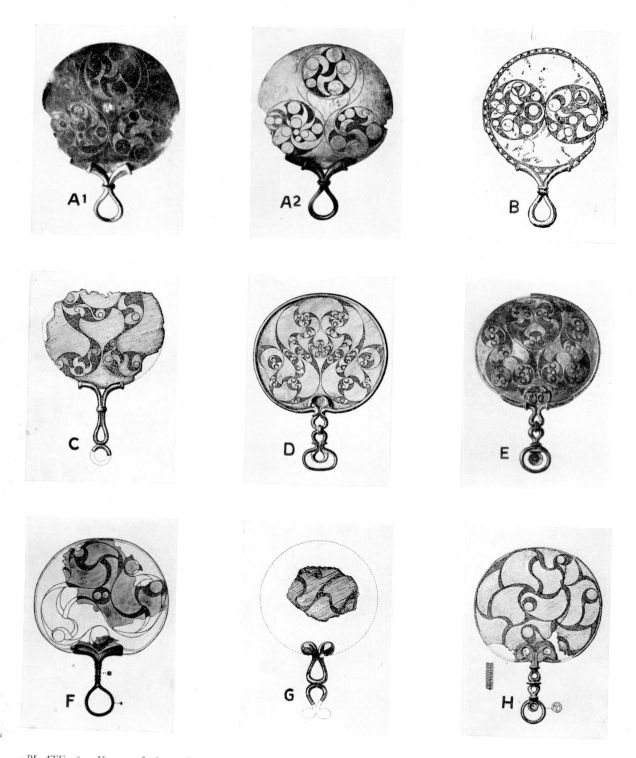

PLATE 56a.—Key set of mirrors (i). a. "Mayer"; b. Trelan Bahow (Cornwall); c. "Gibbs"; d. Desborough (Northants.); e. Birdlip (Glos.); f. Billericay I (Essex); g. "Disney"; h. Old Warden (Beds.). (P. 84 ff.)

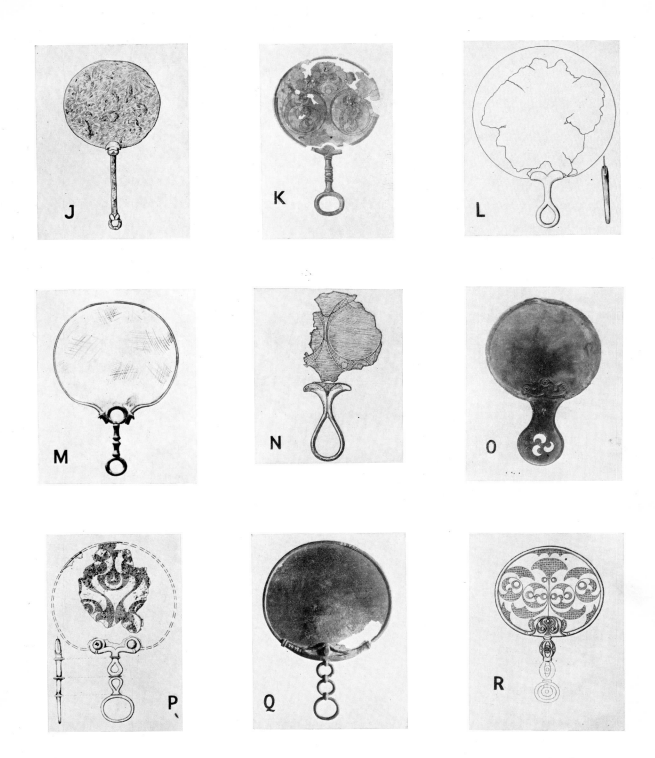

PLATE *56b*.—Key set of mirrors (ii).   *i*. Arras (Yorks.);   *k*. Stamford Hill I (Mount Batten, Devon);   *l*. Billericay II;   *m*. Ingleton (West Riding, Yorks.);   *n*. Rivenhall (Essex);   *o*. Balmaclellan (Kirkcudbrights.);   *p*. Colchester (Essex);   *q*. Llechwedd-ddu (Merioneth);   *r*. Nijmegen, Holland. (P. 84 ff.)

a.

b.

c.

d.

PLATE *57*.—Decorated mirrors (p. 85 ff.). *a.* "Mayer"; *b.* Birdlip (Glos.); *c.* Desborough (Northants.); *d.* "Gibbs".

PLATE 58.

a. Trial hatching under handle of Birdlip mirror, revealed during repairs. (*British Museum.*) (P. 91.)

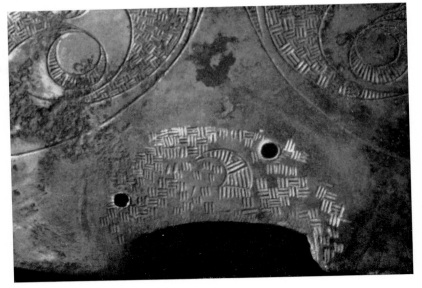

a.

b.

b. Detail of relief on *Ara Pacis Augustae,* Rome. (P. 94.)

_c._

_a._

_b._

PLATE 19.—_a._ Rim of silver dish. _b._ Side of silver bowl : Hildesheim Treasure, Germany. _c._ Handle of silver cup: Bernay Treasure, Eure, France. (P. 94.)

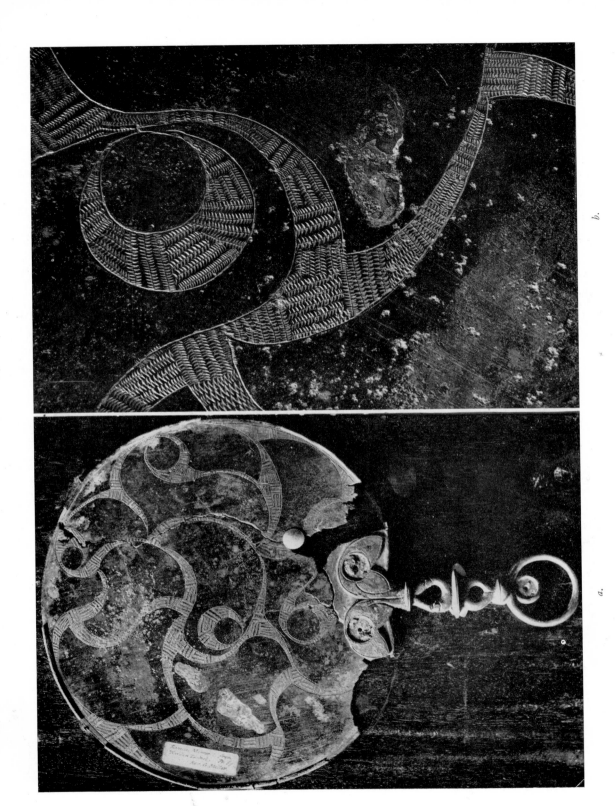

PLATE 60.—(a). Mirror: Old Warden (Beds.). b. Enlarged detail of decoration. (Pp. 94–5, 101.)

a.

b.

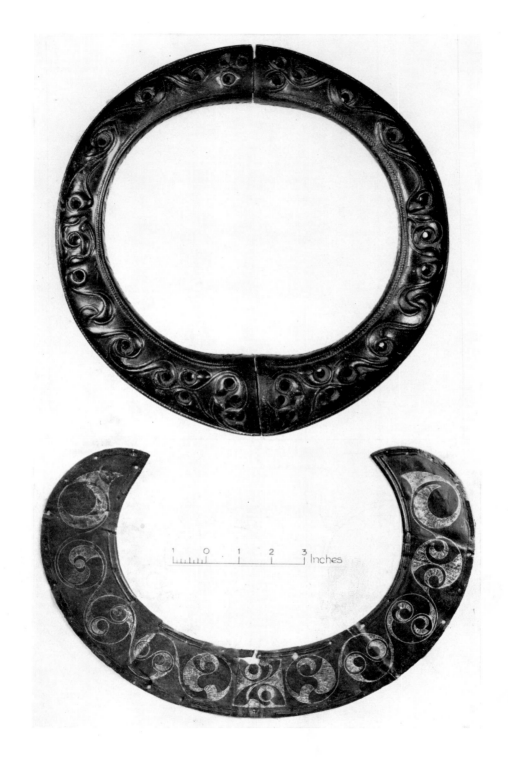

PLATE *61.—a.* Collar: Wraxall (Som.) (P. 106.) *b.* Shield ornament (?): Balmaclellan (Kirkcudbrights.). (P. 116.)

a, and b (inset).

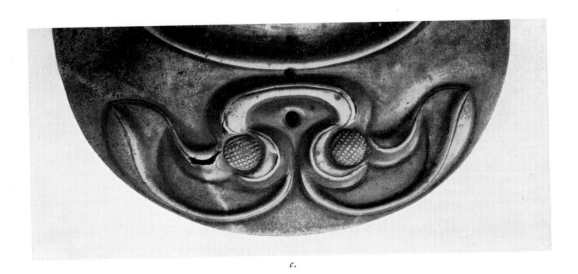

c.

PLATE *62.*—*a.* Collar: Portland (Dorset). (P. 106.) *b.* (*inset*) Collar: Stichill (Peebles.). (Pp. 107, 116.) *c.* Helmet, neck-guard, no provenance. (P. 119.)

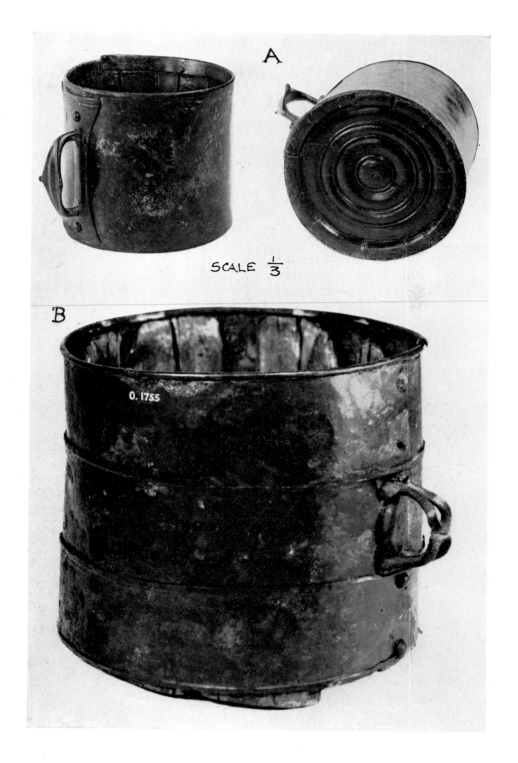

PLATE *63*.—*a*. Tankard: Shapwick Heath (Som.). (P. 108.) *b*. Tankard: River Thames, Kew.
(P. 109.)

PLATE 64.—Tankard: Trawsfynydd (Merioneth.). Hold-fast details. (P 109.).

PLATE *65*.—Tankard: Trawsfynydd (Mer.). *a*. Inside of rim; *b*. base. (P. 109.)

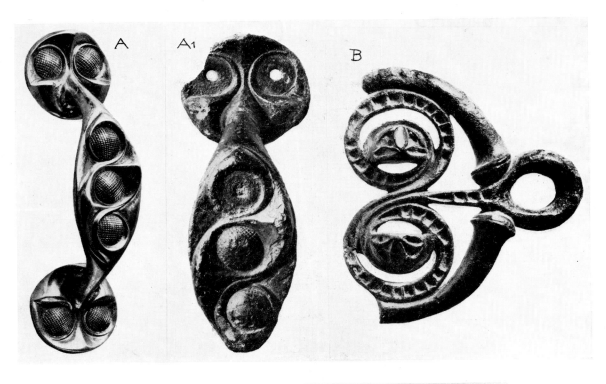

PLATE 66.—*a.* Tankard hold-fast, reconstruction and original: Seven Sisters, Neath (Glam.). (See also Figures 78, 9.) (Pp. 28, 110, 129.) *b.* Harness mount: Seven Sisters. (Pp. 116, 129.) *c.* Harness mount: Rainsborough hill-fort (Northants.). Front and back. (See Figures 53, 4, p. 88 and p. 121.)

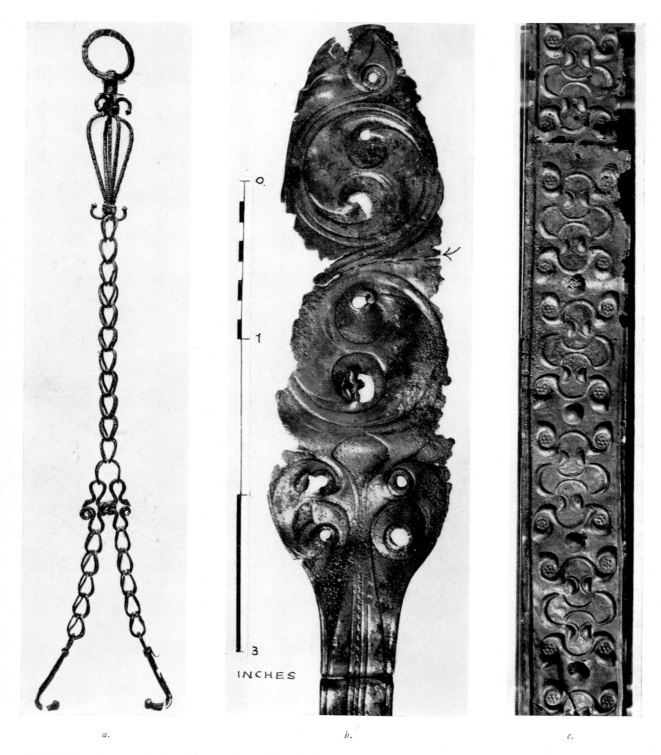

PLATE 67.—a. Iron pot-hook and hanger: Great Chesterford (Essex). (P. 110.) *b.* Terminal of shield-mount: St. Mawgan-in-Pyder (north Cornwall). (P. 115.) *c.* Ornamented strip: Santon Downham (Suffolk). (Pp. 105, 120.)

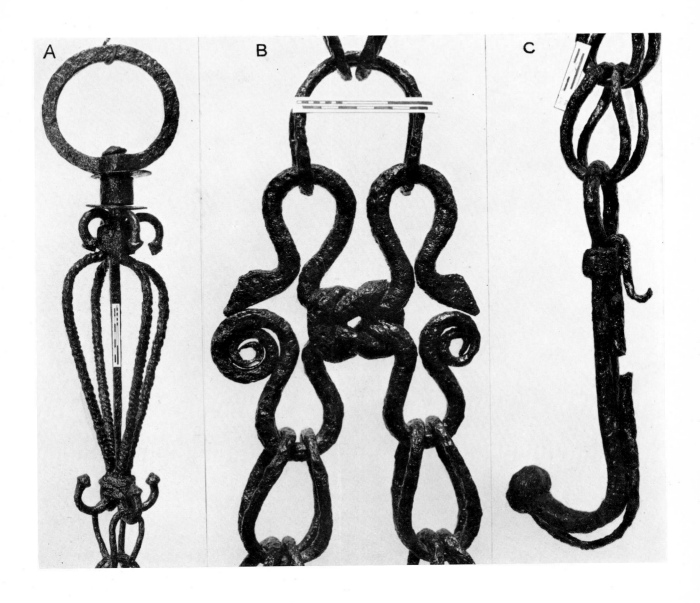

PLATE 68.—Pot-hook: Great Chesterford (Essex). (See *Plate 67a.*) *a.* Swivelled head. *b.* Serpentiform junction of three chains. *c.* A terminal hook. (P. 110.)

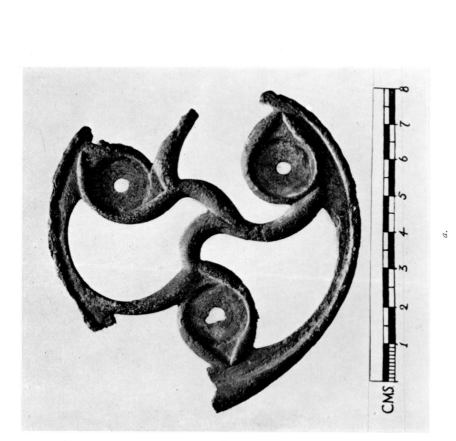

PLATE 69.

a. The Ashmolean triskele.   (See Figure 75, p. 122, and p. 121.)

b. Hame, lower portion of: Suffolk (?).
(See Figure 77, p. 127, and p. 126.)

a.

b.

c.

PLATE *70.*—*a.* Spoons: Penbryn (Cards.). (P. 111.) *b.* Spoon: Cardigan. (P. 112.) *c.* Harness mount, enamelled: Chepstow (Mon.). (P. 129.)

PLATE 71.—*a*. Terret, enamelled (Suffolk). (P. 126.)   *b*. Terret: Ditchley (Oxon.) (P. 126.)   *c*. Terret, enamelled: Polden Hill (Som.). (P. 126.)   *d*. Bridle bit: River Thames (London).   (P. 125.)

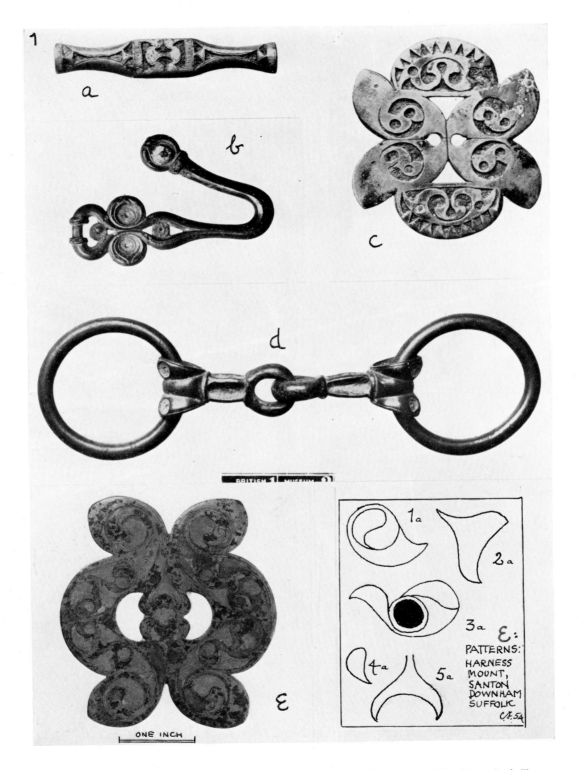

ONE INCH

PLATE 72.—*a–d*. Bronzes: Polden Hill (Som.). (See also *Plate* 73.) *a*. Cheek-piece of bit. (P. 125.) *b*. Trace-hook. (P. 123.) *c*. Harness-mount, enamelled. (P. 129.) *d*. Bridle-bit. (P. 126.) *e*. Harness-mount, enamelled: Santon Downham (Suffolk). (P. 125.)

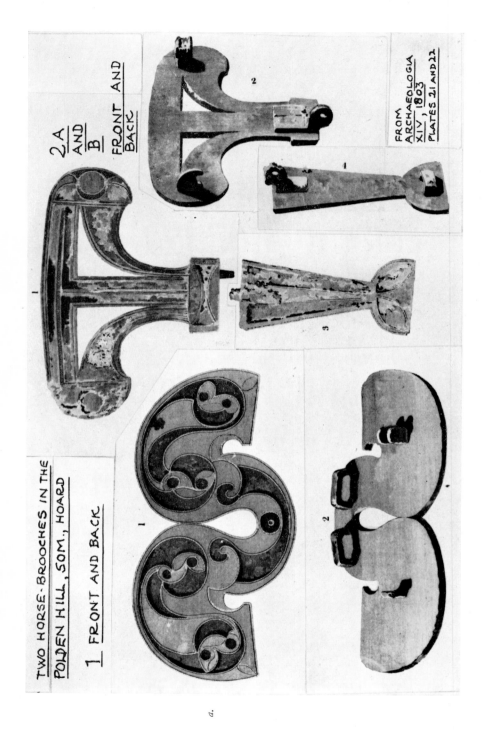

PLATE 73.—a. Horse-brooches, enamelled: Polden Hill (Som.). (See Figure 76, p. 124.) *b.* Scabbard: Northern Ireland.

(Drawn by E. M. Jope.) (P. 43.)

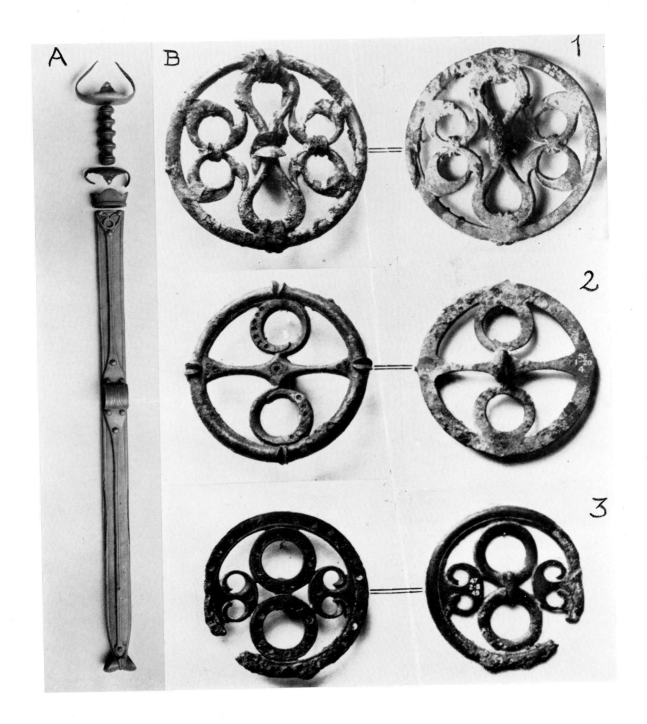

PLATE 74.—a. Sword-hilt and scabbard: Cotterdale (Yorks.). (P. 119.) b. Harness-ornaments: Stanwick (North Riding, Yorks.). (P. 130.)

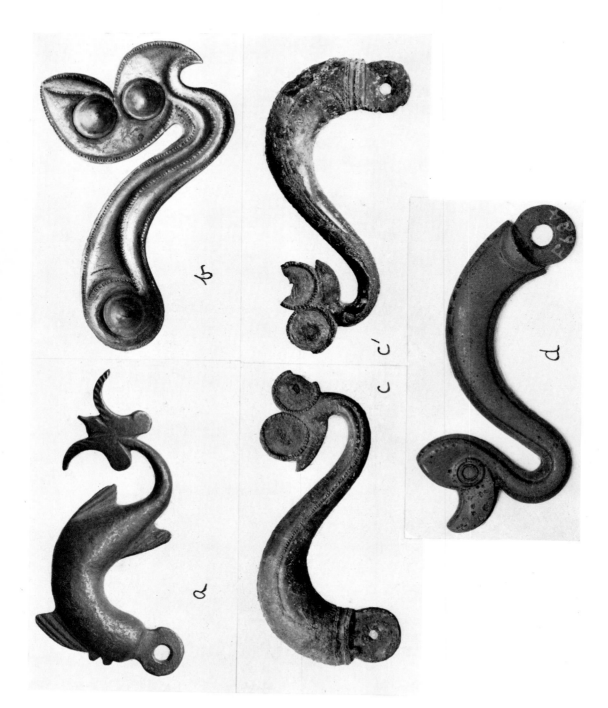

PLATE 75.—"Dolphins": Ornaments for pony-harness (?). (P. 130.)

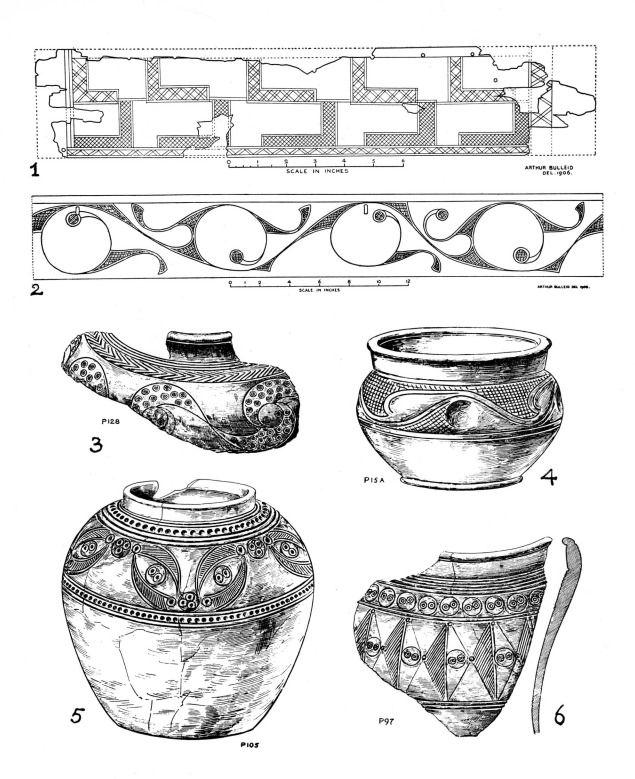

1 SCALE IN INCHES ARTHUR BULLEID DEL. 1906.

2 SCALE IN INCHES ARTHUR BULLEID DEL. 1908.

P128

3

P15A

4

P105

5

P97

6

PLATE 76. 1—2. Ornament on wood-strip and tub; 3—6. Pottery, ornamented. (See also Figures 80–81, pp. 134–5.)
(After *The Glastonbury Lake Village*, Bulleid and Gray. By kind permission.)

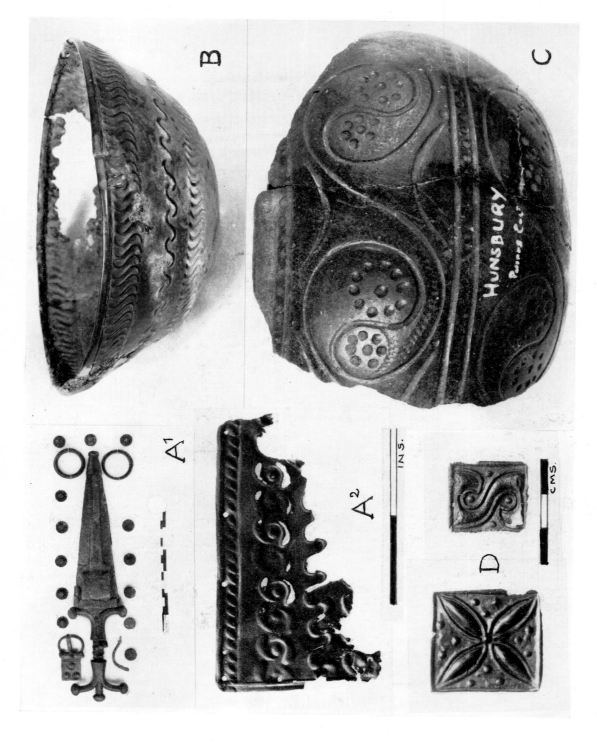

PLATE 77.—a1. Dagger (10-in.) and buckle: Ham Hill (Som.). (P. 119.) *a2.* Ornamented bronze strip: Winchester (Hants.). (Pp. 12, 105.) *b.* Bronze bowl: Hunsbury (Northants.). (P. 12.) *c.* Pottery bowl: Hunsbury. (P. 135.) *d.* Embossed squares, bronze: Silchester (Hants.). (P. 105.)

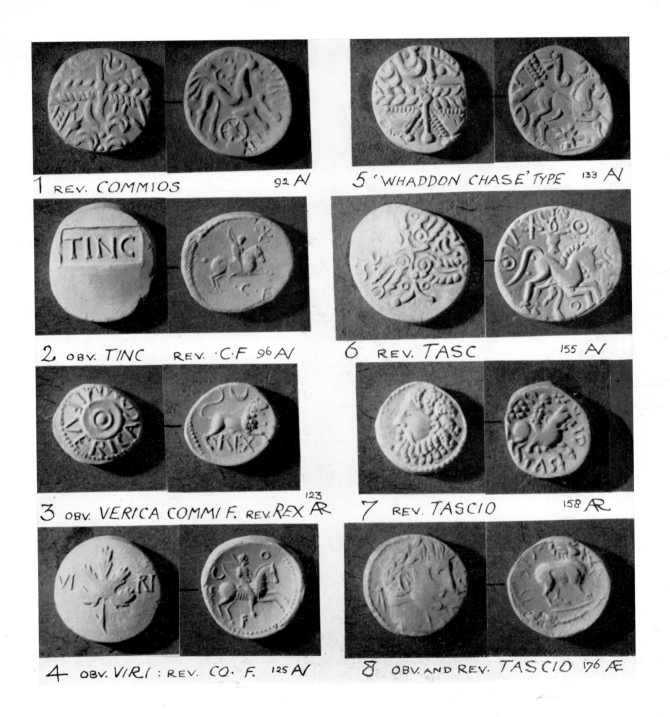

1 REV. COMMIOS   92 A/

5 'WHADDON CHASE' TYPE   133 A/

2 OBV. TINC   REV. ·C·F 96 A/

6 REV. TASC   155 A/

3 OBV. VERICA COMMI F. REV. REX 123 AR

7 REV. TASCIO   158 AR

4 OBV. VIRI : REV. CO·F. 125 A/

8 OBV. AND REV. TASCIO 176 Æ

PLATE 78.—British coins: 1—4. Atrebates and Regni I; 5—8. Catuvellauni. (P. 136 ff.)
(*From casts, British Museum.*)

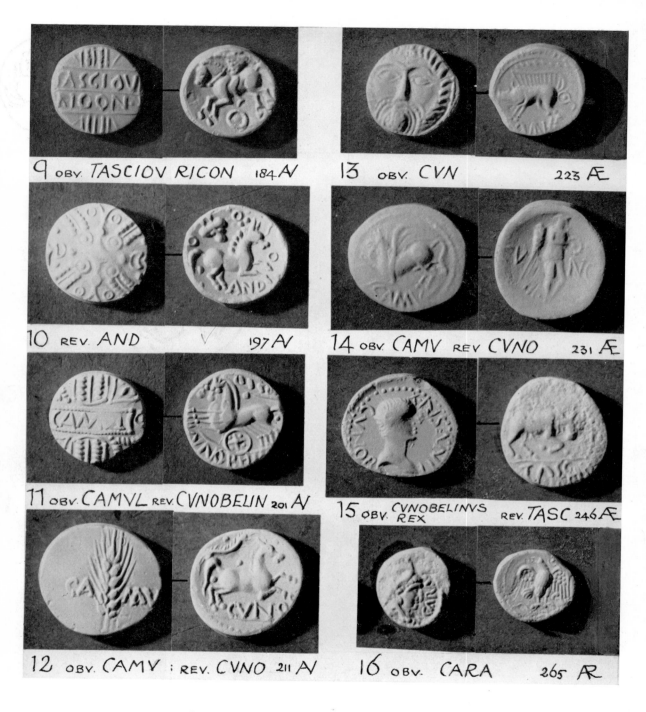

9 OBV. TASCIOV RICON   184 AV

13 OBV. CVN   223 Æ

10 REV. AND   197 AV

14 OBV. CAMV REV. CVNO   231 Æ

11 OBV. CAMVL REV. CVNOBELIN 201 AV

15 OBV. CVNOBELINVS REX   REV. TASC 246 Æ

12 OBV. CAMV : REV. CVNO 211 AV

16 OBV. CARA   265 AR

PLATE 79.—British coins: Catuvellauni. (P. 138 f.)
(*From casts, British Museum.*)

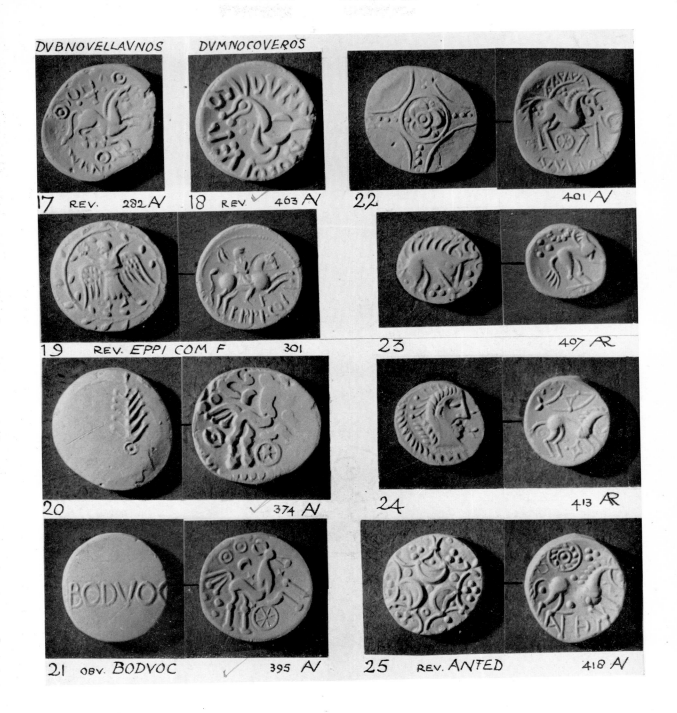

DVBNOVELLAVNOS   DVMNOCOVEROS

17 REV. 282 A̶V̶   18 REV. ✓ 463 A̶V̶   22   401 A̶V̶

19 REV. EPPI COM F   301   23   407 A̶R̶

20   ✓ 374 A̶V̶   24   413 A̶R̶

21 OBV. BODVOC   ✓ 395 A̶V̶   25 REV. ANTED   418 A̶V̶

PLATE 80.—British coins: 17, 19. Cantii (!); 18. Brigantes; 20, 21. Dobunni; 22—25. Iceni. (P. 138 f.)
(From casts, British Museum.)